CHRISTIAN OptiMYSTICS

To my friend Ryan from Dwayne

When we mess up God doesn't throw us out.... Keeps lovin' us and jammin' with us 'til we get it right. Amazing God! God's the WOW! of my story. Praying many blessings for you and your beautiful family.

CHRISTIAN OptiMYSTICS

Running the Rapids of the Spirit

Dwayne O. Ratzlaff

Thomas G. Bandy

CHALICE PRESS
ST. LOUIS, MISSOURI

© Copyright 2006 by Dwayne O. Ratzlaff and Thomas G. Bandy

All rights reserved. For permission to reuse content, please contact Copyright Clearance Center, 222 Rosewood Drive, Danvers, MA 01923, (978) 750-8400, www.thenewcopyright.com.

Bible quotations, unless otherwise noted, are from the *New Revised Standard Version Bible,* copyright 1989, Division of Christian Education of the National Council of the Churches of Christ in the United States of America. Used by permission. All rights reserved.

Quotations marked KJV are from the *King James Version.*

Cover photograph: Getty Images
Cover and interior design: Elizabeth Wright

Visit Chalice Press on the World Wide Web at
www.chalicepress.com

10 9 8 7 6 5 4 3 2 1   06 07 08 09 10 11

Library of Congress Cataloging–in–Publication Data

Ratzlaff, Dwayne O.
  Christian optimystics : running the rapids of the Spirit / Dwayne O. Ratzlaff, Thomas G. Bandy.
    p. cm.
  ISBN-13: 978-0-827205-04-8 (pbk.)
  ISBN-10: 0-827205-04-X (pbk.)
  1. Ratzlaff, Dwayne O. 2. Sexual misconduct by clergy. 3. Reconciliation–Religious aspects–Christianity.   I. Bandy, Thomas G., 1950-   . II. Title.
  BV4392.5.R38 2006
  277.3'083092–dc22
  [B]
                                                                                        2005037539

Printed in the United States of America

*In dialogue with God, leaders navigate the full
diversity of God's white water to transform sin into
forgiveness, guilt into grace, hurt into healing,
despair into hope, and failure into mission.*

■

*Dedicated to capsized leaders
who refuse to stay submerged
in white water
and to prevailing teams
who rescue and reclaim them.*

Contents

Introduction: A Template of Transformation   1
    MEMO: The Template of Transformation, a Spiritual Practice   9

1 Rafting toward a Crisis of Spirit   14
    MEMO: On Experiences of Being Capsized   25

2 Capsized into a Crisis of Morality   27
    MEMO: On Spiritual Warfare   50

3 Submerged within a Crisis of Calling   57
    MEMO: Submerged within a Crisis of Calling   80

4 River-running the Rapids of Spirit   90
    MEMO: River-running the Rapids of Spirit   106

5 River-running the Rapids of Morality   114
    MEMO: River-running the Rapids of Morality   126

6 River-running the Rapids of Calling   132
    MEMO: River-running the Rapids of Calling   150

7 Why I Am an OptiMystic   160
    MEMO: Augustine's Garden   180

Notes   187

INTRODUCTION

In Dialogue
A Template of Transformation, a Spiritual Practice

Journal Writing as Dialogue

My story is a witness to the transformative power of dialogue. It is personal, and it is true. I have kept a journal since I was in seminary. It began when I jotted down a defining moment on a piece of paper. I have that paper today. A spiritual autobiography evolved from that recorded experience. At a time of profound personal crisis, a paradigm shift occurred. The spiritual journal assumed the form of dialogues with God.

I write dialogues as they happen. The spiritual discipline of journal writing has a shaping power that defies calculation. I bring three tools to a spiritual practice: an open Bible, an open journal, and an open heart. On occasion I may bring an open book, perhaps a spiritual classic. I may read a book about vision, leadership, or any growing edge. Then I turn to the scriptures. I read slowly, listen attentively, and write immediately when words come. I meditate on the incoming words and record my response. The incoming word may be just that—a word or sentence, or longer on occasion. The dialogues are to the point. I absorb the word of revelation deeply. An issue of conversation may surface for many months, and writing facilitates the dialogues. This form of dialogue is an ongoing spiritual practice. The pattern is not daily, but it is consistent.

Scripture and Experience in Dialogue

John Cassian (c. 365–c. 435) was among the most eloquent interpreters of Desert spirituality and the monastic movement. Cassian's *Conferences* places scripture and experience in dialogue.

Then indeed the Scriptures lie ever more open to us. They are revealed, heart and sinew. Our experience not only brings us to know them but actually anticipates what they convey. The meaning of the words come through to us not just by way of commentaries but by what we ourselves have gone through...We anticipate its idea instead of following it. We have a sense of it even before we make out the meaning of the words. The sacred words stir memories within us, memories of the daily attacks which we have endured and are enduring, the cost of our negligence or the profits of our zeal, the good things of providence and the deceits of the enemy, the slippery subtle tricks of memory, the blemishes of human frailty, the improvidence of ignorance... Instructed by our own experiences we are not really learning through hearsay but have a feeling for these sentiments as things that we have already seen. They are not like things confided to our capacity for remembrance but, rather, we bring them to birth in the depths of our hearts as if they were feelings naturally there and part of our being. We enter into their meaning not because of what we read but because of what we have experienced earlier.[1]

Modern Research into Dialogue

Flow of Meaning

Dialogue comes from the Greek word *dialogos,* meaning "through the word." Dialogue is a stream or flow of meaning. It occurs as an interplay of words: within, between, and among people. To dialogue is to open oneself to the possibility of new understandings and new creations. David Bohm says two things must happen for this to occur. First, in dialogue we face the pressures of our assumptions and the thoughts that issue from them. Deeply held assumptions can get in the way of communication. Assumptions have a life of their own, injecting their own intentions into conversations. Second, in dialogue we choose to enter an "empty space" where anything can come into conversation. The sole purpose of this emptying and exploring is to communicate the truth that emerges. Dialogue has nothing to do with winning an argument. It allows for the weighing of opinions without choosing.[2]

William van den Heuvel likens dialogue to a dance with the unknown: a creative and unpredictable encounter. New meanings emerge by thinking and talking about the things that "bubble up" during the dance of dialogue.[3] William Isaacs renders John 1:1: "In the beginning was the Relationship (*Logos*)." Isaacs portrays dialogue as a conversation in which two or more people think together in relationship and listen to the possibilities. He defines dialogue as "a shared inquiry, a way of thinking and reflecting together...a living experience of inquiry *within* and *between* people."[4] Relationship is the context of the inquiry.

Building Blocks

William Isaacs presents four skills that form the building blocks of dialogue: listening, respecting, suspending, and voicing. These skills build a new capacity for new actions.[5] Listening is at the core of dialogue, both listening to oneself and to the other. It involves paying attention to one's inner reactions and practicing the art of inner silence. Respecting is about honoring another, even deferring to the other. It includes the respecting of boundaries. Respecting demonstrates a teachable spirit in response to the other. It views the other as mystery in the deepest sense. The respecting skill is possible when one finds a personal center and responds out of that center. Suspending is the ability to loosen one's grip on deeply held assumptions and see things in new ways. It encompasses an ability to allow an idea to be spun out without forming criticism or voicing opinion. Voicing builds on the other three skills. Voicing is courageous speech because it reveals the deep inner self. The words are authentic; the speaker embodies the expression. One has to find one's voice before speaking it by listening in a deep way to one's own voice; then when one speaks, one creates. This is speaking from the center of oneself to the center of the other. The purpose of these skills is to build capacity for authentic actions.[6]

Modern research into the dynamics of dialogue can apply to conversation with God. Each skill is suited for attending to the scriptures and the divine whisper. The listener pays attention to the inner reactions of the self in response to the voice of Sacred Scripture. The reader approaches the biblical text with profound respect in the presence of the divine other, open fully to God's self-disclosure. Suspending assumptions toward scripture and God is as difficult as any human relationship or interaction. The reader gains perspective and an enlarged capacity to see and hear things in new ways. Voicing is the response of the deep inner self to God's self-revealing love. New and authentic actions emerge from the encounter with the inner voice of God mediated through scripture. The four communication skills enhance the potentialities of dialogue.

A Sample of Biblical Dialogue

Dialogue is a template of transformation in scripture. The striking thing about the biblical record is the vast number of foundational events of God's self-revealing that are dialogical in form and substance. Dialogue is too pervasive in scripture and tradition to be reduced to a literary device only. Consider the dynamics of the burning bush dialogue between God and Moses (Ex. 3:1–4:20).

> God called to him out of the bush, "Moses, Moses!" And he said, "Here I am." Then God said, "Come no closer! Remove the sandals from your feet, for the place on which you are standing is holy ground." God said further, "I am the God of your father, the God of Abraham,

the God of Isaac, and the God of Jacob." And Moses hid his face, for he was afraid to look at God.

Then the LORD said, "I have observed the misery of my people who are in Egypt; I have heard their cry on account of their taskmasters. Indeed, I know their sufferings, and I have come down to deliver them from the Egyptians, and to bring them up out of that land to a good and broad land flowing with milk and honey...The cry of the Israelites has now come to me; I have also seen how the Egyptians oppress them. So come, I will send you to Pharaoh to bring my people, the Israelites, out of Egypt." But Moses said to God, "Who am I that I should go to Pharaoh, and bring the Israelites out of Egypt?" God said, "I will be with you; and this shall be the sign for you that it is I who sent you: when you have brought the people out of Egypt, you shall worship God on this mountain."

But Moses said to God, "If I come to the Israelites and say to them, 'The God of your ancestors has sent me to you,' and they ask me, 'What is his name?' what shall I say to them?" God said to Moses, "I AM WHO I AM." God said further, 'Thus you shall say to the Israelites, 'I AM has sent me to you.'" God also said to Moses, "Thus you shall say to the Israelites, 'The LORD, the God of your ancestors, the God of Abraham, the God of Isaac, and the God of Jacob, has sent me to you':

This is my name forever,
And this my title for all generations. (3:4–8, 9–15)

A Sample of Early Church Dialogue

Dialogue is a template of transformation for the formative leaders of the early church. Athanasius's (296–373) *Life of Antony* is considered a masterpiece of history. Dom Leclercq explains the lasting influence of Antony.

> He remained truly the Father of all monks and so in all milieus and in every period of the Western Middle Ages they considered themselves as truly his sons...St. Anthony represents for all, an ideal whose essential characteristic is its potential for realization in different ways. St. Anthony's life, then, for the medieval monks is not simply an historical text, a source of information about a definitely dead past. It is a living text, a means of formation of a monastic life.[7]

The striking thing about the text is that Antony's defining moment is a dialogical encounter. Antony hears the words of Jesus read from the gospels. He responds as if Jesus speaks to him directly. Antony acts. A type of dialogue occurs when Antony obeys the words he has heard.

> Six months had not passed since the death of his parents when, going to the Lord's house as usual and gathering his thoughts, he considered

while he walked how the apostles, forsaking everything, followed the Savior, and how in Acts some sold what they possessed and took the proceeds and placed them at the feet of the apostles for distribution among those in need, and what great hope is stored up for such people in heaven. He went into the church pondering such things, and just then it happened that the Gospel was being read, and he heard the Lord saying to the rich man, *If you would be perfect, go, sell what you possess and give to the poor, and you will have treasure in heaven.* It was as if by God's design he held the saints in his recollection, and as if the passage were read on his account. Immediately Antony went out from the Lord's house and gave to the townspeople the possessions he had from his forebears (three hundred fertile and very beautiful *arourae*), so that they would not disturb him or his sister in the least. And selling all the rest that was portable, when he collected sufficient money, he donated it to the poor, keeping a few things for his sister.

But when, entering the house once more, he heard in the Gospel the Lord saying, *Do not be anxious about tomorrow,* he could not remain any longer, but going out he gave those remaining possessions also to the needy. Placing his sister in the charge of respected and trusted virgins, and giving her over to the convent for rearing, he devoted himself from then on to the discipline rather than the household, giving heed to himself and patiently training himself. There were not yet many monasteries in Egypt, and no monk knew at all the great desert, but each of those wishing to give attention to his life disciplined himself in isolation, not far from his own village.[8]

A Sample Dialogue of the Modern Devotion

Imitation of Christ has proved to be the most influential spiritual classic in the history of Christian spirituality. Although the authorship of the *Imitation* has been contested since at least 1500, many accept Thomas à Kempis (1379/80–1471) as the writer. *Imitation* was written around 1420 and gained instant attention. The devotional classic is a product of the Modern Devotion, a movement started by Dutchman Geert Grote (1384) in the lower part of Germany. The men and women of this renewal movement came to be called the Brothers and Sisters of the Common Life. They formed congregations in cities and towns and lived in shared houses on ordinary streets.[9] John van Engen presents the shape of their spirituality.

> "Imitation" is probably a misleading term for their outlook. Their emphasis fell neither on imitation in a strict sense, nor on "mystic union," as in the teachings of many late medieval authors, but rather on an individual and affective identification with particular moments in Christ's life, chiefly his passion, the result or purpose of which was ideally fourfold: to "relive" with Christ his virtuous life and saving

passion, to have him ever present before one's eyes, to manifest his presence to others, and to orchestrate as it were, all of one's mental and emotional faculties around devotion to him. This emphasis was entirely positive: to have the New Devout live in Christ and Christ in them.[10]

The Imitation of Christ records poignant illustrations of direct dialogues. Christ speaking within the heart is the theme. Thomas writes:

> Our Lord Jesus Christ will come to you and will show you His consolations, if you will make ready for Him a dwelling place within. All that he desires in you is within yourself, and there it is His pleasure to be. There are between Almighty God and a devout soul many spiritual visitings, sweet inward conversations, great gifts of grace, many consolations, much heavenly peace, and wondrous familiarity of the blessed presence of God.[11]

The following dialogue from *The Imitation* brings these "inward conversations" into sharper focus.

> Speak, Lord, for I, Your servant, am ready to hear You. I am Your servant: give me wisdom and understanding to know your commandments. Bow my heart to follow Your holy teachings, that they may sink into my soul like dew into the grass. The children of Israel said to Moses speak: Speak to us and we will hear you, but let the Lord not speak to us, lest perhaps we die for dread. Not so, Lord, not so, I beseech You! Rather, I ask humbly with Samuel the prophet that You vouchsafe to speak to me Yourself, and I shall gladly hear You…
>
> My son, says our Lord, hear My words and follow them, for they are most sweet, far passing the wisdom and learning of all philosophers and all the wise men of the world. My words are spiritual and cannot be comprehended fully by man's intelligence. Neither are they to be adapted or applied according to the vain pleasure of the hearer, but are to be heard in silence, with great humility and reverence, with great inward affection of the heart and in great rest and quiet of body and soul.
>
> Oh, blessed is he, Lord, whom You instruct and teach, so that You may be gentle and merciful to him on the evil day, that is, on the day of the most dreadful judgment, so that he will not then be left desolate and without comfort in the land of damnation.
>
> Then our Lord answers: I have taught prophets from the beginning and I still do not cease to speak to every creature. But many are deaf and will not hear, and many hear the world more gladly than Me, and more easily follow the likings of the flesh than the pleasure of God.

The world promises temporal things of small value, yet is served with great affection; but God promises high and eternal things, and the hearts of the people are slow and dull. Oh, who serves and obeys God in all things with so great a desire as he serves and obeys the world, and as worldly princes are served and obeyed? I believe no one. Why? For a little benefit great journeys are undertaken, but for everlasting life people will scarcely lift their feet once from the ground. A thing that is of small price is many times busily sought, great contention sometimes rises over a penny, and for the promise of a little worldly gain men do not shrink to labour and sweat both night and day.[12]

A Living Human Document in Dialogue
Forces that Shape Life

To be in dialogue is to engage the center of the self with the center of the other. An understanding of what is at the heart of each can only assist the dance of dialogue. Anton Boisen was the father of the clinical pastoral care movement in America. Boisen imaged the human person as a "document" to be read and interpreted. He proposed that the depth experience of persons should be treated with as much respect as the historic texts of the Judeo-Christian faith. Each person is a living text that deserves a hearing in its own right. The pastoral care movement brought respect to each person as a "living human document." The movement acknowledged that the process of engagement with the living text of another person is "inherently dialogical."[13]

In Dialogue with God

Dialogues with God are interactions between God and living human documents. The living texts of these conversations deserve a hearing in their own right. That leads me to a story in which even the past and present tenses are in dialogue.

My story turns on the axis of dialogue like a wheel within a wheel. If the outer wheel is experience, the inner wheel is the experience in dialogue. The story is written in the present tense, and the spiritual journal catches it that way. Dialogues with God give direction, movement, and shape to the story. Many dialogues come from meditation on biblical revelation. Faith seeks direction through them.

Guides from the great rivers of Christian spirituality provide interpretive insights. Spiritual rivers flow down through Christian history. They converge into my story as the evangelical river, the contemplative river, a river through the desert, the stream of social justice, the river of holiness, the charismatic flow, and the incarnational river. The confluence of rivers came to the rescue. The insights are written in the past tense, and faith seeks understanding through them.

Each Christian river has its own stream of energy. Chapter 1 traces the energy of the evangelical river as my river of origin. I raft directly into a crisis of spirit. Chapter 2 retells the crisis of morality. Chapter 3 explores the crisis of calling. The crises swept me down the rivers of Christian spirituality. The crisis of spirit hit me first. It took nearly two years before I could face the pain of the moral crisis. And when the full extent of the moral crisis sunk in, I submerged into a crisis of calling. The experiences of these crises are never separate in reality. Spirit, morality, and calling converge; and dangerous rapids form like the inner dynamics of white water.

Chapters 4, 5, and 6 choreograph the insights earned from chaos. I identify three levels of prevailing teamwork for clergy, congregations, and denominational judicatories paddling together down the rapids of mission. Spirit, morality, and calling influence mission profoundly. Each level of teamwork encounters an increasing gradient and intensity of white water.

Along the way I learned the value of theological reflection. Christian thinking and living are like the two rails of a railroad track. The strength of the ties between the rails make the movement of the train more secure. Similarly, the strength of the ties between theology and life can make the future more secure in the face of evil. Theodicy is the "defense of God's goodness and omnipotence in view of the existence of evil."[14] Can God bring good out of evil choices? Choices enacted on the raging river are brought to chapter 7. I scout[15] the history of two words that trace their origins to the seventeenth century. Can the stories of optimism and mysticism make some sense of chaos? I believe so. The word stories explain why I am a Christian optimystic.

A Witness to God's Creative Love

My story is a witness to God's stubborn persistence and creative love. The odyssey asserts God's incredible mercy and grace. God, the magnificent One, creates rivers of love to reclaim life. God said to me, "Dwayne, you were the paddle captain on many river-runs over my living waters. You put in at your selection, and you chose to take out at your convenience. You enjoyed the adrenaline rush of adventuring. You invited others to join in on the river-runs. Now I am going to show you the real purpose of my rivers of love—not to offer adrenaline rushes, but to love people back to life. Always you were in control. Now you are powerless, out of control, and I will Captain you back to life." I attempted self-rescues, all to no avail. Only then did the Divine Captain take control over my rescue.

It came down to God's refusal to abandon me. Gordon Mursell wrote an epilogue to a majestic story of Christian spirituality, "A Spirituality for a New Millennium." Mursell's words resonate with my story.

> In scripture, life is a journey, frequently (indeed usually) undertaken without any certain knowledge of where we are going, a journey during which we are only briefly and intermittently in control. The experience

of exile and restoration, the collision between past blessings and present sorrows, the tension between the greatness of our vocation and the frailty of our natures—all these are explored in the Bible in ways that are enduringly relevant, and never more so than they are now. But something else is even more relevant: the extraordinary persistence of the God whom Christians believe in, the stubborn refusal of that God to abandon us, irrespective of the number of times we abandon God. The story of Christian spirituality bears witness to the countless ways in which individuals and communities have felt the presence and heard the call of that God, have been disturbed by the divine anger or delighted by the divine beauty, and have felt impelled to give all they had to give in response. The sheer attractiveness of the God who is revealed in Jesus Christ is in itself the strongest case for hope as we set out, like Abraham, not knowing where we are going.[16]

The Template of Transformation

MEMO: January 2005
TO: Dwayne Ratzlaff
FROM: Tom Bandy

Dwayne:

I think the most important thing the reader of this book must understand at the very beginning is that your understanding of "dialogue" is deeper and more complex than anything with which they might readily identify. Most people confuse "dialogue" with "an exchange of information." This has been encouraged by the "dumbing down" effect of contemporary media. Serious dialogue, in which participants "stake" their lives and reveal their deepest attitudes and assumptions, is a rare thing.

One of the most common mistakes modern people make is that they assume they are the ones to initiate the dialogue. They believe it is in their power to start a conversation or remain aloof from conversation. Therefore, every dialogue is like a miniature strategic plan. Your story...and the testimonies from distinct eras in history...reveal that the individual rarely initiates real dialogue. It is initiated from beyond ourselves, thrust upon us, as it were, by unforeseen circumstances, the unpleasant imposition of culture, or the moral interrogation of God. We do not seek dialogue; dialogue seeks us! People are adept at avoiding the conversation, whether in ancient or modern times, but dialogue has a way of catching up with us.

Real dialogue is not therapy, although it may have a therapeutic impact. It is really a joint process of discerning the truth. It is as if two or three people together peel back the layers of an onion. If it makes their eyes water and leaves a perpetual stink on their hands, that is preferable to not knowing what lies at the core. Therapy does not assume a "truth" to be uncovered, only a perspective to be unveiled or a conflict to be resolved. Dialogue is satisfied only with discerning clearly the relative proximity of existence and essence. That may indeed bring healing…but not contentment.

Real dialogue is not collective bargaining, although it may result in a practical plan of action. It is really an experience of mutual mentoring in which two or three people help one another align themselves with a purpose that is larger than they are either individually or collectively. It's not really about tactics or problem solving. It's about being "in sync" with the universe, with the infinite, with a destiny. Most modern debates aim at finding a way each party can fulfill autonomy without getting in the way of anybody else. Real dialogue is satisfied only with the surrender of autonomy to a higher purpose.

As you know, I am deeply influenced by the writings of Plato and the Stoics; Christians such as Origen, Augustine, the Monastic reformers, and Erasmus; and twentieth-century synthesizers such as Alfred North Whitehead, Miguel de Unamuno y Jugo, and my mentor, Paul Tillich. I want to acknowledge this publicly, because you have led the way to acknowledge the historical mentors with whom you are in dialogue. We share common ground as you dialogue with Moses, Antony and Athanasius, Thomas à Kempis, and a host of others.

Yet your description of Thomas à Kempis as a sample dialogue of "modern" devotion and subsequent reference to the therapeutic insights of Anton Boisen and the business insights of William Isaacs surprise me. I suggest that in contemporary times, amid Christian thinkers, the best known advocate of "dialogue" is Paul Tillich (and along with Tillich a host of theologians including H. Richard and Reinhold Niebuhr, and the many feminist and liberation thinkers that they either influenced or frustrated). Allow me to offer an additional context for your dialogue.

Tillich developed his well-known "method of correlation" in between the two European world wars, partly in confrontation with the rising fascism and partly in conversation with the emerging rationalistic culture. "Dialogue" is the natural inclination that makes humans human, the sign that there is more to life than survival, and the bridge to discern an "Ultimate Concern" that stands above, beneath, and beyond ourselves. Existence, through an infinite variety of cultural expressions, asks questions about life, death, meaning, and hope; and Spirit, through diverse expressions of religion, answers.

Yet this eternal dialogue is more complex than this. It is only possible for people to ask questions in the first place because a transcendent structure of Reason lies beneath all predictability and logic. The very fact of "asking a question" suggests that you are already connected with the source of the "answer." The very fact that you can doubt or yearn reveals that you are already one step down the road toward faith and reunion. On the other side of the correlation, Spirit can only "answer the question" through the cultural forms that are the expressions of existence. This means that the very act of intelligibility, understanding, or faith is itself limited and inevitably distorted. The fullness of Spirit simply cannot be contained in words, artistic creations, or technological innovations. Questions always anticipate answers; and answers are always, fundamentally, inadequate.

I hope you will bear with me as I elaborate the significance of all this for theology, religion, and, ultimately, your personal situation. Near the end of his life, Tillich presented the 1963 Earl Lectures to the Graduate Theological Union as a brief synthesis of his theological insights for the church. Even in 1963, observers had clearly identified the emerging postmodern, post-Christendom world emerging on the horizon. His lectures, entitled "The Irrelevance and Relevance of the Christian Message," stand as a bridge between two eras.

In such a dialogue Christian theology can develop in two ways. They are each distinct, yet neither can survive long without the other. The "theology of offense" has its roots in Paul's famous description of the gospel as "scandal and offense" and is articulated by Justin Martyr, the early Monastics, Luther and the Reformers, Karl Barth, Dietrich Bonhoeffer, the neo-orthodox movement, and some expressions of liberation theology today. The answers of "spirit" are "wholly other" than the assumptions of culture and stand in prophetic judgment over against them.

The "theology of mediation" has its roots in Peter's famous speech about God's universal invitation (Acts 10) and is articulated by Origen and Augustine, the later Monastics, Erasmus and the Renaissance, John Wesley, Hans Kung, the Vatican II movement, and some expressions of liberation and feminist theology today. The "answers" of Spirit lie hidden in the very nature and diversity of culture.

Both expressions of theology are legitimately biblical, and both are necessary for a balanced faith. Indeed, the one inevitably leads to the other. The "theology of offense" is not even possible without an accurate and detailed knowledge of the culture that it critiques, and the "theology of mediation" is not even possible without a profound and intimate awareness of the Spirit whom we seek.

One might say that the history of religion (and certainly the history of Christianity) is a tale of constant reformation and counterreformation. Each theology struggles with the other for ascendancy. The "balance" between them is a constant quest, difficult to achieve, that rarely lasts long. For our purposes, however, it would be better to say that the state of our souls—and the careers of our clergy—is a similar tale of constant reformation and counterreformation. Our spiritual lives strive for this same balance. It is difficult to achieve, and it rarely lasts long. No sooner are we satisfied with the state of our dialogue between existence and Spirit than either existence undermines our confidence in Spirit, or Spirit shatters our illusions about culture.

It is in this context that I find William Isaac's description of the four skills that form the building blocks of dialogue to be inadequate to explain the actual experience of Moses, Antony, or Thomas à Kempis. He believes these four skills to be listening, suspending, respecting, and voicing. Of course, he is writing this in a book about *business,* but he wants to extend these skills to be interpretive of *life itself.* In Tillich's perspective, Isaac represents a worldview of "circularity" that has its roots in classical humanism. There is a supernatural component to classical humanism, but it assumes that the gods and humanity are essentially on the same playing field and that they can dialogue pretty much as equals. And so we can listen, suspend judgment, respect the authenticity of our partner in dialogue, and then voice our own perspective in a supreme act of self-differentiation. These are the skills that lead to relativism. There is no Truth, Beauty, or Good to which all of our listening, suspending, respecting, and voicing should point or be judged by. Isaac's "dialogue" has no higher goal than just pragmatically "getting along with" other people so that we can achieve our autonomous goals.

These four skills are not bad things. Indeed, they are very, very good things. It's just that, as dialogue goes (or should go), they are not very comprehensive. The dialogue they shape will not ultimately resolve our profound feelings of guilt and shame, or resolve our profound intuition of alienation and emptiness. Such dialogue will not finally resolve our desperate experience of injustice or explain our deepest desires for love and acceptance. This has always been the problem with classical humanism, from the Stoics to American capitalism. It is merely pragmatic.

Tillich sees two additional conversation partners in the great dialogue between existence and Spirit.

The second conversation partner is the voice of science, technology, and progress. Tillich calls this the "horizontal" line. In contrast to the circularity of classical humanism (listening—suspending—respecting—voicing and then listening some more), the voices of the "horizontal line" are much more results-driven. They believe in inexorable logic and the triumph of human ingenuity. They remain convinced that human progress and cultural advancements will resolve the issues of poverty, hunger, suffering, loneliness, and loss. Existential questions will simply not arise, and therefore spiritual answers will be either irrelevant or reduced to psychotherapy. The voices of classical humanism find such utopianism inconceivably naïve, and yet this confidence in "controlling reason" dominates Western culture at this time.

The third conversation partner is the voice of transcendence that both anticipates and fears the in-breaking of God. Tillich calls this the "vertical" line. Spirit can be anticipated, discerned, and approached through the spiritual disciplines of faith. People will be afraid, surprised, and transformed through the apocalyptic revelation of the True, the Beautiful, and the Good. The voices of verticality discern a God above the gods; an Unconditional Absolute in which all else is conditional, temporary, and inadequate; and an Ultimate Concern that demands allegiance and weighs our best intentions. This Ultimate Concern is scandalous to classical humanism and offensive to controlling reason.

The contemporary church is caught in the middle of this larger, three-way conversation. While we can learn from Paul, Antony, Thomas à Kempis, and many others, our dialogue today is still unique. Our situation is not exactly their situation, and in some ways positively remote from their situation. The more denominations and local churches try relive the dialogue from the past, the more irrelevant they become to the dialogue of today.

Individual pastors and Christians are caught in this contemporary three-way dialogue, whether they like it or not. Their contribution to the dialogue may not be intentional. It may have nothing to do with the content or direction of their preaching and teaching. They contribute to the dialogue in nonverbal ways...how they behave, who they befriend, how they live, where they spend their money, and how they shape their lifestyles. Their moral indiscretions, emotional outbursts, career mistakes, and illegal acts, serious as each individual action might be, are only symptoms that Christian clergy and laity have fallen between the cracks or have failed to keep pace with this greater dialogue. The steady accumulation of all these things leads to a single outcome: irrelevancy.

There is a saying, "There, but for the grace of God, go I." It is condescension disguised as compassion in the heart of church leaders toward colleagues who have "failed." The vertical dimension of Spirit shatters that easy complacency. It would be more accurate for our contemporary situation if church leaders said, "There, in spite of God's grace, we have already gone." There are no innocents in the church. There are no blameless leaders in the church. It is not that one man or woman's failure has reduced the credibility of all, but that any leader's failure reveals the hidden sinfulness of all. God makes no distinction between those who contemplate evil and those who do it.

The circular dimension of classical humanism acknowledges the possibility of failure and the possibility of grace. The horizontal dimension of controlling reason affirms the impossibility of failure and the irrelevance of grace. But the vertical dimension of Spirit reveals the inevitability of failure and the absolute necessity of grace. Classical humanism quests for *phileos,* the perfect harmony of diverse peoples. Modern science and technology quest for *eros,* the autonomous act that creates its own destiny. But Spirit reveals *agape*, the good news that you are accepted *in spite of who or what you are.* Every person of sense eventually asks *where this conversation is going.* The conversation could lead to compromise, and it could lead to competition. Only in the vertical dimension does it lead to redemption.

CHAPTER 1

Rafting toward a Crisis of Spirit
A Metaphor of Life

White-water Rafting

The River Wild[1] is riveted in my memory. The movie has breathtaking white-water[2] scenes. I felt an inner resonance with the incredible white-water flows at a point where three rivers converge. A family sets out on a white-water adventure. The expedition is planned by an experienced rafter. Unexpectedly, they encounter robbers looking to escape by way of the river. The family become captives, and the adventure turns into an odyssey. Awed by the white-water chaos, I thought, "That's my life!" White-water rafting is the visual metaphor of my story.

Pursuing a compelling and absorbing vision is an awesome adventure. Two defining moments at the onset of my river-run stand out. Then, at midlife, I enacted a defining moment in reverse. The crisis changed the adventure into an odyssey[3] with white-water chaos[4] on every side. The experience of chaos is unique to each person. For me, it was like falling into a raging river of despair with only a rescue lifejacket[5] and a helmet.[6] I lost all control over my destiny—or so it seemed. It was a state of utter confusion. I was swept into a crisis of spirit, morality, and calling while river-running[7] God's rapids[8] of love.

The Evangelical River

Shaped by Crisis

Generations will never forget the crisis and chaos of September 11, 2001. It was a defining moment for a President and a nation. Stunned and horrified, I watched the events unfold on national television. People who survived the terror of that hour—and the families of loved ones who did not survive—are shaped by it. We who witnessed the events from a distance are irretrievably changed also. Crisis shapes us at the very core of our being. The heroism that emerged in that hour of attack has penetrated us in profound ways. We grasp for words to express the experience. Most other events appear tame by comparison to 9/11. Crisis and chaos are facts of life. Although sometimes we wish we had faced past trials with present wisdom, none of us is afforded that luxury. We are shaped by these events.

Albert B. Simpson (1843–1919) was shaped by crises that fashioned the very structure of his thought and life. Simpson's spirituality was emerging continually. He called the "hard places" among the greatest blessings of his life.[9] At age fourteen he had his first religious crisis, which threatened his call to be a minister. He called the choice a constraint upon his pleasures. One incident turned out to be the final straw. Buying a shotgun on the sly got him into big trouble with his parents. When his mother discovered the secret, she sentenced him to a "deep humiliation"; he had to return the gun and forfeit the money. The encounter settled the issue of his call to ministry. He gave up all side issues and chose to preach the gospel of Jesus Christ. However, the journey before him was a difficult one.[10]

At sixteen Simpson suffered a nervous breakdown. The crisis precipitated a great struggle of faith. Eventually he fell on his knees and dared a genuine confession.[11] He called it the crisis of his conversion. Although his health returned, a second crisis awaited him. By this time he had been in the ministry for ten years. He was despondent; he doubted his grip on God. This desperate struggle for sanctification began in 1874. It did not reach high water until 1881.[12] He testified:

> I look back with unutterable gratitude to the lonely and sorrowful night when, mistaken in many things and imperfect in all, and not knowing but that it would be death in the most literal sense before the morning light, my heart's first full consecration was made, and with unreserved surrender…Never, perhaps, has my heart known quite such a thrill of joy.[13]

The wonderful discovery of Jesus as Sanctifier changed everything for him. He described the crisis of sanctification (or baptism of the Holy Spirit) as a glorious union with the indwelling Christ (Gal. 2:20).[14]

The third great struggle of Simpson's life involved a complete collapse of spirit and body. He endured two other relapses of long duration in addition to his nervous breakdown at age sixteen. He was depressed. He had worked for years with the aid of medicines and ammonia; a doctor gave him only months to live.[15] At Orchard Beach, Maine, Simpson received Jesus as his Healer.

> [H]e listened to the stories of people who had received the experience of divine healing. It drove him to his Bible to ascertain if it could be so. Now convinced of its accessibility, Simpson raised his right hand to heaven and made "three great and eternal pledges" to God. He

described what happened next, "I arose. It had only been a few moments, but I knew that something was done. Every fiber of my soul was tingling with a sense of God's presence."[16]

Simpson's spiritual discoveries gave birth to a movement of deeper life and missions. It thrived throughout the twentieth century and continues into the twenty-first. When he became convinced of the accessibility of an encounter with God, he put in after it with intense resolve. He was a skilled river-runner over spiritual waters. At the center of his spiritual theology were encounters with Jesus Christ as Savior, Sanctifier, and Healer. He believed that the second coming of Jesus Christ as King could be advanced by taking the gospel to every nation.

Each crisis required the emergence of a new, distinct spiritual river to reclaim him. He was a courageous rafter who often explored alone. He understood that desperate times called for desperate measures. He was an adventurer rafting on the cutting edge. Others called him a "pathfinder" and trailblazer.[17] He was all go with God.

Vision for Adventuring

I soared over white water with Simpson's dynamic spirituality personalized. There were many invitations to encounter the self-revealing God. Simpson revealed the possibilities:

> He wants to reveal to us yet unexplored regions of glorious advances in the life of faith. He wants to call us to higher service, and to show us mightier resources and enablings for the work of life…God's blessing is too vast and our capacity is too great to be filled in a moment. We must drink, and drink, and drink again, if we would know all the fullness of the river of His grace.[18]

I was nurtured by this vision of high expectations and incredible spirit.

My journal records two critical moments that claim me to this day. The first moment graced me with new birth. It began with a family crisis. The death of my grandfather touched me to the core because it was my first real brush with mortality. He had lived a conflicted life, and his entire family felt the resulting wound. The heartache over his death caused me to rethink the direction of my present life and future destiny. The experience continues as a memory of vivid presence.

I am sixteen. It is Sunday evening. A friend and I decide to skip church but change our minds at the last moment. We walk into the service late and take a seat. Something happens that gives shape to the contours of my destiny. An altar call follows the message. I have a lively recollection of that moment. An inner voice says that this is my time for a decision, that God is calling me to choose. The impression is so strong, along with a sense of deep conviction. I respond to the inner call, walk forward, and begin a friendship with Jesus Christ. Attitudes change, as does my outlook on life. Joy surges through me.

I was marked by this crucial event. It was my initiation to the inner voice. That night a relationship began that turned dialogical downstream. A call to vocational ministry followed.

A transforming friendship with Jesus Christ is a gift of the evangelical river. The decision to say yes to the inner voice, to invite Jesus Christ into one's life center, is the most life-affirming decision. Evangelical rafters design rivercrafts to guide people into new life in Christ and to disciple them over this powerful reality. Clark H. Pinnock describes the role of the Spirit in the work of union with God.

> Spirit is leading us to union–to transforming, personal, intimate relationship with the triune God…The purpose of life is a transforming friendship and union with God…Spirit is Lord and giver of life, in creation and new creation. Spirit gives us creaturely vitality and resurrection newness. Spirit indwelling is a mark of a Christian (Rom. 8:9). New life is sharing in the Spirit (Phil. 2:1; Heb. 6:4). Created spirit is touched by uncreated Spirit, who introduces it to the living God…When we say yes to God, Spirit births Christ in us and transformation begins.[19]

There is more. My river of origin called out a unique command to the concept of sanctification. I sought a subsequent experience to conversion, influenced by Albert B. Simpson, one of my founding spiritual guides and a noted leader in the nineteenth-century holiness movement. Sanctification was identified as a death-to-self experience, at which moment the Spirit fills the consecrated believer. I committed to this expectation and embarked on a quest for an encounter with the Spirit. It was focused, intense, and persistent.

It happened late one night. I wrote the experience on a piece of paper that very night. The real-time record of that moment includes these words:

> I have become convinced that the baptism of the Holy Spirit is for me. As I read the book of Acts, I became convinced of it. The last few days I have been rejoicing and praising God in anticipation of the Holy Spirit baptism. At approximately fifteen minutes to midnight I was sitting on the couch, listening to the *Celebration of Hope* (musical) tape. I was not in deep meditation, but I was just waiting upon Jesus. Suddenly, without any warning, the Holy Spirit (a power) entered me; and my whole being quaked (as if electricity shot through my body), my heartbeat increased greatly…Just as suddenly my body relaxed. However, there was a strong tingling sensation in my hands for about ten minutes afterwards. I thought to myself, did it really happen? The tingling was still so strong in my hands I couldn't doubt it…

An awareness of the Spirit's presence and power came from that encounter. All doubts vanished about my call to vocational ministry. I had no idea how critical a role this event would play in the future. The record of this experience served as a continual reminder of that moment when God set me apart for ordained service. The record will resurface as hope when I become desperate for another Spirit touch. This powerful yet gentle energy field returns again.

Simpson connected the mystery of these two critical moments around Paul's startling words about the indwelling Christ (Col. 1:27). Here was an evangelical mysticism for every crisis and all situations, the ever-present presence of the indwelling Christ.[20] The two defining moments of new life in Christ and Spirit-filling for holy living and effective service were fused together by this revelation of the fullness of the indwelling Christ. Simpson presented them as two distinct moments in the life of faith. My experience was consistent with that timeline.

I witnessed to hearing an inner voice at my conversion. I found Simpson's teaching on the inner voice years later. Simpson merged the experience of the indwelling Christ with a message from the Quietists. The synergies came out of his experience. He wrote about it in a tract called *True Peace*. Simpson uncovered "an old mediaeval message" and claimed it as "one of the turning points" of his life. *The Birth of a Vision*[21] includes my written response to the centrality of this turning point as a transformative experience of prayer. It was a message about listening to the "still small voice" of the Spirit and the power of stillness (1 Kings 19:12, KJV).[22] Simpson found a way through the creeds to the inner Christ via the voice of the Spirit.[23]

> It was an old mediaeval message with but one thought, which was this, that God was waiting in the depths of my being to talk to me if only I would get still enough to hear His voice...As I listened, it became to me the voice of prayer, and the voice of wisdom, and the voice of duty. I did not need to think so hard, or pray so hard, or trust so hard, but that "still, small voice" of the Holy Spirit was God's answer to my secret soul, was God's answer to all my questions, was God's life and strength for soul and body, and became the substance of all knowledge, and all prayer, and all blessing; for it was the living God Himself as my Life and my All.[24]

A Center for Renewal

I changed rafts easily. I served as pastor, evangelist, teacher, and author. I got off the raft of teaching in theological education and returned to the raft of pastoral ministry. It was a conflicted decision. I enjoyed teaching future pastors, but the challenge of a new experiment in a historic church won the day. It was a decision that would change many things. My journal entry records the anticipation of the first day in a new ministry.

> A new season of life begins today. This is my first day as Senior Pastor...New beginnings, new seasons of life hold such promise. I have come to this new ministry with high expectations. I come with a deep sense of God's calling. I am here to develop and test a new model of ministry ("cure of souls") and all that pertains to it...

That summer we broke ground for a new church complex in a new suburb. Phase 1 called for a beautiful new sanctuary of worship. Phase 2 envisioned a multipurpose building for family ministries.

I presented a "Challenge for the Future." Below are excerpts from that document.

> The future holds such promises, such hopes for new beginnings. We are at a critical stage in the life of our church…It is imperative that we hurdle the challenge before us. I believe that every major phase of a church's development is precipitated by a crisis, a point of challenge, a decision that involves great risk and faith. It may be a building program, or a decision to enlarge the pastoral staff, or to find new forms of ministry to replace the old ways of doing things. Some churches draw back, because the risk seems too great, too foreboding, too uncomfortable. Often, it takes years for a church to recover from a decision to withdraw from the challenge before her…

We pursued our vision in our new location. Our Statement of Vision was revisited annually and recast by our progress. We formulated one-, three- and five-year goals. The statement began:

> At the heart of our vision is the desire to be a *Center for Renewal.* The Protestant Reformation was nurtured on the vision of the church as a renewed church always renewing. We know that God desires to pour out the new wine of the Gospel through new wineskins in every generation.

The biblical inspiration came from Jesus' kingdom dream (Isa. 61:1–3; Lk. 4:14–21). The vision encompassed renewal through worship, discipleship, personal care, spiritual direction, counseling, outreach, stewardship, modeling, and the spiritual dynamic of the fullness of Jesus Christ. The mission was to reach out to hurting people: to help them find God in the center of their brokenness, to invite them to encounter Christ's healing presence, and to empower them to rebuild their lives.

I was given every edge for adventuring over these powerful rapids. Vision came easily. Creativity was applauded. I resigned as senior pastor after five years and four months of adventuring with a vision, adrenaline rushes, and exhausting river-runs–including two building programs, adjunct teaching, and personal continuing education. The construction of Phase 2, our multipurpose building, had commenced. The cement for the foundation had been poured. I was in shock, in burnout, in a crisis of spirit. It ended with deep shame and humiliation. I never dreamed of such a take-out.

Now overboard, I was protected by two vital pieces of survival gear gifted from the evangelical river: a rescue lifejacket and a helmet. The spiritual equipment that protected me in the struggle for survival were the "breastplate of righteousness" and the "helmet of salvation" (Eph. 6:14, 17). Not mine, but

Christ's own. Christ protected my heart with his incomparable righteousness (Rom. 3:21–26). Filthy rags were all I had to offer. I never lost the memory of the God-graced moments in my life or the experiential reality of the indwelling Christ.

The Source

Similarity and diversity exist within each Christian tradition. The evangelical river is no different. Tributaries of the evangelical river converge and diverge at various points. Timelines about new birth and filling remain a point of divergence.

All evangelicals trace their origins to scripture and search out allies in history. All tributaries of the evangelical river flow through the redemptive work of Jesus Christ, to Paul's conversion on the road to Damascus, all the way through Martin Luther's tower experience. Luther discovered the biblical meaning of righteousness in 1519. In the Reformer's own words:

> I hated that word, "justice of God," which, by the use and custom of all my teachers, I had been taught to understand philosophically as referring to formal or active justice, as they call it, i.e., that justice by which God is just and by which he punishes sinners and the unjust.
>
> But I, blameless monk that I was, felt that before God I was a sinner with an extremely troubled conscience. I couldn't be sure that God was appeased by my satisfaction. I did not love, no, rather I hated the just God who punishes sinners. In silence, if I did not blaspheme, then certainly I grumbled vehemently and got angry at God. I said, "Isn't it enough that we miserable sinners, lost for all eternity because of original sin, are oppressed by every kind of calamity through the Ten Commandments? Why does God heap sorrow upon sorrow through the Gospel and through the Gospel threaten us with his justice and his wrath?" This was how I was raging with wild and disturbed conscience. I constantly badgered St. Paul about that spot in Romans 1 and anxiously wanted to know what he meant.
>
> I meditated night and day on those words until at last, by the mercy of God, I paid attention to their context: "The justice of God is revealed in it, as it is written: 'The just person lives by faith.'" I began to understand that in this verse the justice of God is that by which the just person lives by a gift of God, that is by faith. I began to understand that this verse means that the justice of God is revealed through the Gospel, but it is a passive justice, i.e. that by which the merciful God justifies us by faith, as it is written: "The just person lives by faith." All at once I felt that I had been born again and entered into paradise itself through open gates. Immediately I saw the whole of Scripture in a different light. I ran through the Scriptures from memory and found that other terms had analogous meanings, e.g., the work of God, that

is, what God works in us; the power of God, by which he makes us powerful; the wisdom of God, by which he makes us wise; the strength of God, the salvation of God, the glory of God.

I exalted this sweetest word of mine, "the justice of God," with as much love as before I had hated it with hate. This phrase of Paul was for me the very gate of paradise.[25]

I counted on Luther's discovery when catapulted by the seventh commandment. I did not risk my rescue on anything I had done to deserve the free gift of God's righteousness. My only hope was in God's grace given as gift through the atoning work of Jesus Christ—as declared by Reformation theology—by grace alone, through faith alone, on account of Christ alone. I anchored hope in the God that Martin Luther had discovered to the Reformer's great joy and to my great relief.

Luther's "tower experience" identified the source of the two critical moments of new birth and Spirit-filling that shaped me. Converting grace and sanctifying grace flowed downstream from the eternal spring of God's righteousness. The "breastplate of righteousness" and the "helmet of salvation" were fastened securely to God's justifying grace through faith in Christ. I never lost hope in the source of justifying grace by faith **even though** I struggled to stay afloat, was out of spirit, and could not always see a new future downstream.

The Facts

Here are the details of my story. I served as an ordained pastor within the evangelical river, a river that treats adultery with the utmost seriousness—and I still believe justly so. I fell hard against the seventh commandment (Ex. 20:14). Chapter 2 tells the story of my crisis of morality. I was overboard and empty in spirit. I felt the evangelical river could forgive but not forget. The decision to leave my marriage and continue the relationship after my resignation added to the tension. My river of origin viewed it as a collapse of personal holiness, a desecration of the marriage covenant, and a breakdown of pastoral trust. Going against everything I believed left many personal issues unresolved. I was offered a pathway to reconciliation and healing. The reconciliation of marriage was a central issue. I met with the discipline representative throughout the two-year period. I chose another path in the end. All this while emptied and broken in spirit.

In-between Time

Stuck in an Eddy

I did not know what to do. I was vocationless. I decided to serve as an independent church consultant during this in-between time. It was like being stuck in an eddy[26] without a raft. I found seeds of hope in the thinking of Harrison Owen, the founder of *Open Space Technology,* a work on personal and organizational transformation. Owen was trained as an Episcopal priest.

Owen says that at the core of every person, organization and culture is "Spirit"—a "stream of energy" at the heart of all things. At one point he calls it "pure, raw human energy." Spirit may be "awesome and exciting, but it does tend to make a mess." He contends that a leader must learn how to "work with Spirit." A culture is "the dynamic field within which Spirit is shaped, formed and directed." His concept of "chaos" carries the seeds of new beginnings. Certainly my "mess" left me broken and emptied in spirit. But where was the new? Owen explains:

> Organizations at the edge of transformation are messy. To managers, and others for whom the established liturgy (form and structure) is everything, it is not only a mess, but disaster, for the old form is in disarray. The Spirit of the organization appears as random, disorganized bursts of energy. Chaos. That is the bad news.
>
> The good news is, that for the first time in a long time, Spirit is in evidence. The question is how to convert a mess into an opportunity. Or, how do you bring order out of chaos? The initial response is likely to be an attempt to "slap" some arbitrary structure "on top" of the chaotic Spirit, but the chances that this arbitrary structure will also be appropriate and fit, are not very high.[27]

I wanted to "slap" a quick fix over my chaotic spirit. I contended that a transfer of ordination would be the best fix possible. "Please do not ask me to start all over again," cried my winded and wounded spirit. An initiative was set in motion. Social justice and evangelical representatives exchanged letters over the transfer of ordination. A transfer was denied; I was under discipline. Genuine repentance was at issue, as well as the restoration of marriage. Each river had a different view, so the effort ended. The endeavor underscored the vastly different expectations. Embedded in the exchanged letters was a deep theological impasse over marriage, divorce, and ordination. The social justice river described the offense as sexual misconduct. It viewed the issues as sexual abuse and violation of clergy trust. Reconciliation of marriage was not at issue. Both rivers came to the situation from different angles. The result was two restorative agendas that differed greatly.

Never explored in the institutional exchange was the depth dimension. I had to go deeper. I needed to access the subterranean issues of the heart. A transfer of ordination would have provided structure at the expense of spirit. Owen says we have to return to the "depths" to understand the process of transformation.

> Transformation begins in earnest when Spirit is driven down into the Depths. As the old way disappears and the new has yet to arrive, the experience is that of being down in the Dumps. Despite the pain, it is only from the Depths that one can perceive clearly what is basic and what is incidental. And it is the function of *leadership* to "take point" on the trip. With this perception comes perspective, which in turn

provides the possibility of seeing things in a new way. Hidden potential, previously locked away in the old way of doing business, as expressed by the old Covenant, is unveiled; the seed of a new idea, a new vision. Although it may look very much like the old Vision, it is deeper and richer.[28]

The decision by the evangelical river to refuse the transfer of ordination was a good decision. The subsequent decision of the social justice river to require me to start all over again was another good decision. Both decisions angered me. But the decisions forced me down into the "depths." Or as I experienced it, down into the "dumps." I had to return to spirit.

Returning to the Depths

Can leadership with integrity refuse to work in the realm of spirit? Again, Owen brought clarity to my need to start all over again. I did everything possible to avoid starting over. He claims that the most important task of leadership is to work in the realm of "Spirit."

> I take it as a given that Spirit is the most critical element of any organization. With Spirit of the appropriate quantity, quality and direction almost anything is possible. Without Spirit, the simplest task becomes a monumental obstacle. Furthermore, it is in the Domain of Spirit that leadership operates. While it may be true that Leaders have a multitude of very practical tasks, they have one task which outweighs all others, to empower Spirit.[29]

I spent the first year trying to avoid it. I accepted the inevitable by the end of the second year. I returned to spirit, arguing all the way.

Owen warns about returning to the depths. It is fraught with danger. He tells a tale about a dragon. I did not encounter a dragon in the depths; however, I did come face-to-face with a "Wild Man." I cannot say that I have made friends with him, but I have come to respect the power of his presence.

A Rescue Mission

Harrison Owen gave me new hope and fresh insight into the flow of personal transformation. But it was the salvage mission of multiple rivers of Christian spirituality that made recovery possible. God designed an emergency response team. They did not come to my rescue at once, but moved on different rafts down divergent rivers at different times. Together they breathed new life into my water-logged lungs. Admittedly, I refused a rescue attempt by my river of origin, given the conditions of retrieval.

A Diverse Rescue Team

I would like to say that I navigated the chaos like a skilled paddle captain. I did not navigate well. I would like to report that I acted out the good training that informs a white-water rafter what to do when capsized. I cannot make that claim either. I was in peril. I needed a rescue by the Divine Paddle Captain.[30] I felt unable to act in accord with the manual.

The social justice river came to the rescue with both friendship and process. I engaged ministers from the social justice river through consulting work. Clergy represented a diverse mix of conservative and liberal theologies. Chapter 2 tells my story of hope restored by the social justice river. Other rivers joined the reclamation project.

Each river brought a precious gift. This experiential realization has made me an advocate for the streams of Christian spirituality. All streams are vital to a dynamic Christian spirituality. Jim Wallis claims that a new ecumenical spirit is emerging. In an article entitled "All Together Now," Wallis asserts:

> From the strength of our church traditions has come a new ecumenical spirit for the twenty-first century. Today the denominational ties and loyalties that Christians feel are weaker than ever. Yet never before have Christians been more interested in traditions other than their own. Many people find themselves drinking from the wells of spirituality far afield from where they began.[31]

Richard Foster observes a similar trend:

> Today a mighty river of the Spirit is bursting forth from the hearts of men and women, boys and girls. It is a deep river of divine intimacy, a powerful river of holy living, a dancing river of jubilation in the Spirit, and a broad river of unconditional love for all people. As Jesus says, "Out of the believer's heart shall flow rivers of living water" (Jn. 7:38).
>
> The astonishing new reality in this mighty flow of the Spirit is how sovereignly God is bringing together streams of life that have been isolated from one another for a very long time.[32]

The risks increase in a raging river of converging currents. The water hydraulics[33] become more intense. Rafting skills are put to the ultimate test from the put-in to the take-out. The cause of these dangerous rapids is the diverse positions on theology, mission, and destination. The skill of navigating theological impasse is among the greatest tests. Theology in conflict is no small challenge for the spirit of convergence. Convergence at the precise point of spirituality gives hope for access to the depth dimension of our personal stories.

The Adrenaline Rush

I was a creation of a high-speed evangelical river. The motivational mission was to challenge people with the claims of Jesus Christ and invite a forever friendship with him. No sacrifice was too great for an adventure with so much at stake for so many. The biblical vision gave me a high-speed adrenaline rush. I became an addict, and the addiction contributed to marital neglect and emotional burnout. These factors contributed to my moral breakdown.

Dialogue with God emerged out of the crisis, becoming the form of transformation. But it did not deliver me from my crisis.

On Experiences of Being Capsized

MEMO: January 2005
TO: Dwayne Ratzlaff
FROM: Tom Bandy

Dwayne:

The image of white-water rafting is just as powerful for me as it is for you. I often contrast the experience of an established, traditional church to the experience of an emerging, postmodern church as the difference between canoeing on a misty pond and rafting down the Colorado River during the spring thaw.

Most church leaders are trained to use sixteenth-century technology to paddle out onto a quiet lake with a few intimate friends. There they will eat lunch, engage in polite conversation, contemplate the presence of God, and then paddle home again. They are ill-equipped for the contemporary world of speed, flux, and change. Today they are rafting down a turbulent, uncontrollable river, and their "oar" isn't even in the water 60 percent of the time. Increasing numbers of these leaders are falling out of the boat.

Of course, that isn't the only way church leaders are finding themselves in the water. Many other churches have been sinking lower and lower in the waves for several decades. They have fewer resources, ever smaller crews, empty cargo holds, and are losing momentum. More than one church has simply sunk, quietly and without fanfare, with the captain literally stepping over the railing into a life raft. Unfortunately, the pensions, placement processes, and continuing education opportunities that once stocked the life raft are also disappearing. Leaders are apt to find themselves swimming for their lives with fewer "ships" to pick them up.

Who is to blame for this state of affairs? It is easy to blame changing culture, inadequate seminary training, or insensitive denominational oversight. It is much harder to blame leadership itself, or to address one's own personal failings of faith, attitude, self-discipline, and skills. Yet it is hardest of all to think that the ultimate responsibility for so many sunken ships and capsized leaders is with God. Could it be that behind all the stress of being capsized stands a greater purpose, a larger providence, which is God's own doing? God, after all, is the "Apocalyptic One," always doing the unexpected, always turning us upside down and inside out. True, our moral failures can precipitate us overboard, and we deserve to be blamed. I speculate, however, that if it were not our moral failure that precipitated us overboard, perhaps God would find some other way to do it.

I suspect what we need today is more capsized Christians. We need more Christians who have been precipitated out of their complacency and self-assurance to learn what it is really like to depend on God and God alone. Perhaps if more capsized Christians could then become captains of ecclesiastical ships, they would be less likely to run out of steam or sink in a storm.

You have turned the experience of being capsized into an odyssey of faith. Most Christian leaders today are familiar with only one, or at best two, of the rivers that contribute to the wider ocean of God's mission. And their familiarity all too easily breeds contempt—or at least condescension toward the travelers from other rivers. One benefit of being "swept away" from the river of your content is that it forces you to become intimately acquainted with the peculiar grace discovered in alternate waters.

CHAPTER 2

Capsized into a Crisis of Morality
In Dialogue with the Paddle Captain

A Change of Rafts

I grew up in a loving, faith-filled home that befriended Christ and nurtured a call to ministry in a church noted for great vision and action. All my remembered Christian life occurred between the banks of one evangelical denomination. Not in my wildest imaginations did I anticipate the take-out that would be mine as a pastor of a growing congregation within a dynamic denomination. A doctor of ministry program became one of the watershed experiences of my life. I was introduced to spiritual formation and the morphology[1] of spiritual rivers. The protective shield around my self-identity began to crack. I accepted the pain of being human at a deeper level. The change began with an approach to learning called the case study method. Participants were asked to write out a personal snapshot of a ministry event and submit it to the peer group for counsel. By the end of the cases many presenters needed blood transfusions. The fact that Henri Nouwen's book *The Wounded Healer* became a mentor-friend reveals how the case study method affected me. At the end of the first three-week component of the program I committed to five areas of growth. The first three areas encompassed three new commitments: to nurture my marriage, to cultivate the inner journey of self-understanding, and to risk transparency within interpersonal relationships.

The three commitments never stop tracking me as felt needs for growth. All three commitments confront one another in an extraordinary set of events. I liken it to a perfect storm. Circumstances converge. The raft changes from teaching in theological education to a position of senior pastor in a historic church. I return to pastoral ministry to explore the model of pastor as spiritual guide. I am adventuring over my vision of a *Center for Renewal*. The adventure has been exhausting, but has been accompanied by many adrenaline rushes. The compensation of results and fulfillment has been more than equal to the sacrifices. We achieved goals toward our five-year strategic plan. We constructed a new church complex in a new suburb and celebrated ministry there. However, a pastoral care event set in motion a series of choices and actions that will, over time, lead to my resignation.

Theological education introduced me to the contemplative river. I experimented with *Lectio Divina,* Benedictine, Hesychast, and Ignatian ways of prayer. I saw the potential for a powerful convergence between the evangelical and contemplative rivers. In Ignatian prayer, I saw a way to pay closer attention to the still, small voice that I had heard at my conversion and many times since. Ignatius, a contemplative in action, brought a powerful dynamic of mission to the contemplative experience. I believed the *Spiritual Exercises of St. Ignatius of Loyola* could enhance the possibilities that Albert B. Simpson attributed to the inner voice of the Holy Spirit. I felt that these two rivers together–the evangelical and the contemplative–could open me to real dialogical encounters with the indwelling Christ. The effect would be a deepening of intimacy that would touch me at the marrow of my bones and overflow into mission. Because the inner Christ is made real to experience through the agency of the Spirit, it was my heartfelt desire to live more fully in this reality. I decided to enroll in the *Spiritual Exercises in Daily Life*. The *Exercises* turned a reflective relationship with the Paddle Captain into a dialogical one. The crises of morality and dialogue emerged and converged together.

I retreated at an Ignatian college regularly, and also attended a one-week spiritual retreat based on the *Exercises*. I participated in Ignatian workshops, enrolled in a master of theology program to do advanced study in the spirituality of Saint Ignatius, and taught courses on the *Exercises* and integrated the spirituality into my growth group ministry at church. Yet I felt a missing element. I had never experienced the *Spiritual Exercises in Daily Life* in a director-directee relationship. That missing dimension would be made up through a thirty-one-week experience under spiritual direction.

The Contemplative River
Paddle Strokes of the Exercises

The Contemplative river is about conscious relationship with God. The river encompasses various tributaries or traditions of prayer. These tributaries of interior prayer go very deep to all levels of consciousness. We learn the purpose of contemplative prayer from a make-believe letter of Ignatius of Loyola.

> To help others to experience God directly, and to realize that the incomprehensible mystery we call God, is near…and…we can talk to him. This is the goal of the *Spiritual Exercises* journey. Do you desire that the Father, Son and Spirit share themselves with you? Do you desire to base your life choices and decisions on this personal sharing and communication? Then, by all means, enter into these *Spiritual Exercises*.[2]

The genius behind the *Spiritual Exercises* was Ignatius of Loyola (1491–1556). Born into a family of nobility, he valued honor and chivalry in his chosen military career. He was wounded seriously defending Spain. During recuperation, he read the gospels and *Lives of the Saints,* which opened him to a deep and radical conversion. He denounced wealth and lived in solitude for a time. Ignatius was transformed by a series of mystical encounters with God. The *Exercises* came out of these encounters.[3]

The dynamic movement of the *Spiritual Exercises* leads a person to one particular goal:

> to assist a person's growth into total spiritual freedom, with the unique ruling desire being to choose God, all ways always. Then, a person can live a discerning life–finding God in all things and responding to God's actual word here and now in every concrete situation through all of one's choices and actions.[4]

Discernment Requires a Guide

Contemplative river-running requires discernment. Real dangers lurk under the surface waters. For this reason a guide is essential equipment for running the interior currents of each prayer tributary. We learn the role of a director from the make-believe letter of Ignatius of Loyola to a person who desires to make the *Spiritual Exercises in Daily Life.*

> His very first task is to help you get beyond the barriers that prevent God from being personal with you. This may take a long time or it may proceed quickly; there may be a lot of teaching, explaining, dialogue and possibly some experimenting. However, once you have allowed the Lord to be personal with you, once you are free enough to allow your mystery to be touched by the Lord's mystery, then your guide moves into the second task. His second task is to sit on the sideline and let the Lord lead you.[5]

The prayer guide and retreatant sift through the reactions and spiritual movements with the aid of rules for discerning of spirits.

The *Spiritual Exercises* brought a dynamic change into my relationship with God. Authors who serve as guides over the river, William A. Barry and William J. Connolly, stirred me in the direction of conversation. Their book, *The Practice of Spiritual Direction,* became a mentor on my adventure of dialogical relationship with God. The authors define "Christian spiritual direction" as

> help given by one Christian to another which enables that person to pay attention to God's personal communication to him or her, to respond to this personally-communicating God, to grow in intimacy with this God, and to live out the consequences of the relationship.[6]

According to Barry and Connolly, the "contemplative core of prayer and of all Christian life is conscious relationship with God."[7] To this end there are two fundamental tasks of the director:

First, helping the directee pay attention to God as he reveals himself; Second, helping the directee recognize his reactions and decide on his responses to this God.[8]

The Mystery of Meditation

I raft into the mystery of a dialogical relationship with the paddle of the *Exercises*. The gospels are the primary focus of meditation in this movement toward freedom. The directee is invited to walk in Jesus' footsteps. First, I call to mind the *history* of the scripture passage *to make the past, present*. I read the passage slowly until the imagination grasps the details. The *composition* of the place comes next. As I imagine the place, *the past not only becomes present, but the present becomes part of me*. Then I ask for the *grace* that I seek. The scripture is now present to me, and I to it. I focus on *my particular needs*. I make available to the Lord myself and any particular area of my life that needs to be affected. Then I *listen* and *surrender* to the Lord's presence and words during the *contemplation*. I gaze on that which the Lord reveals to me through the scripture in view of my particular needs. This internal gaze leads to a *response* to what I am hearing from the Lord. I close with a review of prayer. I *reflect* on my experience. I *write* insights into what is happening within me. I record the *dialogue* in my journal.

Conscious Relationship with the Paddle Captain

Dom Augustine Baker (1575–1641), an English Benedictine monk explains the role of spiritual director as "usher."

> The instructor is to behave himself toward them all according to the quality and need of each spirit, always remembering that his office is not to teach his own way, nor indeed any determinate way of prayer, etc., but to instruct his disciples how they may themselves find out the way proper for them, by observing themselves what does good and what causes harm to their spirits; in a word, that he is only God's usher, and must lead souls in God's way and not his own.[9]

I began the *Spiritual Exercises in Daily Life* with an appreciation for the role of a spiritual guide. The guide would usher me into the Ignatian way of prayer. Seeking an experience of the way of Ignatius and the *Spiritual Exercises,* I entered into the director-directee relationship. I began with awareness that some issues could surface, but I recognized no pressing problem. The primary purpose was the experience itself, and through it, a further equipping into my vision of pastor as spiritual guide.

I commence the journey through the first week. The goal of the first stage is

> to be graced with intense sorrow and tears for my sins, while realizing that God loves me nevertheless–just as I am–and forgives me everything through the death on the cross of his son, Jesus Christ. Thus, I realize my own radical incapacity to follow God's call to me,

except in and through Jesus Christ. Defenseless, I stand open before the gratuity of God's love.[10]

Self-knowledge flows deep within the contemplative river. My spiritual director asks me to begin discerning the basic disorder of my personality. Ignatius said that each person needs to identify his or her basic disorder: the hook, Achilles' heel, or point of vulnerability. This is the point where evil can hook us and gain entry.

> The next day I begin the work of identifying my Achilles' heel. I meditate on the first sin, that of the angels—*pride*. I pray for the grace of pure intentions in all things and all things to the praise of God. Is *pride* the basic disorder of my personality, my point of vulnerability, my Achilles' heel, the point where evil enters? Is *pride* the root of my perfectionism, my need for control, my over-conscientiousness, my drivenness, my need to be accepted by everyone, my drive for success and knowledge, my competitive spirit, my need to win?

During open-heart surgery that same day, a member of my congregation dies. I had every confidence she would make it through the operation. That confidence is more than shaken; I am devastated. I had felt a special bond with her because of her illness, engaging spirit, and many visits in the hospital. I write these reflections in my journal the next day:

> I need your merciful love so desperately, Lord. I am devastated today...I am wounded...I have nothing to offer but my hurt right now. (A few days later, I continue to grieve.) My brokenness in church on Sunday, over her death, was a humbling experience. I am unable to get a hold of my emotions in my grief. I like to be in control. It's humbling when I'm not.

Also, I grieve over the sin that I have identified as my Achilles' heel.

> Pride is so deeply embedded in my nature. I do "crave admiration." I work hard to receive it. Pride is a form of "self-worship." Yes, my drive for knowledge and success is self-worship. And then, there is my obsessive-compulsive personality. How difficult it is for me to live with, and how difficult it must be for those who live and work with me. My "over-conscientiousness" is a heavy burden for myself, and others, to carry...Lord, I present my experience of sinfulness to you. I *know* that grace is active in me.

At the spiritual director's session, we co-discern that a convergence has occurred between spiritual and ministry journeys. My director suggests it is time to move to the next stage of the *Exercises,* the Kingdom Exercise,

> "to realize that, in spite of everything, I am called by Jesus Christ to labor with him in accomplishing his mission...I experience as God's personal call...the call of the Holy Spirit deep within me."[11]

I ask of the Lord the grace not to be deaf to his call but to be ready to hear and cooperate with his desires for me.

The contemplative river is an inner movement toward spiritual freedom. I find it difficult to move into the second week of the *Exercises*. I pray for the grace to know Jesus more clearly, love him more dearly, and follow him more nearly. A personal goal is the

> "transformation of my deep operational attitudes into those of Jesus through contemplation of his life, so that I will follow him unconditionally in the particular way to which he calls me…"[12]

A perfect storm begins to form. I have to deal with the deaths of five church members and friends over three months. I submerge in grief-work. Also, I continue to lament over how infected I am with pride. And then this thought from my journal:

> "Periodically, through the week, I have been fearful that the Lord might put me through some painful experience to teach me humility. But then I say, 'The Lord is not like that.'"

At a session with the spiritual director, I refer to a good intention hooked away. I reflect on my awareness of an emotional bond with a female member of my congregation. It is the result of mutual grief over her mother's death, one of the deaths cited above. I express the thought that the Lord is at work within me through these unexpected feelings. Journal meditations turn to my discomfort with emotional vulnerability. I return to the Kingdom Exercise to pray for the grace to hear and follow God's call in the concrete circumstances of my life. I follow Jesus with less spiritual freedom than when I began the *Exercises*. A journal entry records the struggle clothed in the words of spiritual warfare.

> Again, the word of the Lord to my heart is "Follow me." I am not following with the same *weightlessness* that I was only a short while ago. I asked the Lord to be patient with me while I worked my way through this situation, and especially, to keep me from falling. Before, Satan was on the outside, looking in. But now, unexpectedly, he has entered the walls of my fortress. He has caught me off guard. Completely unexpected! We are looking at each other, "eyeball to eyeball," inside the fortress of my life. Never has he been so near me, nor I so vulnerable to him. I feel the pain and struggle of the encounter. I need the Lord to keep me from falling in order that I may continue to follow Him in His kingdom work. I will to follow you Lord.

I meditate on the call of Jesus to "Follow me." Crisis and dialogue emerge and converge together.

I ask Jesus, "Are you Lord of my circumstances?"

The answer: "I am Lord of all."

At a session with my spiritual director, our co-discernment is that I stand on holy ground at this point in the *Exercises*. My journal records a collage of reflections.

> This is holy ground! The Lord is at work through this! You are where you need to be–in touch with your humanity–in the journey of the *Exercises*. There is also mystery here! The Lord will show the way. I am under attack by Satan. A graced ministry experience becomes the hook–the insidiousness of Satan! I am where I need to be in handling the issue. Don't do anything that Jesus isn't calling you to do. Remain in the eye of the storm.

The movement of the second week ushers me into the temptation of Jesus. I am into the seventeenth calendar week since I began this contemplative journey. My feelings range from sheer agony to wonderment that my life experience and flow of the *Exercises* could be in such synchronicity. I am fearful to tell any other person about the emerging crisis. I decide to raise the "Standard of Christ." My journal records this decision as a "turning point" for "flowing in grace." At a session with the spiritual director, we discern that "relationship is both gift and hook. It will always need discernment to remain gift…"

Another dynamic of the contemplative stream is the confrontation with personal evil. The goal of the Two Standards (Christ and Satan) within the second week is "to realize that laboring with Christ to bring the kingdom to be demands direct confrontation with the active forces of evil in myself and in the world."[13] Meditating on the Two Standards, I choose to raise the Standard of Christ for my life now and for the future. I am aware that water hydraulics are all around me. I am vulnerable, and I do not like it. I am determined to keep the Standard of Christ with the Paddle Captain's help. I reflect on the first two stages (weeks) of the *Exercises*.

> The first week…put me in touch with my pride, so deeply rooted within me. During the second week…I have been seeking the grace of humility. I never realized how close a companion humility would become. I realize now, that given the right circumstances, I am capable of anything–thinking of doing the unthinkable! This has been a humbling experience. I cannot prevail on my own. My dependence on the Lord is real if I am to live the Standard of Christ. To be so vulnerable to the enemy's schemes is very humbling. It causes me to cast myself upon the Lord for His help. Also, to respond to those who fail, with love and compassion.

A new discernment emerges at the session with my spiritual director. It continues with me through the remainder of the *Spiritual Exercises in Daily Life* and beyond: "Flow in grace, not ahead of it, or behind it." Spiritual friendship centered in Jesus is discerned as holy ground. I sense a return to equilibrium and the flow of grace.

I enter week three, where the goal is "to deepen personal love and compassion for the suffering Jesus, so that I desire to go all the way to Calvary with him."[14] I meditate on Jesus' suffering in the Garden of Gethsemane. I reflect:

> There is a "cross" involved in being faithful to one's calling: a faithful Christian, husband, father, and pastor. I feel that…I have been under severe attack from the "enemy." He wants me to be unfaithful to my calling. I have been attacked emotionally, mentally, and physically. I have been attacked to the core of my being. I have shuddered under the severity of it. I have experienced so many emotions these past few months. So many new lows, so many occasions when I felt my life was falling apart. Lord, as I journey with you through your passion, help me to be in touch with my own, that I might feel yours more deeply.

I feel that I am flowing in grace. Henri Nouwen's book *Compassion* becomes a mentor-friend. I celebrate intimacy with Jesus.

I enter Week Four, and my twenty-ninth week in spiritual direction, where the goal is "through contemplation of the Risen Jesus to become able always to see his victory in the cross."[15] The stages close with Contemplation to Attain Love of God. The goal of the "entire movement of spiritual growth is to be able to live ongoing discernment of God's call to me in every event of daily life and, so, to find God in all things."[16] I conclude the journey through the *Exercises* in the thirty-first week. I write a reflective letter.

> I have the deepest conviction–feeling that the Lord has been my "Counselor" through the experience of the *Spiritual Exercises*. Repeatedly…He has offered counsel each step of the journey. It has been a painful journey–"painful giftedness"–is the appropriate way to capture it. As I draw this period of my life journey to a close–the taking of the *Exercises*–I could not have experienced more deeply the truth reality of Jesus as my "Counselor." Lord, our love and intimacy is a gift beyond measure. Please, guide me deeper into this journey of communion with you.

The *Spiritual Exercises in Daily Life* ended, and with it the director-directee relationship.

In Dialogue over Paddle Strokes

The template of dialogue becomes more prominent as the moral crisis deepens. I am warned about the possibility of excluding myself from all that has been entrusted to me. *Discernment* winds through the tributaries of the contemplative river. Each feeling and act has a direction toward *consolation*[17] or *desolation*.[18] The wrong paddle strokes in dangerous white water can bring disaster.

"I am holding your life together, Dwayne."

Lord, only you can hold it together right now.

"I have given you so much to give, Dwayne. Don't exclude yourself from giving it."

[During the meditation I am reminded of a rule for discernment: "A decision made in consolation should not be reversed during desolation." This is not a good time to make a major decision.]

Lord, my only hope right now is that you will hold it together!

The "spiritual warfare" has become intense. I meditate on Mark 1:21–28, the cure of a demoniac. In dialogue,

"You are in a spiritual warfare, Dwayne…The enemy will surprise you, like he did with me in the synagogue. You must act decisively against the evil one."

The enemy has surprised me already. You know that, Lord. You have enabled me to withstand the evil one's powerful attack. He is back to subtler ways again, but very much at work. He is out to create violence.

"Continue in the path I have set for you. I have a special plan for you. Don't let the enemy discourage you. I am with you."

Although no longer in a relationship of spiritual direction, I returned to the *Spiritual Exercises* when the desolation came. I was able to overcome the desolation and to reaffirm obedience and mission. However, I am at burnout. I am in conflict to the core of my being. I pursue the vision of *A Center for Renewal*. I attempt to cope with the issues of my personal life. Over the next several months, the Lord continues to speak to me about being faithful to my callings and covenants, obeying God's voice, and assuring me of God's presence. I return again to the *Spiritual Exercises* and to the rules for the discerning of spirits. I revisit the Two Standards and reaffirm faithfulness.

I capsize within months. I am overboard into chaos. From a dialogue on spiritual retreat:

I have shed so many tears here, Lord. I have come to you with a broken heart again and again. I have agonized in prayer. I have failed. No one will know the tears I have shed, or the desire to be faithful…Lord, I have disobeyed. I have fallen. I have sinned.

"I will use you in the future. Tomorrow is another day. We will start new."

I confess to the sin of adultery. I resign, a spent and burnt-out pastor.

Streams in the Desert

Capsized into the Abode of the Demons

I capsize into the abode of the demons. Special skills are required for the undertow. A capsized rafter has to overcome the inner demons of the chaos. The rapids are fierce. The undercurrents can swallow and refuse to release a wounded rafter. The river is a desert experience. It was here that

> the desert Fathers [and Mothers] lived in silence and solitude, conscious of the severe temptations which the desert environment itself held. For these waste regions were the abode of the demons and the forces of evil, and so they saw their life as one of ascetical conflict, the life of Christian athletes. In the deserts, at the margins of human society, they sought God, and their own inner identity.[19]

The reality of the new river came suddenly. All that gave definition to my identity for all my adult life was swept away by the undertow of the moral fault, private confessions, and public record. The inner demons were unleashed with such force it would take many months for me to master them. I was propelled into chaos. The pain I had endured so far only remotely compared to the agony-filled waters in front of me. I will attempt to describe the desert streams before saying more about the inner struggle.

Mastering Chaos Overboard

Being on a raft in white water is very different from being in white water without one. You face both the physical and the mental challenges of survival. Mental black holes lurk on every side. It is warfare with the awesome elements of nature; it is a descent into hell. Spiritual warfare is a central reality of desert spirituality. Mastering inner demons with interior prayer is at the heart of the desert experience, particularly in the elusive world of the heart and mind.

How are we to understand evil in the world of the twenty-first century? Christian spiritual traditions agree on the reality of evil but disagree in their account of it. Walter Wink, a writer in the social justice stream, gives this account:

> I prefer to think of the Powers as impersonal entities, though I know of no way to settle the question except dogmatically...Generally, I have bracketed the question of the metaphysical status of the Powers, and have instead treated them phenomenologically–that is, I have attempted to describe the experiences that got called "Satan," "demons," "powers," "angels," and the like. Thus I speak of "demons" as the actual spirituality of systems and structures that have betrayed their divine vocations. I use the expression "The Domination System" to indicate what happens when an entire network of Powers becomes integrated around idolatrous values. And I refer to "Satan" as the world-encompassing spirit of the Domination System. Do these entities

possess actual metaphysical *being,* or are they the "corporate personality" or ethos or gestalt of a group, having no independent existence apart from the group? My main objection to personalizing demons is that they then are regarded as having a "body" or form separate from the physical and historical institutions of which, on my theory, they are the actual interiority. Therefore I prefer to regard them as the impersonal spiritual realities at the center of institutional life.[20]

C. Peter Wagner, a writer converging the evangelical and charismatic streams, traveled to Argentina to explore the dynamic spiritual renewal among the people. His observations about the spiritual awakening are in contrast to Wink's theory. Wagner identifies three levels of spiritual warfare at work in Argentina, as responses to personal beings of evil:

1. Ground-level spiritual warfare. This is the ministry of casting out demons.
2. Occult-level spiritual warfare. It seems evident that we see a kind of demonic power at work through shamans, New Age channelers, occult practitioners, witches and warlocks, Satanist priests, fortune-tellers and the like.
3. Strategic-level spiritual warfare. Here we contend with an even more ominous concentration of demonic power: territorial spirits… (Eph. 6:12).[21]

M. Scott Peck, a psychiatrist, provided a fascinating study into human evil. Peck did not believe in a personal devil, but as a Christian he did believe in human evil. When he could avoid the issue no longer as an open-minded scientist, he searched out an opportunity to observe an exorcism firsthand. As a result of his personal involvement in two cases, Peck concluded,

In both cases I was privileged to be present at their successful exorcisms. The vast majority of cases described in the literature are those of possession by minor demons. These two were highly unusual in that both were cases of Satanic possession. I now know Satan is real. I have met it.[22]

The drama of evil has to take into account all the data on human evil, including Paul's experience of inner conflict (Rom. 7:19). There is wisdom in the convergence of the diverging views among the traditions. I refer to the inner demons as aspects of the self-addictions that afflict me. A day of great liberation arrived when I accepted full responsibility for those self-destructing addictions, although it took time for me to arrive at that destination.

If it is true that malevolent beings employed the addictions to destroy me, it is equally true that I presented an inadequate counterattack. I have serious demon-busting ahead of me. The desert river forces a capsized rafter to confront the evil within. Life in the desert exists at the point where the forces of evil, and the redemptive power of God meet. Kenneth Leech explains the encounter at the depths of the desert river.

> [T]hat encounter with evil calls forth from all of us the resources which only the desert can give: the resources of spiritual renewal, the fruit of purification, of wrestling, of confronting ourselves against the stark reality of God. The life of the hermit points to a permanent need in the Church if it is to be a pilgrim Church, a wilderness people.[23]

I battled the evil within and was defeated. I am about to wrestle with evil again.

Dangerous Rapids

Evagrius Ponticus (345–399) was the first to write extensively about the spirituality of the desert. He settled in Egypt and lived as a monk. His eight thoughts, when allowed to linger, stir up our passions.

> There are eight general or eight categories of thoughts in which are included every thought. First is that of gluttony, then impurity [lust], avarice [greed], sadness, anger, acedia [noonday demon], vainglory, and last of all, pride. It is not in our power to determine whether we are disturbed by these thoughts, but it is up to us to decide if they are to linger within us or not and whether or not they are to stir up our passions.[24]

Evagrius presented a synthesis of *apatheia,* the right ordering of passion and agape, or spiritual love, as a remedy for the soul. Bamberger notes, "Purification of passions supposes love. Love fully flowers only when the passions are put in order."[25] Evagrius understood the context for this proper reordering, "You have been brought into apatheia by the mercy of Christ."[26]

Two weeks prior to the grief work that triggers an emotional bond, during the first week (of *Spiritual Exercises*), meditations invite me into an encounter with my personal sin history. The grace I seek is a heartfelt knowledge of my sins and faults–the hidden disordered and sinful tendencies underlying my decisions and actions, and the influence of the world on all this. At a meditation on the sin of Adam and Eve,

> I was captured by the aspect of Adam and Eve's sin that involved the sensual. The fruit was "a delight to the eyes" (Gen. 3:6). I was in touch with my own sensual attractions. I felt that the sensual within me was like a wild beast. It is well contained, controlled by discipline, but if I ever released the reigns, I would be capable of things that would lead to shame and confusion. Lord, I surrender my attractions to you.

The passion of lust, though present, was contained by discipline.

If the moral crisis had simply been the acting out of sexual fantasies, the appetites would have been satisfied long before the burnout phase of my ministry. One contributor of the sheer exhaustion was the emotional energy I expended in walking the path of integrity as I understood integrity at the time.

It can be argued justly that allowing another emotional bond to compete with the marriage bond is a breakdown of integrity. Many choices are made before bonding becomes adultery. The spiritual and emotional adultery come first. And then physical lust is satisfied.

Before the grief work that forged the emotional and spiritual bond, my journal reveals the disordered passions that concern me most. First week meditations reveal "excessive devotion to work and productivity" that track me for most of my ministry along with "over-conscientiousness." I live a life of extremes rather than balance. I describe myself as "obsessive-compulsive." My drive for "success," pursuit of "knowledge," concern for "reputation," need to be "one step ahead of everyone else–one-upmanship–competition in ministry (hidden, but real)"–all are named. As I reflect on the "seven deadly sins: sloth, lust, anger, pride, envy, gluttony and greed," I identify pride as the basic disorder of my personality. So much of my service is infected by pride, a form of self-worship. I grieve over how much I "crave admiration." I feel deep pain about my thirst for admiration in terms of caregiving. My journal reveals deep hurt over my pride, "so deeply embedded in my nature." Evagrius observes:

> The demon of pride is the cause of the most damaging fall for the soul. For it induces the monk to deny that God is his helper and to consider that he himself is the cause of virtuous actions. Further, he gets a big head in regard to the brethren, considering them stupid because they do not all have this same opinion of him.
>
> Anger and sadness follow on the heels of this demon.[27]

Anger follows hot on pride's heels. Evagrius continues:

> The most fierce passion is anger. In fact it is defined as a boiling, and stirring up of wrath against one who has given injury–or is thought to have done so. It constantly irritates the soul and above all at the time of prayer it seizes the mind and flashes the picture of the offensive person before one's eyes. Then there comes a time when it persists longer, is transformed into indignation, stirs up alarming experiences by night.[28]

The "fierce passion" of anger consumed me. It infiltrated all aspects of my life and infected all my relationships.

Debriefing a Disastrous River-Run

Occupied with the issues of survival, I look for self-rescues away from my calling. I live from place to place. I do not allow myself the luxury of therapy yet because I am not ready to submerge in the painful process of counseling. I need the little emotional reserve that remains to re-deploy in the workplace. Just keeping emotions in check during an interview is a major accomplishment. I decide to apply skills of vision, leadership, and strategic planning to a consulting ministry and to target non-profit agencies and churches. On the first anniversary of my resignation I obtain the first contract. I agree to lead a client through a seven–step vision-mission process. A seed of hope is planted.

I begin therapy. I attend the first of four counseling sessions offered and paid for by my denomination of origin. I am ready to move beyond survival needs. The therapist leads me through a timeline leading up to the moral crisis, the events surrounding the crisis, and all that has transpired since.

The assignment was to consider a possible distinction between "sin" and "woundedness." The second session led me through a systemic perspective of "family of origin" issues in both my birth family and my marriage within it. The assignment was to write observations about my family of origin. Also, I identified issues from my marriage. The focus turned to the "being" of Dwayne in the third session. I observed that my self-identity came through doing. Positive strokes came through accomplishment. I considered that it was easier to bond with women than with men and that I received considerable recognition and affirmation from women around doing. I acknowledged my "playfulness with women." [I now own up to it as "flirtatiousness."] The assignments invited reflection on two questions: (1) Who is the "being" of Dwayne? (2) What "boundaries" or "safeguards" are required? I devoted significant time to these two questions. I brought the answers to the final counseling session. I committed to six "safeguards" to prevent another crisis of morality and to to an orientation of life and service that evolve around "being," not "doing." "Doing" evolves around the axis of work and busyness. The desert streams call busyness a form of "moral laziness." James Houston explains:

> The Desert Fathers (a protest movement against worldliness in the early church) spoke of busyness as "moral laziness." Busyness can also be an addictive drug, which is why its victims are increasingly referred to as "workaholics." Busyness acts to repress our inner fears and personal anxieties, as we scramble to achieve an enviable image to display to others. We become "outward" people, obsessed with how we appear, rather than "inward" people, reflecting on the meaning of our lives.
>
> Busyness also seems to be a determination not to "miss out on life." Behind much of the rat-race of modern life is the unexamined assumption that what I do determines who I am. In this way, we define ourselves by what we do, rather than by any quality of what we are inside. It is typical in a party for one stranger to approach another with the question "What do you do?" Perhaps we wouldn't have a clue how to reply to the deeper question, "Who are you?"[29]

The therapist assigned two books: *Iron John* (Robert Bly) and *Generation to Generation: Family Process in Church and Synagogue* (Edwin H. Friedman), both of which offered deep insights into my adventure turned odyssey. In reflecting on the therapeutic work, I have a deepening awareness that I am standing on "holy ground," that my "descent" is filled with holy purpose.

The Wild Man in the Water

A far deeper work circled downstream. The greater fears came from all that lurked under the chaotic waters. I recall my fear of descent into the emotional aspects of pastoral care. This was my deepest fear, expressed only weeks before returning to parish ministry. The fear was not the capacity for compassion. My mission evolved around the axis of compassion and the mission of Jesus. I had genuine capacity for expressing compassion. The descent into compassion frightened me because it made me feel vulnerable and out of control. Strength and control had always been essential to my persona. An emotional bond shaped by grief work activated the descent into my deepest fears of parish ministry. I was destined to meet the "thing" that lived in the dark deep of the waters at some point. As hard as I fought the descent, and I struggled sincerely, the unyielding commitment to the emotional bond served as the channel of descent to the "thing."

In the dark deep of the desert streams, capsized and fighting for survival, I met the deepest fear in my emotional psyche—a "red horse." Robert Bly explains:

> Each man is given three horses that we ride at various times of our lives: we fall off and get back on...We need three skills, for each horse has its own sort of gait; each horse shies at different things, responds to a rider differently...Teachers and parents often tell us to skip the red horse. Some men did not live through the red in adolescence. Such a man then will have to go back to red later, learn to flare up, and be obnoxious when he is forty. Ministers often find themselves forcibly confined to white because they skipped red, and their congregations won't let them go back to it. But then they can't go forward into black...When a person moves into the black, that process amounts to bringing all of the shadow material, which has been for years projected out there...back inside. That process could be called retrieving and eating the shadow...When he does find those parts, and retrieves them, other people will begin to trust him.[30]

Riding the "red horse" was the "Wild Man." Bly continues:

> The Wild Man's energy is that energy that is conscious of a wound... The Wild Man's qualities, among them love of spontaneity, association with wilderness, honoring of grief, and respect for riskiness, frightens many people. Some men, as soon as they receive the first impulses to riskiness and recognize its link with what we've called the Wild Man, become frightened, stop all wildness, and recommend timidity and collective behavior to others. Some of these men become...Protestant ministers.[31]

I had never met the "Wild Man" until he called for me at midlife. Oh yes, there had been signs of his activity I was never prepared to accept. My love for risk-taking, adventuring, the flirtatious side of my persona, and the enjoyment of female affirmation—all pointed to the "Wild Man" in waiting. I never wanted to go down to encounter him because I was afraid of all that might be unleashed. So I waited, so to speak, until I was at the top of my vocation. Exhausted, obnoxious, rebellious, angry, and self-intoxicated (I did not care anymore), I swept away my covenants. I faced the "Wild Man" at that price. I accept the "Wild Man" as part of me now. I do not want to be the "Wild Man" again.

Emotional Triangles among Rafters

Insight continued when the therapist introduced the theory of emotional systems and the power of emotional triangles. The words of Edwin H. Friedman hit home with force.

> The emotional processes in a family always have the power to subvert or override its religious values. The emotional system of any family, parishioner or congregational, can always "jam" the spiritual messages it is receiving.[32]

I received clear guidance from the still, small voice, but was unable to retain it and felt helpless to follow. God's call was to stand faithful to all my covenants.

I was unaware of the power of emotional triangles. One of the most "pervasive" triangles for all clergy encompasses "the clergy's own personal family, the congregational family itself, and any family within the congregation."[33] Grief work forged an emotional triangle. Friedman's seven laws on emotional triangles revealed the futility of efforts to resist or suppress an emotional bond. The strategy to work with it only deepened it. Laws 1 and 3 address this opposite effect:

> 1. The relationship of any two members of an emotional triangle is kept in balance by the way a third party relates to each of them or to their relationship. When a given relationship is stuck, therefore, there is probably a third person or issue that is part of the homeostasis [balance].
>
> 3. Attempts to change the relationship of the other two sides of an emotional triangle not only are generally ineffective, but also, homeostatic forces often convert these efforts to their opposite intent.[34]

The discernment to commit to my marriage and continue the friendship failed. The strategy to apply a corrective to the emotional bond only deepened the bond. I strove to manage the three emotional systems: congregational, marriage, and friendship. I moved toward burnout and hit the wall of exhaustion. In desolation, nothing mattered to me anymore. The emotional processes subverted my core values. The discernment should have been a closure of spiritual friendship at the point I realized something critical: that I had developed a deeper emotional bond with a female member of my congregation than with my own spouse. The choices to manage the relationship were entirely mine. I was the pastor, the person entrusted to care with integrity.

I learned the dangers of secret keeping. After my spiritual direction ended, I kept the struggle a secret; and the secrecy added to its power. One of my "safeguards" is to find a safe outlet to share personal things. John Cassian (365–435), a desert father, addressed the great danger of evil thoughts kept secret. Evil thoughts need to be "brought out into the open."

> An evil thought sheds its danger when it is brought out into the open, and even before the verdict of discernment is proffered the most foul serpent which, so to speak, has been dragged out of its dark subterranean lair into the light by the fact of open avowal retreats, disgraced and denounced. Its dangerous promptings hold sway in us as long as these are concealed in the heart.[35]

Turning in the Paddles

I remember the day I came to the end of self-rescues. I gave up. I prayed for the grace of a "sign" to proceed. I capitulated. At a meditation on John 19:

> Lord, I feel like I've come to the end of myself and my future. I give you myself and my future. If there is any future for me at age forty-three, you are going to have to build it! I await your response. Come to my aid, O Lord…
>
> I pray for the grace of purpose, mission, and meaning.
>
> Meditating on Acts 4:23–37, I pray for the birth of the new world–energized by your Spirit. "Lord, you are carrying me. It's time to release it!"

A new world was about to birth, but not before the old was turned in. I had been a fool. I had faced demons with my own paddles of anger and argument. It would take time to complete the handover. Fortunately, the Paddle Captain is a relentless lover. From a mentor-author, Henri Nouwen:

> That is the struggle. It is the struggle to die to the false self. But this struggle is far, far beyond our own strength. Anyone who wants to fight his demons with his own weapons is a fool. The wisdom of the desert is that the confrontation with our own frightening nothingness forces us to surrender ourselves totally and unconditionally to the Lord Jesus Christ…Only Christ can overcome the powers of evil.[36]

Compulsion was at the center of the old ways: the compulsion to perform, to succeed, and to crave affirmation. Nouwen exposes the root cause of compulsion.

> The compulsion manifests itself in the lurking fear of failing and the steady urge to prevent this by gathering more of the same–more work, more money, more friends.

> These very compulsions are at the basis of the two main enemies of the spiritual life: anger and greed...What else is anger than the impulsive response to the experience of being deprived? When my sense of self depends on what others say of me, anger is a quite natural reaction to a critical word. And when my sense of self depends on what I can acquire, greed flares up when my desires are frustrated. Thus greed and anger are the brother and sister of the false self fabricated by the social compulsions of an unredeemed world.[37]

The compulsion was the steady urge for more work, more knowledge, and more affirmation. The fierce passion of my anger was a response to the deprivations of self-addiction. I capitulated! I turned in my paddles. The Paddle Captain took control of my rescue from the dangerous rapids. The rescue is a process, not a moment. The inner demons are overcome, but not overnight. The demons are contained, but not eradicated. The demons are brought to "apatheia, a state of abiding calm deriving from full harmony of the passions."[38] The proof of "apatheia" is

> "when the spirit begins to see its own light, when it remains in a state of tranquility in the presence of the images it has during sleep and when it maintains its calm as it beholds the affairs of life."[39]

The Social Justice River
In Dialogue with the Paddle Captain

I walked away from my calling. I lost all hope of new beginnings. I viewed the moral crisis as unforgivable on my river of origin. Everything within me said, "I am finished." I could not imagine restoration in view of the serious nature of adultery. I had no reason for hope. Nevertheless, I began to sense new stirrings of calling about five months after my resignation. I prayed for a deeper trust in God's care for me. At a meditation on Isaiah 41:9, a dialogue stirred me:

> "You are my servant. I have chosen you and have not
>   rejected you...
> You will proclaim my name again."
> When and where, Lord?
> "Soon...My glory will return."

Praying Matthew 27:45–28:20, a deeply meaningful image returned to me. I was surprised by its coming into awareness and wondered about the meaning of its return.

> The image of the risen Lord standing over me, with his hands on my head, while I kneel in front of him, returned. It has symbolized the anointing of the Spirit on my life.

"What are you saying, Lord?"

Reflecting on John 11:1–44, and the words, "I am the resurrection and the life," I was buoyed by the words,

> "Dwayne, I am resurrecting you from the ash heap of failure. You will rise again to serve me. I have called you and anointed you."

I was rescued by the unconditional love of the social justice stream. Searching for a new career during an economic contraction, I began a consulting service to congregations. I made a decision to visit ministers of mainline congregations. I telephoned churches, asked to speak to ministers, and requested appointments to explain a seven–step vision-mission process. I met two ministers from the same mainline denomination among the first churches visited. They gifted me with the embrace of compassion in action. One minister gave me my first consulting contract and involved me in a community of prayer that encompassed the streams of Christian spirituality. The second minister provided a church home and a map to a new beginning. Both ministers breathed new hope into my hope-less heart. I decided to respond to God's stirrings of calling. My network of support was threefold: an ecumenical community of mainline church ministers who met for weekly study, an outreach prayer ministry with whom I had begun a consultative relationship, and a mainline congregation that committed to sponsor me through the candidate for ministry process leading to ordination.

Rafter Solidarity

A network of rafters on the social justice river rescued me. Christians from mainline churches embraced me and showed me compassion in action. They demonstrated the meaning of human solidarity. I scouted the river that adopted me. The source of the river is rooted in justice, kindness, and humility (Mic. 6:8). Walter Rauschenbusch (1861–1918) is recognized as the "founder" of the modern "Social Gospel" movement in America.[40] Stephen R. Graham delineates the convergence of two rivers in the spirituality of Rauschenbusch.

> Despite the growing rift between the revivalists' emphasis on personal conversion and the focus of religious liberals on social concerns, Rauschenbusch kept the two firmly joined. He was convinced that social changes would only be lasting if they were nourished by "deep wells of personal religious life." He drew on many spiritual classics of the Christian tradition, including Augustine's *Confessions,* Thomas à Kempis's *Imitation of Christ,* John Bunyan's *Pilgrim's Progress* and Richard Baxter's *The Saints' Rest*.[41]

The social reformer believed that the Holy Spirit is the source of the church's power to fight social injustices.

We must open our minds to the Spirit of Jesus in its primitive, uncorrupted, and still unexhausted power. That Spirit is the fountain of youth for the church. As a human organization it grows old and decrepit like every other human organization. But again and again it has been rejuvenated by a new baptism in that Spirit.[42]

Rauschenbusch claimed the Lord's Prayer as "the great charter of all social prayers."[43] The father of the social gospel said that when Jesus addressed God as "Our Father," he

spoke from that consciousness of human solidarity which was a matter of course in all his thinking. He compels us to clasp hands in spirit with all our brothers and thus to approach the Father together. This rules out all selfish isolation in religion. Before God no man stands alone. Before the All-seeing he is surrounded by the spiritual throng of all to whom he stands related near and far, all whom he loves and hates, whom he serves or oppresses, whom he wrongs or saves. We are one with our fellow-men in all our needs. We are one in our sin and our salvation. To recognize that oneness is the first step toward praying the Lord's Prayer aright. That recognition is also the foundation of social Christianity.[44]

Human solidarity does not wink at sin. Rather, it causes us to see the sin of the other in ourselves. It does not position us as adversaries against one another. It places us side by side. We do not separate the need of the other from our own need; we are in it together. Human solidarity sees through the sin to the value of the person. My adopted denomination restored my sense of value. After I had battled shame, guilt, isolation, and diminishments for months, someone recognized God's ministry in me, not as past, but as present. Hope resurrects!

Temptation has a whole new meaning for me. There is great wisdom on the broken side of temptation. Without its wisdom, and given the same set of circumstances, would the outcome be different? I would like to think so. Yet I doubt a different outcome. Rauschenbusch is on the mark.

In the prayer, "Lead us not into temptation," we feel the human trembling of fear. Experience has taught us our frailty. Every man can see certain contingencies just a step ahead of him and knows that his moral capacity for resistance would collapse hopelessly if he were placed in these situations. Therefore Jesus gives voice to our inarticulate plea to God not to bring us into such situations.[45]

Even to read these words gives me a sense that another understands. "Certain contingencies" came against me, and in the end I collapsed. These contingencies are not an excuse for clergy sexual misconduct. I feared a humbling, and the fear actualized. Mystery remains for me. Asking for the grace to see Jesus more clearly, love him more dearly, and follow him more nearly, I meditate on John 13:36–38, in which Jesus predicted Peter's denial.

> Jesus predicted Peter's failure therefore Jesus knew of it in advance. Jesus knew of my failure in advance also. I understand it from the perspective of my weakness. I don't understand it from the perspective of *providence*!

"You will."

Often I wished to be delivered from the set of circumstances that came against me. I have learned much from a painful humbling. I needed these lessons, but did I need to inflict so much pain on myself and others to learn them? As to the Lord's Prayer, the representative of the social gospel continues:

> The words "Deliver us from the evil one" have in them the ring of battle. They bring to mind the incessant grapple between God and the permanent and malignant powers of evil in humanity. To the men of the first century that meant Satan and his host of evil spirits who ruled in the oppressive, extortionate, and idolatrous powers of Rome. Today the original spirit of that prayer will probably be best understood by those who are pitted against the terrible powers of organized covetousness and institutionalized oppression.
>
> Thus the Lord's Prayer is the great prayer of social Christianity. It is charged with what we call "social consciousness." It assumes the social solidarity of men [and women] as a matter of course. It recognizes the social basis of all moral and religious life even in the most intimate personal relations to God.[46]

Human solidarity against the evils that overcome us is the difference between despair and hope. Embracing the powerless with compassion in action is an incredible gift, rooted in God's embrace of compassionate love.

When the rafters of social justice embraced me out of the chaos, they made me feel that my problems were their problems too. They invited me onto their rafts. They handed me an oar to make me feel useful again. And they never announced judgment or acquittal over my moral sin. I was the recipient of the gift of human solidarity, of compassion in action.

Solidarity with the Paddle Captain

Divine solidarity, "God-with-us," is a mystery beyond our grasp. God is the source of human solidarity and compassion in action. Henri Nouwen brings the contemplative and social justice rivers together. He touches the deep of God's compassion with these words:

> The compassion that Jesus felt was obviously quite different from superficial or passing feelings of sorrow or sympathy. Rather, it extended to the most vulnerable part of his being. It is related to the

> Hebrew word for compassion, *rachamim,* which refers to the womb of Yahweh. Indeed, compassion is such a deep, central, and powerful emotion in Jesus that it can only be described as a movement of the womb of God. There, all the divine tenderness and gentleness lies hidden. There, God is father and mother, brother and sister, son and daughter. There, all feelings, emotions, and passions are one in divine love. When Jesus was moved to compassion, the source of all life trembled, the ground of all love burst open, and the abyss of God's immense, inexhaustible, and unfathomable tenderness revealed itself.[47]

Jesus Christ revealed the fullness of God's compassion in specific, concrete ways. Nouwen, McNeill, and Morrison breathe hope into the hearts of all people crying out for help.

> To us, who cry out from the depth of our brokenness for a hand that will touch us, an arm that can embrace us, lips that will kiss us, a word that speaks to us here and now, and a heart that is not afraid of our fears and trembling; to us, who feel our own pain as no other human being feels it, has felt it, or ever will feel it and who are always waiting for someone who dares to come close–to us a man has come who can truly say, "I am with you." Jesus Christ, who is God-with-us, has come to us in the freedom of love, not needing to experience our human condition but freely choosing to do so out of love. (Phil. 2:6–8).[48]

I experienced the intimacy of divine solidarity throughout my odyssey. I felt God's presence in the rivercrafts always. Even capsized, I felt buoyed by God's presence beside me, sustaining my head above the waters. In no way was the experience of divine solidarity a blessing on my choices. God's compassion in action was not a confirmation of my decisions. I never confused them. God was with me in my anguish as I attended to the crisis of morality. The Divine Lover connected me with people who breathed into me a future with hope. Rafters on the river of social justice embraced me out of the chaos. At the convergence of divine and human solidarity, I received the gifts of compassion in action: a network of caring people, acceptance and friendship, a $4,500 bursary to cover the cost of the five required courses, tangible gifts of groceries and money, several consulting projects, and a route into a new future with hope. Agonizing personal decisions waited downstream. Among them, I chose divorce over reconciliation.

Downstream in the Direction of Hope

A little church with a large heart accepted a risk. Still hurting from the aftermath of my moral crisis and still working through unresolved issues, I began as a supply/interim minister in a church that became my healing community. Three years after my resignation from my denomination of origin, two years into my three-year journey back to ordination in my adopted denomination, I began anew. I was a candidate for Order of Ministry. I returned to my pastoral calling. I received a gift–the gospel of the second chance. A special congregation presented me with a second chance to live out my calling. We began rafting downstream together, with many deep issues still heavy within my heart. River-running in the same rivercraft, we paddled together in solidarity, even through the adjustments ahead.

I receive a fresh invitation from the "still, small voice." I have served for about five months in my new parish ministry. It is about six months before my remarriage.

"Discover again the spiritual resources that are yours, Dwayne."

Still hurting deeply, I take no action on this word. I have another powerful dialogue several months later. It is an invitation, to "rediscover prayer," and a promise: "you will recover passion." The words flow effortlessly, accompanied by deep feelings.

> "Dwayne, rediscover the power of prayer.
> For your children rediscover prayer…
> For your marriage rediscover prayer…
> For your ministry rediscover prayer…
> For your ventures rediscover prayer…
> I will make myself known through you…
> Remember the days of old
> Did I not manifest my power?
> Did I not reveal my life?
> I will do so again in the latter days.
> You are my channel.
> Do not let the past disarm you.
> Awake to the future.
> A double portion of my Spirit will rest upon you
> To accomplish what I intend through you.
> The latter will outgrow the former.
> You will seek out a people for my name.
> Rediscover prayer, and you will recover passion.
> Fear not. I am with thee.
> Pray."

I take no action in spite of its deep, affective impact upon me. Most unusual, my journal records only one dialogue entry over the next seven months.

Two inner demons will not let me go. They are the deep wounds of shame and guilt. I am bound by them. They question my call to mission. Discipline does not free me. Counseling does not free me. A parish does not free me. Remarriage does not free me. Reordination does not free me. A deeper work awaits me downstream. Something within resurrects on Easter weekend. A corporate form of dialogue with God emerges at the mouth of the charismatic river. Here, I meet the transforming power of prophetic presbytery.

On Spiritual Warfare

MEMO: January 2005
TO: Dwayne Ratzlaff
FROM: Tom Bandy

Dwayne:

In several ways your story is as compelling as the "confessions" of Augustine, the "mortifications" of Antony, or even the anguished journals of John Wesley. Indeed, the pride and pain, transformation and hope, of your spiritual journey is reminiscent of the writings of many historic church leaders.

You are remarkably, perhaps even ruthlessly, and some might say morbidly, honest. Such honesty is rarer today than in times past, due to the relativism of our culture; but it reveals how the Unconditioned God of the vertical dimension still speaks in our heart of darkness.

You go deep into the history of theology and philosophy searching for clues to your own struggle and the human condition in general. Such breadth of inquiry is also rarer today than in past times and demands a power of synthesis foreign to scientific analysis.

You are extraordinarily eclectic in your choice of dialogue partners. Such openness is rare today, as people prefer the security of their restricted reading and learning choices. This is simply a matter of existential courage—"the courage to be." Many in your situation would have given up and begun selling insurance. You did not.

You approach spiritual analysis with the spirit of the former military commander and later spiritual guide, Ignatius of Loyola, whose "discipline" you found so helpful. This militant attitude toward sin and salvation leads naturally to the metaphors of "spiritual warfare" that were so prominent in the Middle Ages and that are so resurgent in contemporary American culture. Such passion could be abused. Loyola's discipline was later subverted to become inquisition; Calvin's institutes were later subverted into revolution; and it is not difficult to see contemporary holiness subverted into moralistic judgementalism.

Indeed, to some extent you are the victim of just such an evolution of ideas. If you feel anger toward the inflexibility of denominations and the exclusivity of their policies today, you would have fared worse among the Jesuits in the sixteenth century or the English Protestants of the seventeenth century. The point of my observation is that the insights that have helped you experience acceptance and renewed self-esteem are the same insights that gave birth to your erstwhile judges. This is the paradox and ambiguity of dialogue. We discover that the prisoners and the judges all spring from the same soil, and it is but a blink of the eye that will cause them to change places.

The crux of your story, at this point, is your experience of spiritual warfare. If the formative spiritual moment of your life was *only* your initial conversion and call to ministry, I doubt that it would have come down to "spiritual warfare." It would have been "spiritual confusion," or perhaps "emotional immaturity," or even "career doubt." Many clergy (and prominent lay church leaders!) today have been guilty of moral indiscretion, but it did not lead to spiritual warfare. It led them to continuing education, or counseling, or alternative careers—and in the best scenario it also led them to greater intellectual clarity, healthier intimate relationships, and a more satisfying employment. Of course, that is also true for you—except that this is not the whole story. There was greater trauma for you, a more profound existential crisis.

It was your second formative spiritual moment that set the stage for spiritual warfare. I like the simple way you have described this baptism of the Holy Spirit: "spirit filling for holy living." It is this seamless union of faith and lifestyle that sets the stage for the future crisis. The "Holiness Movement" has always been countercultural because of it. Both classical humanism and scientific progressivism separate faith and lifestyle. One's convictions remain "personal," adored in the inner sanctum of the soul; but one's public behavior can be remarkably utilitarian, pragmatic, and self-serving. For example, one can still believe in the sanctity of marriage, and even romanticize the notion of eternal love, and at the same time divorce with relative ease and have multiple sexual encounters with very little guilt. Once faith and lifestyle become seamless, however, a breakdown in behavior implies a break with Spirit itself.

I want to comment on the spiritual warfare that you (and others who unite faith and lifestyle as you do) experienced. However, before I do, it is valuable to first explore the "terrain" and understand the "combatants" through which this spiritual warfare takes place.

The "terrain" on which this spiritual warfare is fought is culture itself, but not just the objective culture in which we give and take, manipulate and are manipulated. It is also the subjective experience of culture, the manner in which we have embraced culture in the shaping of our mindset and soul. This is not just an external struggle, but an internal struggle that shapes even how we interpret and understand the external struggle. Contemporary American dualism (whether in the guise of popular television programs about the supernatural or popular fundamentalist preaching about the end of the world) deals only with the external struggle. It largely ignores the internal struggle and uncritically applies subjective assumptions to the interpretation of external experience. By ignoring subjective assumptions, the "battle" has already been lost, because any conclusions about the turmoil or direction of life have already been warped and limited. The transcendent God of the vertical dimension in life judges first the *hearts* of men and women—and the hidden assumptions of their mentors—before the course of history is judged. This is the underlying message in H. Richard Niebuhr's whole interpretation of Luther in *Christ and Culture*.

Among the five typologies Niebuhr used to study "holiness" (for that is what he was doing—examining the interface of faith and lifestyle), you have focused on two and placed them in opposition: Christ transforming culture versus Christ of culture. It is the opposition that Niebuhr and I myself would question. Insofar as the Gnostics represented the "Christ of culture" and Augustine represented "Christ transforming culture," these are opposites. In the history of Christian thought, Augustine's viewpoint won. Yet the very fact of incarnation implies a deeper connectedness between Spirit and culture that cannot be ignored. As many ancient commentators observed, God *chose* to be born in a stable and not in the inn, and certainly not in the palace. There was a deliberate choice of cultural forms. Culture might be a greater or lesser vehicle to reveal the Holy. For Jesus to be fully human, and to literally suffer and die, the cultural forms of trials and nails became necessary. But the miracle of incarnation implies something more. For Jesus to be fully divine, and to literally connect with the world and the human beings therein, the cultural forms of church and communication become necessary.

A better knowledge of the "terrain" helps us better understand the nature of the "combatants." Christian faith has always believed that history is caught up in a greater struggle between good and evil, God and Satan. Orthodox Christianity, however, has always distinguished "Satan" from "culture." The Gnostics of Augustine's era, the Manicheans of the medieval era, and many dualists of the modern era do not make such a distinction. That is their error. They believe culture—the world itself—to be inherently evil. "Culture" and "Satan" become virtually synonymous. Orthodox Christianity, however, realized that such a conviction undermines the saving significance of Christ. If culture cannot be used—transformed—to become portals through which God can reach humanity, then the incarnation did not literally happen; and the chasm between God and humanity cannot be crossed.

More than one desert hermit (or "spiritual isolationist" to place their behavior in contemporary context) fell victim to this error. The criticism of those of orthodox faith was not that they were extreme in their behavior, but that they ended up denying the absolute victory of the cross. God and Satan became equal adversaries; humans became victims of their strife; and salvation became a reward for an elite. That is gnosticism with a vengeance! One has only to watch modern television programs about the supernatural to see its enduring attraction. Christianity always opposed it.

The "desert fathers" that have been so significant to your assessment of this "spiritual warfare" also opposed such dualism. They retreated from *one kind of culture* to create *an alternative culture*. It was not just a matter of simpler living, but of aligning lifestyle around the sole purpose of finding unity with God through intimacy with Christ. All those stories about monks wrestling with sexual temptations are really metaphors to describe the overall purpose of aligning all of one's love, passion, and yearning for intimacy to Christ and Christ alone. I am struck by your comment that your attitude toward culture became a "high-speed adrenaline rush" to which you became addicted. That is language the desert fathers would understand! It is misplaced eros. Dante observed that "lust," in and of itself, is not bad. It is the *object of lust* that causes one's downfall. The Christian needs to thirst, yearn, or "lust" for Christ and Christ alone. Not for converts. Not for sexual relationships (even marriage was a sidetrack!). Not for power over others. The adrenaline rush should be reserved for Christ alone.

The spiritual warfare described by Evagrius and the desert fathers is very different from the warfare described by the other writers you quote. It is not just "an alternative" viewpoint; it is a categorically different standpoint vis-à-vis the victory of God.

Walter Wink is a good representative of the liberal point of view that demons are systems, structures, or persons that have betrayed their divine purpose. Capitalism can be demonic, and so also the institutional church, or cultic personalities, or the Internet, or anything that sidetracks or subverts the quest to realize the kingdom of God. Spiritual warfare is about the use or abuse of power. The war is fought on an economic, political, and sociological battleground. The antagonists are corporate and political leaders who wield power for self-interest or the public good; demographic groups who invest or spend money in ways that influence the capitalist economy, or who vote in or out politicians who shape public policy; and microcultures of powerlessness that organize to protest victimization and take immoral power-brokers to court.

There are weaknesses in this view of spiritual warfare. "Divine purpose" is remarkably transparent to human minds and tends to get lost in strategic planning. The god that transcends the battlefield begins to resemble faith in the legal system of democracy. The perpetual sinfulness of human nature dooms any demonic or divine victory temporary at best.

M. Scott Peck is a good representative of the psychological point of view that demons are perversions of the human psyche that literally possess and twist a person to do things against their nature. As you point out, these are no mere addictions or neuroses, but are tantamount to possession. Otherwise good-natured people become unrecognizably evil characters. Spiritual warfare is about the health or corruption of the individual. The war is fought on a psychological and behavioral battlefield that may be reduced in scope but is radically intense and frightening in relationship. The antagonists are demons and exorcists, each striving to manipulate the mind and individual behavior one way or another.

There are weaknesses in this view as well. Although both Satan and God are "real," it is a reality that is remarkably unempirical and depends as much on the subjectivity of the observer as on the behavior of the one under observation. The difference between addiction, neurosis, and radical possession seems to be a matter of degree rather than category; and this suggests that discernment of the devil in people is left to the determination of the chosen exorcist rather than God.

C. Peter Wagner is a good representative the global view that demons are supernatural beings outside the order of creation working to invade, subvert, and enslave the world in both its individual/internal and corporate/external aspects. He connects the perversion of institutions and the corruption of individuals in a larger conspiracy that involves non-human, supernaturally guided, strategic plans for good or ill. The war is fought in the human psyche, among the world religions and diverse spiritualities, and in the socioeconomic politics of board room and state capitals. The antagonists are parallel armies of supernatural demons or angels into which human beings may be recruited.

There are weaknesses in this view, too. The larger synthesis that explains the diverse extremes of evil in the world demands a hypothesis of various levels of demi-gods that sounds more gnostic than Christian. Paradoxically, the view that renounces other spiritualities in pop culture as demonic appeals to the very pop culture that is enthralled with supernatural warfare. The implicit dualism does not leave a clearly definable place for God who is above all gods, providence that is in control of history, or Christ as the center of God's redemption.

All three of these perspectives are more alike than their advocates may wish to admit. They emerge from, and appeal to, the circularity of classical humanism. Human beings participate in a complex and multitiered world of fact, emotion, and power—individual and corporate, local and global—in which the gods and man have relative powers to determine the future. They acknowledge the horizontal line of scientific progressivism by accepting the linear course of strategic planning that will eventually lead to an end time, but the immanence of that end is obscure. The war between good and evil goes on forever. Dualism is the result. Jesus may be the divine CEO or paradigm for the perfect union organizer; or the chief exorcist and divine clinician; or the generalissimo of the divine forces. But there is no God above all gods, no decisive place for incarnation, no mystical participation in Jesus, and no decisive salvation in the cross once for all.

This is why the perspective on spiritual warfare for Evagrius, the desert fathers, and the early monastic movement is in a very different category to these other viewpoints. The clearly vertical dimension is inserted into the dialogue between classical humanism and scientific progressivism and carries the interpretation of spiritual warfare in a different direction. The war is won. No matter how painful our experiences may be, we are essentially living in the aftermath. The wreckage may still abound, and the fights may still break out. Individuals like you may still be harmed, but the essential battle has been fought and won by Christ. The final victory is assured.

This abstract digression has a personal point. Those who are capsized into moral chaos (or any kind of chaos) may well need therapy to exorcise the demons from their habitual behavior and will give thanks to Christ the healer. They may well discern that their condition has been influenced by systems, institutions, and policies of self-interest that need to be challenged and will give thanks to Christ the advocate. Both will offer a *conditional* acceptance. You have experienced all of that. What remains, however, is an *unconditional* acceptance. An unconditional acceptance can only be offered by the Unconditioned God above gods, and it can only be experienced across the gap of infinity through the intersection of culture and Spirit in the incarnation of Christ. That is the hope toward which Evagrius points.

You already mention that Evagrius identified eight ways in which the human spirit is subverted or sidetracked from unity with Christ. These were later refined into the "seven deadly sins" of pride, covetousness, lust, envy, gluttony, anger, and sloth. They were matched with the "seven lively virtues" of faith, charity, prudence, hope, temperance, justice, and fortitude. Part of the spiritual discipline of mentoring in the monastery was that spiritual guides and pilgrim companions could inquire of one another, or critique one another, as to how addicted they were to the deadly sins or how aligned they were to the lively virtues.

Evagrius' synthesis for the right ordering of passion and spiritual love (eros and agape) lies at the core of the monastic faith community as an alternative cultural form. It began as an alternative *to the world,* but it did not take long before it was perceived as an alternative *to the institutional church.* I find it interesting that your first response to being "capsized into a crisis of morality" was to turn to other denominations. You looked within the established church and quickly found it to be inadequate for your personal redemption. Eventually you stumbled upon (or were led into) the contemplative stream of faith and discovered Evagrius. You had to get to the desert to find an oasis.

I think many of your readers will ask this question: *How exactly did you survive in the water?* They see how and why you were "capsized," and they begin to see how you explored various "rivers," dialogued with an eclectic diversity of "river rafters," and eventually found new hope. But they are wondering how you survived in the water. Perhaps that is where your readers already find themselves. They are "capsized" for any of a number of reasons. They are in the river, and they may or may not have the "life jacket" of biblical training and historical knowledge that kept your nose above the water. They are flailing about, clutching at straws, and near despair.

The clue to your immediate survival is found in the monastic discipline into which novices were invited by the desert fathers. Not everyone could accept that discipline, but some are predisposed to it because they are knowledgeable enough, inclined that way, or simply desperate to try anything. The basic principles of survival are these:

Obedience to a larger biblical vision of salvation; to the literal historicity of the incarnation of Jesus (fully human, fully God, infinite paradox, crucial for salvation) as articulated by the ancient Confession of Chalcedon; and to authentic spiritual guides who can mentor you through the ambiguities of life.

Whether or not you are young or old, a veteran of the church or a newcomer to ministry, highly educated or a high-school dropout, or of one personality type or another—all are irrelevant to your survival when you have been capsized. It is this obedience that will keep you from going down. Stability is found in simplifying and reshaping your lifestyle around the principles of moderation, cooperation, poverty, chastity, and fidelity. Turn your back on the paraphernalia of life, the expectations of institutions, and the trappings of success. Such stability is extremely countercultural. The world does not generally endorse moderation. Baby boomers are not known for their ability to cooperate. Capitalists flee from poverty. The media mocks chastity. Failure to remain loyal to your covenant relationships is often the very thing that pushed you overboard to begin with. But this "renunciation" of self and worldliness is crucial to survival. When you are in the water, you need to divest yourself of expensive clothes, kick off your shoes, let go of your attaché case, and allow the water to wash away the lipstick.

You must have courage to strive to live faithfully in troubled times; to risk keeping your life unstable as you listen for God, resisting easy answers and shallow options; and to humble yourself to search for truth wherever you might find it.

This is what Paul Tillich first described as "the courage to be": to simply survive, exist, and deny despair. There are more ways to commit suicide than by killing the body. Perpetuating addiction to self-destructive habits is the real suicide. Dante's inferno is populated not by people who did wrong, but by people who found ever more ingenious and self-deceiving ways to keep doing wrong.

In the end, Dwayne, you confronted the particular demons that had thrown you overboard and that pursued you even while you flailed in the water: lust, pride, and anger. You finally gave up struggling and surrendered to Christ, which is the whole goal and object of the mentoring of Evagrius. Paradoxically, redemption is only found when you stop trying to redeem yourself.

The experience of unconditional love can be found in all of the rivers of which you speak. You found it first in the social justice stream. Many never find it in that stream because it, too, is burdened by tasks, obligations, and a hidden conviction that humanity is "justified by works" rather than faith. All the theological rivers carry that burden, and also the potential for grace. As I said before, the church is caught in the dialogue among the circularity of classical humanism, the horizontal dimension of scientific progressivism, and the verticality of Ultimate Concern; and each voice shapes the church as we know it.

Your journey, however, is not over. I note that with particular interest. Even after forgiveness and acceptance has been offered, it is more difficult than we think to accept the fact that we are accepted. Shame and guilt remain. You began life with *two* transformational experiences. It seems that there are *two* stages to redemption. You have been "converted" all over again have and refocused your sense of call. Yet you need to be blessed with a new spirit of "holiness," and this "baptism" will take longer.

I have the sense that your experience of spiritual warfare at this stage in your spiritual journey has brought you a sense of *conditional* acceptance. You have been accepted—feel better about yourself, have more confidence in your calling—*on the condition* that you have submitted to counseling, reprioritized your life plan, and retooled your career path. Yet there lingers the shame and guilt, and this is a sign that *unconditional acceptance* lies yet ahead.

CHAPTER 3

Submerged within a Crisis of Calling
Paddle Strokes of Desperation

Desperate Rapids

Something within resurrects on Easter weekend. It has been three months since the dialogue that left a residue of powerful feelings. I have not acted on the inner voice drawing me to a rediscovery of lost spiritual resources. I reflect on the invitation:

"Rediscover prayer, and you will recover passion."

I long for a reassurance that God can still use me. I meditate on the great commission (Mt. 28:16–20). I hear words I never anticipated.

> Instead of "Go," I hear "Wait—until you're equipped with power from on high."
>
> Lord, I need a new equipping, a new empowering from on high. I long for a new anointing, a new reassuring.
>
> I am counseled, "Come aside awhile. Wait. Sit at my feet. Discover Mary again. Love me more—than these."

I return to the Acts for meditation. I recall the touch of the Spirit at seminary when I needed a confirmation of calling. God touched me in my desperation. I am desperate again for another encounter with the Spirit as I meditate on Acts 2–4.

> Lord Jesus,
> I long for such a primal experience of your Spirit-fullness:
> speech, piety, and hope.
> Lord, I need your Spirit-touch.
> May your "dove" land upon my head anew!

> Inner vision:
> Kneeling in front of Jesus,
> Jesus has his hands on my head.
> He says,
> "Come, Holy Spirit."

Desperation is expressed in the language of my personal Adam-and-Eve experience. I have eaten the forbidden fruit. My eyes have been opened. Something deep within needs to be touched. Guidance comes through these words:

> "Dwayne,
> Put yourself where the wind of the Spirit is blowing.
> Hoist your sail."

I knew of a place in Toronto, Canada, where the wind of the Spirit was blowing. The renewal was called the "Toronto Blessing." I was a stranger to the happenings at the Toronto Airport Vineyard Church (now the Toronto Airport Christian Fellowship). I had heard of "weird goings on" at the church. Could this be the place where I was to hoist my sail?

Reordination approaches. I have been an interim minister for nineteen months. I have an unforgettable dialogical encounter six months before my ordination.

> During prayer and meditation I see myself
> face-to-face with the Spirit-Dove.
> Me to Spirit-Dove:
> "Infiltrate all my psychic energies."
> Wings Flutter–Feel Breeze.
> In the Spirit-Dove's eyes I see:
> Compassion…
> Fire…
> Knowledge…
> Power…
> Healing…
> Spirit-Dove to Me:
> "In me, they are yours."
> Spirit-Dove flies into my head.
> Comes in.
> Infiltrates me.
> From within the Spirit-Dove says:
> "I infuse you now.
> All your energies are My channels.
> All your powers My containers.
> Spread your wings now, Dwayne! It's time!"
> Awesome!

I am ordained on June 2, 1996, into the Order of Ministry. Years earlier, September 7, 1979, I had been ordained into the Gospel Ministry. I have been ordained twice. The preordination prayer is an "awesome" experience. The primal encounters that follow are even more so.

The Charismatic River

The Genius of the River

The movement of the Spirit over the past hundred years can be scouted as three powerful waves over the pentecostal-charismatic river. The first wave began April 9, 1906, on Bonnie Brae Street in Los Angeles. It was Easter season. Something extraordinary happened in a house that night. William Seymour (1870–1922) and the overflow crowds moved to the Azusa Street Mission, giving birth to the pentecostal movement. Today there are more than fourteen thousand pentecostal denominations throughout the world.[1]

The second wave saw pentecostalism overflow into the mainline churches.[2] In Van Nuys, California, Dennis Bennett, rector of St. Mark's Episcopal (Anglican) Church, encountered the Spirit in 1960. The charismatic movement within Protestant mainline churches is in flow. In 1967, Duquesne University, Pittsburgh, students and faculty encountered the Spirit, and the Catholic charismatic movement is on the move. Killian McDonnell and Leon Joseph Cardinal Suenens provided leadership.[3]

The third wave of the Holy Spirit began at Fuller Theological Seminary in 1981 inside the classroom of John Wimber, founder of the Association of Vineyard Churches. Vinson Synan describes the third wavers.

> This "wave" was comprised of mainline evangelicals who experienced signs and wonders but who disdained labels such as "Pentecostal" or "Charismatic." The Vineyard was the most visible movement of this category. By 2000, the third wavers, also called "neo-charismatics," were credited with some 295 million members worldwide.[4]

The genius of the pentecostal-charismatic movement is its powerful capacity to penetrate the deep inner core of human experience. Harvey Cox calls the river a "primal spirituality" in three dimensions: "primal speech," "primal piety," and "primal hope." In these three ways pentecostalism taps into the "deep substratum of human religiosity."[5] Traumatic cultural shifts gave rise to the movement. In response to these shifts, conservatives insisted on dogmas while liberals absorbed culture's rationality. Both groups lost their "spiritual appeal."[6] Pentecostals found another way. Cox explains:

> They rebelled against creeds but retained the mystery. They abolished hierarchies but kept ecstasy. They rejected both scientism and traditionalism. They returned to the raw inner core of human spirituality and thus provided just the new kind of "religious space" many people needed.[7]

Pentecostalism has ravished the souls of many individuals. Yet the primary purpose of the Spirit's visitation is "to gather up and knit together the broken human family."[8]

I am rafting with a loving church community. I have celebrated ordination with the friends who accompanied me on the way. The new future with hope has come to birth. I am dreaming of river-runs again. And yet, inner demons continue to pursue me. I am harassed by shame, guilt, and the fear that God cannot use me anymore. My river of origin declared me disqualified for ordained ministry. My adopted stream declared me fit for ordained ministry. I am desperate for a sign that will settle the issue from God's point of view. I need an inner confirmation of call that will heal the deep hurt in my heart. I cannot reach it.

The Third Wavers

I decide to scout the third wavers of the charismatic river. I do not know what to expect on the eve of attending a renewal meeting. Synan explains:

> In 1994 a new chapter of the charismatic renewal began at the Airport Vineyard Church in Toronto, Canada. The Vineyard is a network of charismatic churches not connected to any historic denomination. The phenomena experienced there have become known as the "Toronto blessing." Dramatic and controversial effects of a revival there included holy laughter, falling and barking, in the context of healings, speaking in tongues and evangelical preaching.[9]

I visit the renewal meetings nearly three months after ordination. I am reading Acts again. I hear inner words and receive an inner image while listening to Acts 5:12–42.

> "I am in it!
> Hoist your sail."

> I see an image of a person with a sail or chute on the edge of a cliff. He takes a run and jumps off the cliff. The wind catches the sail/chute, and the rider glides through the air. I am the glider. It takes a risk–a faith move–that when I leap over the cliff the wind will catch the sail and propel me forward.

> I must *accelerate* and *leap*!
> Lord, I pray for the grace!

I accept the words as a prompting from the inner Guide to move onto the river of charismatic renewal.

I attend the First Pastor's Conference. It is a "primal" experience in every way. I respond to the altar invitation. The events at the altar bring the charismatic and holiness rivers together. The invitation is directed to all pastors tempted by sexual unfaithfulness. I need to respond to the past. I move to the altar. From my journal:

> I saw…(the Senior Pastors of Toronto Airport Vineyard Church) nearby praying for people. I went over to…and asked if (they) would pray for me. In fifteen seconds I shared my story with him. He said he'd pray. He laid hands on me–with catcher behind me–and began praying for:
>
> the inner child that needed love,
> freedom from the bondage of guilt and shame,
> healing of the man,
> that whatever made me vulnerable would be healed,
> protection for the future,
> filling and anointing.
>
> …(He) had his hands on my head. (She) came and touched my pulse area. I was aware of her energy field–felt it–my ankles became light–moving up my legs a loss of feeling (like my legs became air) and I gently fell backwards. The experience was gentle and natural. I was fully conscious at all times. When (she) came over, I felt the force, the energy, the impact of her presence (or the Spirit's presence in and through her). Her presence was brief–and she returned to the others on the floor–but in those few seconds there was power present! I was over on my back although gently and slowly. I feel a deep cleansing, though exhausted.

I am touched to the core.

Paddling through an Energy Field

I had experienced the same type of energy field years earlier. I was calm. I was waiting on God alone in the living room. With no prior experience or knowledge of an energy field and no expectation of one, an electric-like current shot through my body. Now in a community experience of waiting on God, I encounter the energy field again.

Tom Harpur, a respected writer on religion and ethics, gives credibility to the energy-field experience. As a skeptical newspaper journalist, Harpur was assigned to cover a Kathryn Kuhlman healing service held in Toronto. He observed people collapse as they approached her for healing. Kuhlman came over to meet Harpur during an intermission. She had been informed in advance that a reporter from the *Toronto Star* would be present. Harpur recalls his experience.

> As she came towards me, she spoke my name and, holding out her hands, took both of mine. As she smiled up at me, she said, "Welcome," and kept her grip while we exchanged a few words.

I will never forget the experience. The nearest I can come to describing it is to say that it was like holding on to the terminals of a strong battery or being plugged into some other source of electrical current. There was an unmistakable—and, for me, quite unexpected—surge of an electric-like current into my hands and up my arms. At six feet four inches in height, I towered over this elderly, petite woman. Yet she seemed at the center of a force or energy field that was palpably alive and much stronger than I was.[10]

Back Paddling

I turned to a respected author among Catholic charismatics for understanding into the phenomenon of falling backward. Francis MacNutt explains:

Personally, I believe the symbolic meaning of resting in the Spirit is that God is doing something in our ministry that knocks the props out from under us, literally and figuratively. It is not something that the person who falls is doing by his or her own effort, still less anything initiated by the one who prays. It is God taking charge at a time in history when there is much concentration on human effort—self-improvement courses, salvation by education, the limitless possibilities of our liberated humanity. The New Age movement proclaims that we are gods who can do anything we set our minds to. And here is God knocking people off their feet and saying, in effect, "Oh no, you can't!"[11]

I was back paddling. I was on my back "soaking." I was paying attention to thoughts, words, feelings, and images.

In charismatic spirituality, the twofold purpose for soaking is healing and intimacy. Carol Arnott explains how intimacy and healing occur together.

Soaking in His presence opens up the heart and soul to Divine romance and intimacy. It allows the Lord to love you and you to love Him, much like a couple in love find that their love and intimacy deepen as they spend more and more time together. This is one missing piece of the Christian experience that God has come to restore in this move of the Holy Spirit.[12]

Prophetic Team Dialogue—1

I was invited to sign up for personal prophecy at the pastor's conference. I had never before been the subject of personal prophecy. Anglican bishop David Pytches describes the gift of prophecy in these terms:

The gift of prophecy (1 Corinthians 12:10; 14:1) is the special ability that God gives to members of the Body of Christ to receive and communicate an immediate message of God to his gathered people, a group among them or any one of his people individually, through a divinely anointed utterance.[13]

I gathered with other participants to receive personal prophecy. Each one was assigned to a team of three persons. The team had no prior knowledge of me. They did know my name and the city where I lived. Below is the dialogue of the prophetic team.

Team Member: Now, Dwayne, I just want to make sure I'm on the right track here. Have you just come out…Are you in an abusive situation?… Faintly, I say "Yes, that I had an affair…" OK. I have just seen you…a real heaviness upon you. And I also see heart changes that the Lord has been doing. He's been really shaking you, really, really shaking you deep down inside. I see the heart changes, and I also see the heaviness that's been upon you. I really believe He wants to lift that right off. He's raising you up. That's the word. He's raising you up. It's not over. It's not finished. It's not dead.

Team Leader: This is the season in which God is using broken people. Look at…They're both the products of broken marriages and failed home situations…I want you to look at the life of Peter. How broken he was. And really at the absolute end of himself when He came to death of self. He thought it was all over and he went back fishing. That's when the Lord called him and said, "Feed my sheep."

I sense that the Lord is bringing closure on the past. And he wants you to bring closure. It's time for closure… "I'm the God of the second and third chance. I don't put anyone on the ash heap…I'm a God of restoration…" Like this church is an amalgamation of broken people. We're all rejects that somehow ended up on the same garbage dump. And God somehow turned the garbage into something beautiful…So Father, we take the ashes of his life and we speak beauty into it. Yeah. Thank you, Lord. I sense he's going to recommission you and just in the right season…Hopelessness goes, and hope displaces hopelessness…

Team Member: …As a mother of Christ, I would like to say, "You are forgiven, son. And welcome home. Welcome home." *Team Leader:* The Father's blessing. The Father's blessing. Not for what you do but for being a son. He says, "Enter into the fullness of your sonship."

Team Member: …When you first sat down the word *eagle* came to me…I just see you soaring up…I see evangelism. Do you have a heart for evangelism? But what I got was a sense when you were younger…I've seen a real fire when you were a younger man…That flame is getting fanned again…I pray life back into that vision again…I also see you as an "eagle" just soaring up…"I'm even going to use your brokenness."

...There was one time in my life where somebody actually did something and said something over me and it broke...I really believe He's nudging me to do that over you. Is that OK? (I gave permission.) I just see these cords around you. The Lord wants you to just break them off. All these cords that have entangled you, He's breaking off right now. He's loosening you from these cords so that you may be free...We just take those cords right off...right off. Those cords of condemnation. Unwrap his heart...his mind. We're just going to unwrap these cords symbolically right off you right now because what we do in the natural we do in the Spirit.

Team Leader: We need to unwrap some grave clothes here because the enemy had you buried...your ministry buried...And we say, "Dwayne, come forth in the name of Jesus!"

The revelations were accurate: my dependence on training, need for understanding, situation of abuse, passion for evangelism in younger years, loss of hope, heaviness of guilt, emotionally desperate for a word of absolution, need for recommissioning through a Spirit-touch, a breaking of the cords that had bound me, and the image of the soaring eagle (the image of God's promise to me months earlier). I had been a complete stranger to the prophetic team. I placed four markers on my odyssey the last day of the conference: I rededicate myself to uphold the standards of the heart! I take faith and release fear! I take forgiveness and release rejection! I take blessing and release hurt!

A Hurting Rafter Finds Heart Healing

Although active in the ministry of inner healing, I did not realize how difficult it would be for me to enter it personally. The act of soaking prayer and the prophetic team's dialogue accomplished a deep work of heart healing within me. Francis MacNutt explains inner healing.

The basic idea of inner healing is simply this: Jesus, who is the same yesterday, today and forever, can take the memories of our past and (1) *heal* them from the wounds that still remain and affect our present lives; (2) *fill with His love* all those places in us that have so long been empty, once they have been healed and drained of the poison of past hurts and resentment.

...This involves two things, then: (1) *Bringing to light* the things that have hurt us... (2) *Praying* to the Lord to heal the binding effects of the hurtful incidents of the past.[14]

The encounters changed me. God set me on the path to freedom from shame, guilt, and deep woundedness. God gave me the Spirit-touch I needed, the reassurance and recommission in my calling. I was free from the chains that had bound me. I received a new freedom to serve. I returned to the congregation that gave me a second chance.

The Holiness River

From my journal:

Invitation to healing for pastors who have/are tempted by sexual unfaithfulness...I felt I needed to deal with the past at that moment *at a deeper level*...I was on the floor for a long period of time–fully conscious–dealing with the issues with the Lord. Rehearsing all that happened from first inappropriate feeling to divorce to remarriage...A deep response–*a deep repentance*–with sincere tears–before the Lord... Asking forgiveness–seeking a new anointing from the Lord. Asking the Lord about *restitution*.

So began the paddling upstream to the places I had never anticipated a return to. I went back in response to the One who asked it of me.

A Convergence of Rivers

God is active as I raft over the converging rivers of divine love. In the evangelical stream, I claim Martin Luther's discovery that I am a sinner saved by grace alone, through faith alone, on account of Christ alone. I choose to live out of a transforming friendship with Jesus the Christ. In the contemplative stream, I fall overboard and flow into a dialogical relationship with God. In the desert stream, I struggle with the disordered passions of the false self so deeply embedded in my personality. I commit to being over doing as a new axis of life and service. In the social justice stream, I learn the profound meaning of human and divine solidarity. Out of this womb births a restoration of call and a new future with hope. In the pentecostal-charismatic stream, I receive a primal healing of the heart, freedom from the past and a recommissioning of the Spirit. And in the holiness stream, I recommit to the virtues of health and wholeness and receive the gift of reconciliation.

The Paddle of Sanctification

I am a complex set of motives. Any claim to the moral notion of holiness as entire freedom from self-promotion is beyond my grasp. The only hope is to have an alien righteousness living in and expressing through this Christian. The apostle Paul wrote about Christ being formed within (Gal. 4:19). The Christ within birthed and nurtured by the live-in Spirit is the sole hope of holiness. It is his righteousness alone and not my own self-endeavors. As I nurture relationship with God by listening more attentively and following more closely, his life can grow in and through me. Kenneth Leech scouts the holiness river.

> So in its origin holiness is a metaphysical rather than a moral notion. That which is holy is that which is set apart for God, and therefore shares something of the mystery and power of the divine. It is "a relationship more than a quality." Places, objects, times of the year, and people were only capable of partaking of holiness in so far as they were related to God, for he was holiness itself...

It is this sense of the otherness, the mystery, the transcendence of God to which the idea of holiness testifies. There is none like God, magnificent in holiness (Ex. 15:11), none holy as Yahweh is holy, and no one beside him (1 Sam. 2:2).[15]

I came to value John Wesley's wide-ranging synthesis of Protestant, Catholic, and Eastern Christianity.[16] Wesley shaped a powerful tributary called the Methodist movement. Downstream Methodism gave birth to the nineteenth-century holiness movement, one of the streams flowing through my denomination of origin.

John Wesley and the Methodists gathered in conferences to craft theology. At a conference on June 25, 1744, they agreed that sanctification is, "To be renewed in the image of God, *in righteousness and true holiness.*"[17] At another conference on August 1, 1745, they spoke of sanctification as follows:

Q. When does inward sanctification begin?

A. In the moment a man is justified. Yet sin remains in him; yea, the seed of all sin, 'till he is *sanctified throughout.* From that time a believer gradually dies to sin, and grows in grace.[18]

For Wesley and his movement, sanctification occurs in an instant ("in one moment"[19]) at some point after justification by faith, and then it continues as a process of growth in grace.

I believed and taught similarly. I identified the moment of sanctification as the evening I was branded by the Spirit during my final semester at seminary. The experience dissolved all doubts about my call to vocational ministry. All that led up to the Spirit-touch of that night was a type of death-to-self. From that day forward I sought sincerely to live out the process of abiding in Christ by the power of the Spirit. At least the process of sanctification encompassed a continuing decision to die daily to self at the center. Now I am on the verge of returning upstream to repent over the utter failure to live out this experiential doctrine of sanctification.

Sanctification Strokes

The central issue of my restoration from the viewpoint of my denomination of origin was the matter of repentance, an essential stroke for navigating the holiness river. The judicatory felt strongly that I had not arrived at a genuine repentance over my moral fault. The proof of an inadequate repentance was my unwillingness to end the "adulterous" relationship and take steps to restore my broken marriage. At the altar I rehearsed all the choices from first to last. I was moved to a response of deeper repentance while soaking in prayer. I asked the Lord about appropriate restitution. The answer came through a deep impression and an inner picture. I obeyed the inner revelation to accept full responsibility and seek reconciliation with my divorced wife, even after remarriage.

John Wesley addressed the issue of repentance in a published sermon. Wesley traces the passages into sin.

> (1) The divine seed of loving, conquering faith, remains in him that is born of God. "He keepeth himself," by the grace of God, and "cannot commit sin." (2) A temptation arises; whether from the world, the flesh, or the devil, it matters not. (3) The Spirit of God gives him warning that sin is near, and bids him more abundantly to watch unto prayer. (4) He gives way, in some degree, to the temptation, which now begins to grow pleasing to him. (5) The Holy Spirit is grieved; his faith is weakened; and his love of God grows cold. (6) The Spirit reproves him more sharply, and saith, "This is the way; walk thou in it." (7) He turns away from the painful voice of God, and listens to the pleasing voice of the tempter. (8) Evil desire begins and spreads in his soul, till faith and love vanish away: he is then capable of committing outward sin, the power of the Lord being departed from him.[20]

The description retraces my odyssey into adultery from a holiness perspective. There is no place to hide and no one to blame. God was faithful in the warnings. At various times I saw that sin was near, yet I allowed the temptation to gain power over me. I turned away from the voice of obedience repeatedly. I placed myself on the road to burnout and adultery. I chose to put myself through a painful humbling. All the while, God's repeated call was to be faithful to all covenants.

At all times I was embraced by divine love even as the power to obey diminished within me. I felt powerless and permitted the temptation to gain power over me. An act of obedience in the right direction would have strengthened the power to obey and diminished the temptation. Each time I put off the call to covenant-keeping, the strength of temptation intensified. Over time I led myself to powerlessness, burnout, confusion, and adultery. So all the more amazing is God's abiding love to one such as me.

Renewed faith comes through the waters of repentance. Wesley is blunt, yet on the mark.

> Wilt thou say, "But I have again committed sin, since I had redemption through his blood?" And therefore it is, that "I abhor myself, and repent in dust and ashes." It is meet that thou should abhor thyself; and it is God who hath wrought thee to this self-same thing. But, dost thou now believe? Hath He again enabled thee to say, "I know that my Redeemer liveth"; "and the life which I now live, I live by faith in the Son of God?" Then that faith again cancels all that is past, and there is no condemnation to thee.[21]

Faith is alive, sin is cancelled, and condemnation is gone. Of such is the fruit of repentance.

Eastern Christianity has a word for this change of heart. Eastern spiritual writers call it compunction, or "the gift of tears." It is indispensable to the spiritual life, a gift sought with fervent heart. Without it, there is no true repentance. Symeon the New Theologian (949–1022) held that "the divine fire of compunction effects with tears, or rather by means of them," the transformation of the soul and "produces virtues."

> Compunction is the fruit of practice and the means whereby the fruits are obtained. Or, rather, it produces virtues, it creates them...Therefore he who wishes to rid himself of passions or attain virtues must diligently seek compunction before all [other] good things and together with all the virtues. Apart from it he will never see his own soul purified...No one will ever prove from the divine Scriptures that any person ever was cleansed without tears and constant compunction. No one ever became holy or received the Holy Spirit, or had the vision of God or experienced His dwelling within himself, or ever had Him dwelling in his heart, without previous repentance and compunction and constant tears ever flowing as from a fountain. Such tears flood and wash out the house of the soul; they moisten and refresh the soul that has been possessed and enflamed by the unapproachable fire.[22]

But repentance as "the gift of tears" is a work of the Spirit, not self-induced. It is encompassed in the larger Spirit actions of sanctification. Exploring the movement of the Spirit in the ecumenical church, Thaddeus D. Horgan explains:

> The transformation of life effected in and by the Spirit is what Scripture refers to as "sanctification." In our finite grasp of this it is only possible to express what this means through a series of phrases or images which even then do not fully capture the depth and extent of the life-transforming change the Spirit works in us and through the church. For instance, Scripture speaks of this in terms of the Spirit's exposing (throwing light on) the sins of the world, of leading people to ask God's forgiveness and truly repenting, of enabling people to turn in forgiveness, love, compassion, and service to their neighbor, of coming to ever fuller knowledge of the truth, of becoming a more faithful servant of the living God, and of exercising the gifts of ministry "bestowed on us by God" (1 Cor. 12:4ff.).[23]

Another rafting mentor over the river of holiness was Thomas Merton. God's holiness unmasks sin for what it is. There is no "saving face," only "saving grace" in the presence of God. There was no place to hide from the record of the raw data of the deep impression of sin that I received in soaking prayer. Sin was unmasked. Merton describes sin for all that it is.

> Sin is the refusal of spiritual life, the rejection of the inner order and peace that come from our union with the divine will. In a word, sin is the refusal of God's will and of his love. It is not only a refusal to "do"

this or that thing willed by God, or a determination to do what he forbids. It is more radically a refusal to be what we are, a rejection of our mysterious, contingent, spiritual reality hidden in the very mystery of God. Sin is our refusal to be what we are created to be–sons of God, images of God. Ultimately sin, while seeming to be an assertion of freedom, is a flight from the freedom and the responsibility of divine sonship.[24]

Even more so is the call to holiness a "solemn obligation" upon persons who have taken "religious vows" and thereby "have bound themselves to take the basic Christian vocation to holiness especially seriously."[25] The call to holiness is the "solemn obligation" of ordained ministry. Obedience is the heart stroke of holiness.

Impossible! That was my immediate response to an inner picture that invaded my consciousness in worship at the Freedom Conference (TACF). An inner picture confronts me along with the words,

"I want the [denomination of origin] to bless you."

I did not make light of the encounter. It was a moving experience. I dismissed it as an impossible scenario. It was one thing to move upstream to my divorced wife to seek reconciliation as a heartfelt act of obedience; it would be something else entirely to expect my former denomination to bless me.

The possibility of "rebuilding some bridges to people in my past" held sway on my mind. Douglas John Hall speaks to the "Christian perspective on the future."

> When our eyes are opened to *God's* possibilities [Mk. 10:27], we may discover within ourselves, as they did, enough trust to choose the way that wasn't there before, and enough imagination to make it a truly *viable* way. It is never an *easy* choice. It is after all always some variation on…"the Way of the cross." But it is a way, an access to the future beyond the impasse of the present; and if we do not choose it when it presents itself to us, there is no guarantee that it will continue to be there.
>
> There is thus a strange and never quite "reasonable" interconnection between the recognition that God alone determines the future and that God makes us responsible for it. "…[W]ork out your own salvation with fear and trembling; for God is at work in you…" [Phil. 2:12]. The possibility of getting into the future beyond the cul-de-sac of the present is always a matter of "sheer grace" and "sheer faith" [*sola gratia, sola fide*]. But *obedience* to this possibility and necessity calls for decision and imagination.[26]

God's invitation to "take action" was repeated. I decided to test the words of the divine whisper, "I want the [denomination of origin] to bless you." I acted on it. A meeting was granted, and a representative group of the judicatory was present. I prepared a written statement of repentance, not wanting to leave words to the inspiration of the moment.

I could not control my emotions as I drove onto the site of the district office. Even after reordination in my adopted denomination, I was a prodigal son returning home to take responsibility and seek reconciliation. I was confronting so many dreams, memories, losses, and much hurt, as well as the end of so many relationships. I wept. I was able to gain control of my emotions sufficiently to enter the office, enter the room, and greet former colleagues. The moment I began to read the prepared statement, a flood of emotion overcame me. Tears flowing, reading was difficult. It took me more than an hour interspersed with emotions of brokenness to complete the reading.

Members of the judicatory asked several questions as they sought to discern the sincerity of repentance. The most important question they asked of me was to respond to their decision to uphold the discipline, a decision that denied the transfer of ordination to my adopted denomination. I answered in support of their decision. The members gathered around me, laid hands on me, and blessed me in prayer. Here was the blessing that the Lord desired for me. I received letters from the judicatory of the denomination and the official board of my former congregation accepting my repentance as genuine and granting forgiveness.

Nouwen, McNeill, and Morrison write openly about the negativity evoked by the word *obedience.*

> [T]he word *obedience* is often tainted by many feelings of hostility, resentment or distance. It nearly always implies that someone is in a position to impose his or her will on others.
>
> None of these negative associations, however, belongs to the obedience of Jesus Christ. His obedience is hearing God's loving word and responding to it. The word obedience is derived from the Latin word *audire,* which means "to listen." Obedience, as it is embodied in Jesus Christ, is a total listening, a giving attention with no hesitation or limitation, a being "all ear." It is an expression of the intimacy that can exist between two persons. Here the one who obeys knows without restriction the will of the one who commands and has only one all-embracing desire: to live out that will.[27]

The outcome of obedience included an unexpected miracle. Excerpts of the statement of repentance were read at the national assembly of the denomination during a session of corporate repentance. Reflecting on all these events, I stood amazed.

Candace R. Benyei is right when she points out that discernment is "hardly an exact science."

> Listening to God is a delicate and sometimes arduous process. Because God no longer writes out his or her will on stone tablets, the determination of what that will is must be made through a process of

spiritual discernment. In time-honored fashion, this discernment has involved the authority of the religious tradition and/or scriptures, the input of the community of believers, and perhaps, in cases pertaining to individual matters, the counsel of a practiced spiritual mentor. This discernment is necessary because the needs and neuroses of the human ego are loud and legion and must be separated from the still small voice of the Holy. Discernment, however, is hardly an exact science and at best is an ongoing process.[28]

I contemplate one final step. Should I make an offer of restitution? At times the voice of God turns out to be more oneself than God. In my journal are statements of guidance that I believed to be the voice of God. I discover later that the guidance was my own voice. I seek counsel on the matter of restitution, which is another stroke for river-running the holiness stream. For me, it would be an offer to submit to obedience and accept a secondary role in the denomination of origin. Can I be at peace with my past without this step of closure? Do I need to come full circle?

I take the final step that will bring the white-water odyssey full circle. I make an offer of restitution.

A White-water Surprise

God has a wonderful way of sharing a smile when it is least expected. The smile occurred around the time that I was waiting for a response from my denomination of origin regarding my offer of restitution and full reconciliation. It began with a telephone call from a member of my congregation in my adopted denomination. She informed me that a church member had been released from the hospital and sent to the Rosslyn, a care home for seniors. I thought, "Not there." The Rosslyn was renovated from my old church. We had sold the building years earlier, lifted the dedication, and relocated to a new church complex in a growing suburb. A developer had gutted the interior, constructed three floors of apartment units, and built a new entrance. It was still the old church to me, the building that once was home to the congregation that called me. I had not returned since the day we relocated.

I felt goose bumps on my body as I walked into the building. So many memories flooded my mind as I found the way to her room. I knocked on the door, waited for an invitation, and entered. We engaged in a brief chat. I told her that the building was a church once, that I had been the last senior pastor and had vivid memories of preaching there. It became apparent that she was in great pain, emotional and physical. In fact, the mental and physical anguish was so great she begged me to pray that God would take her life then. We talked about the immediate care she needed and how to address it. I was not going to pray that God would take her life. I read scripture and prayed for healing. I told her I would return soon. As I was about to leave, she asked me to come, hold her hand, and pray Psalm 23 aloud with her. I did.

I returned to the Rosslyn to visit her again. From the moment I walked into the room, I knew everything had changed. She was sitting up. Her frame of mind was transfigured. I was amazed. I asked her what had changed. She said that by the time we had finished praying Psalm 23 together during the previous visit, she knew that something wonderful had happened. During the reciting of Psalm 23, an electric-like energy had passed through her body, and she was healed from the mental and physical anguish. She returned home soon after my second visit. She was not healed of all her physical challenges, but she was healed of the mental and physical anguish that had led her to beg God to take her life. To this day she testifies to the miracle that God did for her as we recited Psalm 23. She had planned to take her own life that night, but God had something far more wonderful in mind for her–a miracle of healing. We have celebrated that moment together on many occasions.

I knew that regardless of the answer yet to come from my denomination of origin, God had confirmed me again to the divine calling on my life. God's reconfirmation came in the very building to which I was called as senior pastor, to serve a congregation among whom I would fall into moral sin. I have had no reason to return to the Rosslyn since.

Prophetic Team Dialogue—2

As I continued to wait for a decision from my denomination of origin, I accepted the invitation to participate in another prophetic session. I attended the Sixth Annual Pastor's Conference, Toronto Airport Christian Fellowship. A light was about to break out. Among many images and words, this image of hope was spoken over me:

> *Team Member:* I saw a big light cloud around you like a mist, a grayish color. It started to dissipate little by little. It started to open up, and open up, and open up. And then the big bright rays came upon you and you were standing up in a splendor, like out of you would come rays of light that would go here and there, here and there. All around you people will be touched by the light that was in you as the cloud dissipates completely.

A letter came from the serving president of my denomination of origin. He wrote words of forgiveness and reconciliation. It was a letter of closure that said that my work of reconciliation was complete. The cloud had dissipated. The long, arduous journey had come full circle. The words of the inner Guide, "I want the [denomination of origin] to bless you," had found another fulfillment. Although the letter reaffirmed that I did not qualify for ordained service in my denomination of origin, I was grateful for these words: "We are content to see you enter ministry in another denomination without a judgmental spirit, but with good wishes and blessings." I was free to serve again, free to give myself fully to my adopted denomination, no longer a prisoner to the past.

Embodying God's Presence in the Material World
A New Calling for a New Future

I have caught the current of a new future. I am reclaimed, recalled, reconciled, and recharged. I am a "project" of God's amazing grace, and I cannot express the gratitude that overwhelms my heart. God did not abandon me to a humbling crafted by my own choices. From the day I capitulated, the true Captain took charge and transformed personal chaos into divine design. I meditate on Romans 9 and pray for the grace to be a carrier of God's presence in the world. I see

> A picture of Jesus washing my feet
> in the waters of mercy.
> I sink into the experience.
> I feel accepted, loved, forgiven, and understood.
> Deeply affected by the experience.
> Gratitude.

All doubts vanish about my destiny. Being is the new axis around which this destiny turns. Doing is not excluded, only reoriented. I seek to be faithful to the new calling. I have no reputation to defend, no ladders to climb, nothing to prove. I raft into a new future with a new calling and a new commitment. As to the calling, I hear,

> "Dwayne, I place a new calling on your life…
> to be a pastor of my presence
> You will pastor people into my presence
> You will pastor people from my presence.
> This is your new calling and your new commissioning.
>
> Wherever you go, you will carry my presence with you—there is no greater destiny. I seek those, like you, who will be my presence-bearers. Carry my presence with you, and I will show myself to be with you. Live out of this destiny, and you will be blessed."

Guidance comes while listening to Romans 5 and praying for the grace to hear and follow in the present circumstances of my life. I hear,

> "You are prepared for usefulness, Dwayne…
> It will be in the ways I have loved you back to life…"

As to the commitment, while engaged in meditation on John 1:1–18 and 1 John 1:1–4, I hear,

> "Share your experience of me.
> Trust it."

As I discern the invitation of the inner Guide, it is apparent that the Shepherd of Love has imparted a new calling into my life: to be a pastor

(=shepherd) of the presence. A new thing on the white-water odyssey is the linkage of shepherding with the presence of God. The call is to shepherd people into God's presence and from God's presence. A second descriptor of call came as presence-bearer. There is a word of guidance as to embodiment: "It will be in the ways I have loved you back to life." God loved me back to life over the converging rivers of the evangelical, contemplative, desert, social justice, pentecostal-charismatic, holiness, and incarnational traditions. A second word of guidance as to embodiment: "Explore the invocation of my presence."

God's love was enacted in the world of the material. God's love came as embodiment of people, words, processes, and places. Human love in action over all the rivers mediated God's captaineering love, reclaiming a lost rafter. I have little sense of where my life would be today if these acts of reclamation had no material expression. People, words, processes, and places were incarnate mediators, containers of presence, enfleshments of God's mercy and grace. My odyssey has led to the deepest appreciation of love, embodied and enacted, in the concrete circumstances of life. Always I felt the love of the compassionate Shepherd as presence and promise. The incarnational river is the container of convergence for all the rivers of divine love.

I discern that the call encompasses an experience of God's presence as active in every person, over-against, alongside, indwelling, out there, right here, manifest, destiny-altering, gracious gift, defying magic, revelatory, illuminating, emanating energy, and nurturing simultaneity. To seek the presence of God with this enormity is an awe-inspiring thought. To be a carrier of the presence of God to this breadth and depth would be a breath-taking reality. The incarnational river holds all these possibilities within its waters.

The Incarnational River

Jesus' declaration of messianic vocation (Isa. 61:1–3; Lk. 4:18–19) is the mainstream of the incarnational river. The rivers of God's love converge at the incarnational river, which is about the presence of God in the material world, the intersecting of the spiritual and physical for the reclamation of life to God's design. Kenneth Leech writes about incarnational faith.

> The incarnation…is more than an assertion about the reality of the flesh and materiality of Christ; it is a governing principle of the Church's life, of God's relationship with the world, of the structure of all spiritual life and experience…
>
> A major consequence of taking incarnational faith seriously is that the spiritual person, far from despising or fearing or withdrawing from the world, needs to be inflamed by a passionate and intense love of the world, seeing in the material things of the world that handiwork of God, and in the people of the world the face of Christ.[29]

Jesus' incarnational declaration was my biblical mandate before my humbling. It is so today. What is distinct in the new call is the new sense of carrying the presence of God as Jesus carried the presence of God. To fulfill the call to be presence-bearers requires that which only the Spirit can give in every sense. Clark H. Pinnock speaks to the Spirit's role.

> It was evident that the power of the Spirit was on him for the benefit of the world. Jesus came as the Anointed One, preaching the gospel of the kingdom and performing signs of new creation. He proclaimed good news to the poor, mercy to the sick, liberty to captives, sight to the blind. By the power of the Spirit, Jesus announced a God who wills human wholeness. Therefore he went not to the righteous but to the sick and the outcast, to gather them under God's wings. By the Spirit he set people free from entrapment. He brought them hope and liberated their relationships. Demonic powers were driven out and creaturely life was restored. All this happened because the energies of the life-giving Spirit were at work in Jesus.[30]

Presence-bearers will continue the mission of Jesus in all its fullness. They will possess Jesus' promise of "greater works" that encompass all the rivers of God's love (Jn. 14:12–14).

Rivercrafts

I call these greater works rivercrafts. A variety of white water calls for a variety of raft designs. Selecting a rivercraft requires knowledge of the type of water: small, steep, large, or high-volume. The rivercrafts reclaimed my life. Each river of God's presence has its own distinct characteristics.

> To scout the rivercrafts for running the rapids over the rivers of God's love will propel me to the destination and take-out. Two phrases of guidance: (1) "It will be in the ways I have loved you back to life..."; and (2) "Explore the invocation of my presence." Each river hosts many rafts. I focus on the rivers and the rivercrafts over which God transformed my personal chaos into divine design.

EVANGELICAL RIVERCRAFTS

The evangelical river designs rivercrafts that take the form of theological reflection, faith-life shaped by the Word, faith-sharing the good news of Jesus Christ, and mentoring people in the Christian way. These evangelical rivercrafts guided me into God's gift of a transforming friendship with Jesus Christ. The decision to say yes to the inner voice—to invite Jesus Christ into my heart to be my Savior, Lord, and personal Friend—is the most life-energizing decision I have ever made. All the wonderful acts of transforming love occur within the context of friendship, including conversion.

CONTEMPLATIVE RIVERCRAFTS

The contemplative river designs rivercrafts that take the shape of spiritual direction, meditative writing, living in the present moment, and sacred silence.

Contemplative rivercrafts guided me into God's gift of dialogical relationship with God. The *Spiritual Exercises* taught me to listen and respond to the voice of God in words, feelings, and inner pictures. I first rode the contemplative river with the Quaker spirituality of Richard Foster's *Celebration of Discipline*. Another Quaker, Thomas Kelly, and his marvelous classic *Testament of Devotion,* with its concept of "a Divine Center," left a deep impression.

> Deep within us all there is an amazing inner sanctuary of the soul, a holy place, a Divine Center, a speaking Voice, to which we may continuously return. Eternity is at our hearts, pressing upon our time-torn lives, warming us with intimations of an astounding destiny, calling us home unto Itself...
>
> But the living Christ within us is the initiator and we are the responders. God the Lover, the accuser, the revealer of light and darkness presses within us, "Behold I stand at the door and knock." And all our apparent initiative is already a response, a testimonial to his secret presence and working within us.[31]

A potent dynamic exists when attention to the divine whisper converges with the discipline of listening to scripture. Paying particular attention to the foundational events of God's self-disclosure has inspired generations of seekers. Eugene H. Peterson calls for a return to "contemplative exegesis."

> We read Scripture in order to listen again to the word of God *spoken,* and when we do, we hear him *speak*. Somehow or other these words *live*. ...When we listen to the word of God in Scripture, listening for what God is revealing out of himself, a story is shaped in our hearing; and the fact that it is story and not something else—systematic theology, moral instruction, wise sayings—has powerful implications for exegetical work. For just as words have a revealing quality to them, so stories have a shaping quality to them.[32]

Words shaped into story when I read sections of my journal that comprised periods of time. Whether it was the story of calling, the story of divorce and remarriage, the story of repentance and reconciliation, the story of personal friendship with God, the story of a healing congregation, or the story of the new future, all parts connected to the larger story of my life. Peterson describes this shaping dynamic.

> Words are sounds that reveal. Words make stories that shape. Contemplative exegesis means opening our interiors to these revealing sounds and submitting our lives to the story these words tell in order to be shaped by them. This involves a poet's respect for words, and a lover's responsiveness to words.[33]

Desert Rivercrafts

The desert river designs rivercrafts of solitude, contemplation, spiritual conversation, spiritual warfare, and intentional therapy to engage the eight passionate thoughts. These rivercrafts lead to apatheia and God's gift of being as the axis of life.

The desert forced me to enter my wounds. Encounter in the desert is described as living in a furnace of transformation. I confronted the resident evil so deeply imbedded in my personality. So much of my life and service evolved around the axis of doing, pleasing, and craving affirmation. Stripped of the false self, I committed to begin again around the axis of being. Henri J. M. Nouwen spoke to my wound.

> For as long as you can remember, you have been a pleaser, depending on others to give you an identity. You need not look at that only in a negative way. You wanted to give yourself to others, and you did so quickly and easily. But now you are being asked to let go of all these self-made props and trust that God is enough for you. You must stop being a pleaser and reclaim your identity as a free self.[34]

Social Justice Rivercrafts

The social justice river designs rivercrafts that take the shape of reclaiming the dignity of the human person, deeds of compassion, nurturing social consciousness, and prophetic ministries of restorative justice. Social justice rivercrafts have a common theme: They are shaped for the express purpose of aligning the present order of things to the reign of God. They represent a radical discontentment with what Walter Wink calls "domination systems" and the institutional evil that marginalizes, suppresses, and abuses people for ends that are self-oriented. Systemic evil is seen as the primary cause of human suffering. These rivercrafts guided me into God's gift of compassion in action, out of which a new future came into being.

The rafters of social justice gave me non-anxious presence. They helped to restore dignity after the public humiliation of being a pastor who broke the public trust of so many. Their gift of compassion was not a blessing on my moral fault but a valuing of human dignity and worth. Because they were non-anxious about my wound, they were able to give me time to reorient and heal without condemnation. They could affirm the gifts and calling of God on my life. Marcus J. Borg, an influential rafter on the social justice river, says that spirituality is about the process of opening the heart to God.

> The fruit of this process is compassion...Compassion is not simply a means for the self's transformation but also the end or goal of such transformation. God's will for us–the goal of the working of the Spirit within–is to become more compassionate beings. Such was Saint Paul's point when he spoke of the greatest of the spiritual gifts as love, his more abstract term for what Jesus meant by compassion. If spirituality–a life of relationship with the Spirit of God–does not lead to compassion, then either it is life in relationship to a different spirit or there is a lot of static in the relationship. The absence or presence of compassion is the central test for discerning whether something is "of

God." As the primary gift of the Spirit, compassion is the primary sign of spiritual growth.[35]

Compassion, as fruit and goal of transformation, propels God's dream for the world.

Pentecostal-Charismatic Rivercrafts

The pentecostal-charismatic river designs rivercrafts that encompass powerful experiences of worship. These rivercrafts seek the manifest presence, Spirit-baptism, impartations of spiritual giftings. Such giftings serve as portals to signs, wonders, and healing ministries; to power/presence evangelism; and to the use of prophetic symbolism to penetrate into the deep substratum of persons. These rivercrafts guided me into God's gift of Spirit-energy zones of healing. When I entered one of these zones, everything changed. The outcome was deep inner healing and recommissioning by the Spirit. Tommy Tenney names it: "the residue of God on a person creates a *divine radiation zone* of the manifest presence of God, so much so that it affects those around you."[36] These divine energy zones of the manifest presence have a purpose—to fulfill the mission of Jesus (Lk. 4:18–19).

Holiness Rivercrafts

The holiness river designs rivercrafts to inculcate spiritual virtues; grow the fruit of the Spirit; and advance personal sanctification, repentance, restitution, and reconciliation. These rivercrafts guided me into God's gift of obedience as loving response to the moral character of God. I have learned the consequences of disobedience and the blessings of obedience. The negative feelings toward obedience have to do with the implication that "someone is in a position to impose his or her will on others."[37] Presence-bearers do not bring these negative associations to the virtue. They are carriers of the obedience of Jesus.

The Quakers possess a vision for "complete obedience," an obedience that will go the second half: "Commit your lives in unreserved obedience to him."[38] Thomas R. Kelly claims four steps to this "holy obedience":

> [T]he first step to the obedience of the second half is the flaming vision of the wonder of such a life, a vision which comes occasionally to us all...But whatever the earthly mystery of this moment of charm, this vision of an absolutely holy life is, I am convinced, the invading, urging, inviting, persuading work of the Eternal One.
>
> The second step to holy obedience is this: begin where you are. Obey *now*.
>
> And the third step in holy obedience, or a counsel, is this: if you slip and stumble and forget God for an hour, and assert your old proud self, and rely upon your own clever wisdom, don't spend too much time in anguished regrets and self-accusations but begin again, just where you are.

> Yet a fourth consideration in holy obedience is this: Don't grit your teeth and clench your fists and say, 'I will! I will!' Relax. Take hands off. Submit yourself to God.[39]

Obedience is not about trying harder. It is about listening to God attentively and yielding completely.

These are the ways God loved me back to life over the rivers of divine love. The rivers of God's love are the reign of God infusing the material world. God's reign is embodied in and through the church. These rivercrafts guided me into God's gift of the church as embodiment of the life, death, resurrection, and reign of Jesus the Christ.

Ecclesial River-running

Karl Rahner envisioned that the spirituality of the future will be threefold in character: It will be mystical, prophetic, and ecclesial. Mary E. Hines fleshes out the implications of Rahnerian spirituality.

> [T]he original experience of faith becomes fuller and more concrete as it is reflected on, put into words and acted on in the community of faith. Christians…find this universal experience confirmed in the life, death and resurrection of Jesus the Christ and continue to reflect on it in the community of the church. For the Christian, spirituality has to do concretely with discipleship of Jesus lived out in the church with its traditions, dogmas and doctrines.[40]

The white-water odyssey was ecclesial in nature. The river-running experiences were connected to "the community of faith" at all points: as to leading, governance, teaching, service, discipline, alienation, and restoration. My story puts models of the church in tension. Avery Dulles advances our understanding of the church and revelation.

> Because the mystery of the Church is at work in the hearts of committed Christians, as something in which they vitally participate, they can assess the adequacy and limits of various models by consulting their own experience…The Church exists only as a dynamic reality achieving itself in history, and only through some kind of sharing in the Church's life can one understand at all sufficiently what the Church is. A person lacking this inner familiarity given by faith could not be a competent judge of the value of the models.[41]

Here is the tension: Both my denomination of origin and my adopted denomination trace the roots of faith to God's self-revelation in the life, death, and resurrection of Jesus; yet both live out of diverse models of revelation and the church. Both denominations adhere to a "zero tolerance" position on clergy sexual misconduct but differ as to the limitations and possibilities of restoration to ordained service. There is particular disagreement when the outcome of the misconduct is divorce and remarriage. I am no longer eligible for licensed ministry at any level in my denomination of origin. Yet in my adopted denomination, with full knowledge of my odyssey, I have been restored and ordained, and I serve as a minister in good standing.

Acting out of differing models, both denominations have been faithful and consistent in their actions toward me. Both denominations, as human embodiments of the church, remain faithful to their "theory and practice." Both denominations seek to be "a dynamic reality achieving itself in history." Both models of church and revelation, and the ways they responded to my story, "illumine the mystery of the Church."[42] I rafted over the diverse mystery of the church. Reclaimed by and serving fully in my adopted denomination (social justice), I was able to return upstream to repent, to reconcile, to offer restitution, and to bring a biblical closure with my denomination of origin (evangelical). The evangelical model illumines the sanctity of marriage among the ordained, as example to all, within and beyond the church. Certain choices against this sanctity carry consequences for ordained ministers that are irreversible. On the other hand, the social justice model illumines the reinheriting of the disinherited, the depths of God's grace to restore the fallen fully to ordained service. I have river-run the mystery of the church as participant, fallen, and restored.

God transforms personal chaos into divine design. The lessons earned from chaos are multiform. I submit them to the collective wisdom of clergy, congregations, and judicatories.

Submerged within a Crisis of Calling

MEMO: February 2005
TO: Dwayne Ratzlaff
FROM: Tom Bandy

Dwayne:

The transition of your thinking from the crisis of morality and grace to the crisis of calling is a significant departure from much of the literature of "biographical brooding" that is so popular among baby boomers today. It reveals the depth and urgency of your spiritual quest. It is so remarkably similar to the desert fathers to whom you refer, and so remarkably foreign to the modern "churchmanship" that postmodern people have grown to disrespect and distrust.

Most "enlightened" people would be satisfied with restoration of social acceptance and personal equanimity. Psychotherapy became acceptable as part of the daily "grooming" habits of modern people in the 1960s—along with coffee addictions, retirement planning, and planned parenting. Spirituality became acceptable as part of the annual rituals of postmodern people in the late 1990s—along with cocaine addiction, x-treme sports, and the mystical pronouncements of movie stars receiving their Oscar. Your exploration of the crisis of calling is like wearing a "hair shirt" at the mall and opting to eat locusts and honey in the food court. It stands out.

It is the *relentlessness* of your self-examination and the *persistence* of your quest that will most offend the readers of your book. After all, 50 percent of the adult population in North America has already committed a moral indiscretion, and the other 50 percent have either tried and failed or are thinking about it now. From their point of view, you have already attained "OK-ness." They are puzzled about what this "salvation" might be that you still seek. There is something more, but most contemporary people (and contemporary clergy) aren't sure what it is.

Before I comment on some of the details of your quest, let me say a further word about its conclusion. Although you do not explicitly say it, you have learned the difference between a career and calling. Throughout your story about the "rivers" flows an "undercurrent" of longing for an institutional reconciliation with your denomination of origin. Even your eventual acceptance by another denomination holds a nuance of career preservation. It is as if, for all your spiritual brooding, the course of your living has still been dominated by the very practical desire to make a living as a parish minister. Job security, professional identity, and income from an ecclesiastical source have lurked in the eddies of your struggle. Indeed, my perception is that however different the various rivers of spirituality are, they are all alike in one thing: They are all, ultimately, institutionalized. They all end up with salaried staff, property, and program budgets. The reality is that most modern clergy who transfer from one stream to another do so more from a desire to have a better pension plan than from a desire to get closer to Jesus.

The miracle at the end of your story, I think, is that finally you eschewed career and surrendered fully to calling. You write:

"All doubts vanish about my destiny. Being is the new axis around which this destiny turns. Doing is not excluded, only reoriented. I seek to be faithful to the new calling. I have no reputation to defend, no ladders to climb, nothing to prove. I raft into a new future with a new calling and a new commitment."

These words are reminiscent of the liturgy from Wesley's Watch Night Service:

"I am no longer my own, but thine. Put me to what thou wilt, rank me with whom thou wilt; put me to doing, put me to suffering; let me be employed for thee, or laid aside for thee; let me be full, let me be empty; let me have all things, let me have nothing; I freely and heartily yield all things to thy pleasure and disposal."[43]

This is indeed a manner of rafting into a new future. It may be that the Spirit wanted you to be blessed by your denomination of origin, but I suspect it was so you could finally step beyond any dependence on any denomination for the authentication of your spiritual life.

This, of course, goes beyond interest to clergy alone. Any Christian (paid or unpaid, ordained or lay) will find this an important insight. Charismatic experience, more than any other stream of Christian spirituality, blurs distinctions between clergy and laity. Each stream seems to isolate the preacher, priest, or professional as uniquely relevant to God's calling, and each stream tends to define clergy as being "called out" from the general "body of Christ." The charismatic movement, on the other hand, goes the other way. It deliberately breaks down any differences based on certification or training and defines the deepest spirituality as being "called into" the experience of Christ. The charismatic movement has always been a great "leveler" in the church.

The typology Harvey Cox offers in *Fire from Heaven* helps interpret charismatic experience in general and your situation in particular. It also represents a considerable reversal in perspective from Cox's work thirty years earlier—*The Secular City*. Originally Cox predicted the triumph of secular materialism and godlessness and the demise of the sacred, but in fact what happened was the triumph of spirituality and the demise of the secular. Even now it catches people by surprise. When I served in the national office of the United Church of Canada in the 1990s, I would get calls from the media asking my opinion of the Toronto Blessing. They expected a liberal diatribe against manipulative, emotional religion and were surprised by my perception that the "Blessing" was connecting with a deeper, existential, "primal" yearning of the general public for whom secularity had proven bankrupt. Indeed, your story is not unique. I have talked to many an established mainstream or evangelical pastor who spoke of personal transformations at the "Toronto Blessing"—and begged me not to tell their bishops and presbyteries, lest it negatively impact their careers.

You might say that the charismatic movement cuts through a lot of ecclesiastical and theological futility to get to the real heart of the matter. *Heart* is the operative word. Much of established religion today is a "head trip": a well-managed, controlled, intellectual, abstract enterprise in which anything out of the ordinary in worship is dismissed as sociological or psychological aberration. People intuitively know that there is more to religion than this.

"Primal speech" is really more than speaking in tongues, having uncontrollable tears or laughter, or shouting until the roof falls down. It is more akin to the voice from the burning bush that announces "I am who I am." It is a defiant declaration of being over against nonbeing, of purpose over against purposelessness, of infinite value over against relative value. It is like shouting "God is!" or hearing God shout back "Here I am!" It is probably the simplest and most direct way of stepping back from the brink of nothingness.

"Primal piety" is really more than a redefinition of rules for behavior along conservative lines. It is a reshaping of lifestyle to align oneself with God's will. This is what Paul means in Romans 12 about refusing to be conformed to the world, but being transformed by God's grace. It is a shift from one kind of habitual behavior pattern to another, revealed both in the spontaneity and the daring of daily living:

Christian Behavior	Worldly Behavior
Honest self-assessment	Delusions of grandeur
Living spiritual gifts	Pursuing a career
Genuine love	Manipulative emotion
Familial affection	Competitive collegiality
Honorable action	Pragmatic self-advancement
Enthusiastic service	Grumbling duty
Liberal hospitality	Selective welcoming
Persistent optimism	Persistent cynicism
Empathic relationships	Self-centeredness
Respectful humility	Judgmental arrogance
Ready forgiveness	Ready vengeance
Peaceable living	Angry living
Desire for goodness	Desire for success

Lifestyle is one of the most "primal" ways to define life. It is not abstract, theoretical, or even voluntary. It is not chosen, just lived. The evangelical and social justice rivers understand these alternative behaviors to be a matter of decision, for which the individual human being will be held accountable. The charismatic, on the other hand, understands this alternative behavior as the inevitable result of being "swept away" by the Spirit. There really is no decision—nor any accountability—involved. It is, or it isn't. It is because the individual was "touched by the Holy," whether or not he or she was looking for it. It is radical grace.

"Primal hope" is more than an eschatological expectation of the consummation of history in justice and judgment. It is more personal than that. Your own story illustrates the point. You knew you were accepted, and you knew that God could still use you for good purposes, but you yearned for more than that. You yearned for a deeper cleansing of the spirit. It is one thing to remove the guilt, but quite another to remove the shame. It is this dichotomy that Paul Ricoeur sought to interpret in his well-known book *The Symbolism of Evil*.[44] The mark of evil is more than moral culpability; it is a kind of existential uncleanness that even liturgical confession cannot erase. Roman Catholic orthodoxy has always been suspicious of the charismatic movement for this reason, just as Protestant orthodoxy is suspicious because the movement suggests that therapeutic counseling and good words are not enough.

I suspect your speculations about the meaning of "falling backward" strike both Catholic and Protestant ears strangely. Why would you read anything further into the experience other than a psychological glitch resulting in a physical weakness? Yet the experience of power and comfort that surrounded the experience does suggest a deeper significance. It is akin to the team-building exercise that builds trust, in which people allow themselves to fall backward, *trusting* that their partners behind will catch them before they crack their heads.

The "primal" experience described by Harvey Cox is ultimately one of *radical trust*. You stake everything on an irrational surrender to a Higher Power whose existence cannot be proven. Such is the offense to the "secular city."

It seems to me that you have missed two preconditions to the charismatic experience, which are essential to your understanding of this as a genuine Christian movement. Without these two assumptions, I think your readers will be mystified as to why the charismatic river has been so powerful for you.

The first precondition is prayer—and a specific understanding about prayer. It is obvious that you treat life itself as a prayer, and that the moments when you actually "pray" in any traditional sense of that word are really only "spikes" of soulful intensity in a life already sensitized to the holy. You see God everywhere, in everything, through every relationship, hidden behind every object. It is what my mentor (Tillich) might have called an attitude of "belief-ful realism," in which life itself has become sacramental. Infinite spirit permeates the finite world, and it only takes a blink or a breath for you to cross the threshold.

Although a surprising number of pagans share this view of the world, many Christians do not. Mainstream evangelicals and social activists, for example, generally perceive a wide gulf between personal and daily experience on the one side, and divine and eschatological purpose on the other. The former requires the medium of biblical knowledge to cross that gulf, and even then Christ tends to be a principle of salvation rather than a traveling companion. The latter requires the medium of ideological clarity or psychological health to cross that gulf, and even then Christ tends to be a template for behavior rather than personal savior. The charismatic movement uniquely appeals to those people who see a potential "burning bush" in every azalea.

I think it is revealing that your language about prayer is both sensual and sexual. This is certainly true to ancient and medieval experience, although it is unsettling to modern people. Prayer really is a function of eros more than agape in the sense that it is an expression of the desire of the finite to become united with the infinite. Paul expressed this kind of desire, asking to know nothing except Christ, to participate in Christ, to share in his sufferings so that he can share in his resurrection. Dante and other late-medieval Christians did not really disapprove of lust in the way the later Puritans did. The only problem with lust was that the object of desire was misplaced. You follow truth with the same passion with which Dante followed Beatrice through hell.

The second precondition is the Bible—and a specific treatment of the Bible. It is obvious that you are biblically *conversant* and not just biblically literate. This may be due to your experience as a seminary teacher, but I think it has more to do with immersing yourself in biblical metaphors and stories subsequent to your initial baptism of the Spirit. You filter daily experience through biblical phrases, stories, ideas, and events. In this sense, your approach to scripture resembles the allegorical method of the ancient church more than the critical method of the modern church.

Although many Christians (particularly evangelical Christians) will identify with this treatment of the Bible, many pagans certainly will not. The death of Christendom has meant that many of the stories, metaphors, and concepts that were implicitly Christian have been forgotten from cultural memory. Postmoderns are as likely to attribute experiences of the supernatural to Zeus, Thor, or an unknown Higher Power as to Jesus Christ or the God of Abraham and Sarah. The charismatic movement only succeeds as an expression of Christianity when it is experienced through the interpretive filter of scripture.

I think this is particularly important to your discussion of spiritual and emotional healing. As I said before, this connects with the "primal hope" to be cleansed of shame as well as forgiven of sin. The healing of which you speak is interpreted or focused by your particular understanding of scripture and not especially by any understanding of depth psychology. I mention this because it shapes your expectations for the outcome of healing. What are the marks of healing? How do you know you are "healed"? Because your own quest for healing had to do with issues of intimacy, marriage, and self-esteem, you tend to measure success against the fairly conservative Roman and Jewish expectations of family and marriage that are assumed by scripture. To what extent Paul *prescribes* specific behavior patterns regarding family and marriage as intrinsically Christian, and to what extent Paul *assumes* specific patterns as normative based on Roman cultural experience, is an area of some controversy today.

You tell a powerful story about visiting the senior woman released from the hospital to a temporary residence in Rosslyn, the former church building that had been renovated for convalescent care. You tell the story primarily to illustrate a step in *your* healing—divine confirmation of your calling as a pastor. Yet the story bears another interpretation. It is a story of being used as a mediator of grace to bring healing to this woman of *anguish,* although not of *infirmity.* Spiritual healing had more to do with peace of mind, or serenity of heart, than any particular change in physical health. Depth psychology might interpret this to mean an acceptance of loss and new strength to live within limitations. Your biblical template of thought, however, interprets this as a divine intervention that gives her faith and takes away pain.

What does "healing" look like? How does cleansing "feel"? How can one be confident that the restoration of wholeness you claim is in fact a reality of grace, and not a self-delusion or personal excuse? The truth is that I have met all too many "charismatics" who claim to be healed and cleansed, but who really seem to be making excuses for themselves and escaping reality. On the other hand, I have met all too many "seekers" who yearn to be healed and cleansed, but who in reality cannot get beyond their personal self-recriminations to accept the fact that they are already accepted by God.

I think this is the context in which your reflections on Wesley's doctrine of sanctification should really be developed. Wesley is perhaps clearer in describing the steps through which believers fall from grace than he is describing the steps through which believers are restored to grace. I think it is somewhat the same for you—and indeed, for anyone. We are much clearer about how we got into this predicament than we are about how we will get out of it. The journey from "I repent in dust and ashes" to "I know that my redeemer lives" is marked by specific measurements of success.

Sincere repentance: The individual faces the truth of self-destructive behavior; alienation from God; and hurtful, abusive, or immoral behavior. The individual turns away from evil habits, and dedicates himself or herself to a new way of life.

Intentional atonement: The individual specifically sets out to right wrongs, seek forgiveness from injured parties, engrain new and healthy habits in living, and commit to a spiritual discipline designed to know Christ. The individual develops a credible pattern of observably healthy, faithful behavior.

Radical surrender: The individual accepts ultimate inability to erase the shame of the past or to right all the wrongs committed. The individual surrenders all pride and choice to God and dedicates himself or herself solely to companionship with Christ and to a lifestyle shaped by the Spirit.

Fruits of the Spirit: The individual gradually demonstrates more and more completely the "fruits of the spirit": love, joy, peace, patience, kindness, gentleness, fidelity, meekness, temperance, endurance, and so forth. The individual seeks and accepts the reproof and correction of peers and searches for divine guidance.

Discernment of Call: The individual receives and clarifies a personal mission that reaches beyond self to serve strangers by doing beneficial deeds and sharing Christian hope. The call may vary from person to person, but is the final sign of Christian maturity.

The first two steps remind one of traditional twelve-step recovery programs, but the peculiarly Christian character of sanctification soon emerges. One of the things about your story is that you have pressed the process of healing or sanctification far beyond stage two. One can see how each of the spiritual rivers you discuss impacts the process of sanctification at various points. In the end, the final mark of healing is calling. The healed become healers.

Your brief mention of the early eleventh-century Eastern rite monk, Symeon the New Theologian, is particularly apt in this context and is worth further exploration. He belongs within the "charismatic stream" of Christian spirituality because of the unique synergy he described between divine grace and human freedom and because of his emphasis on mystical union with the divine through prayerful repetition of the name of Jesus. This synergy earned him the antagonism of Western, anti-Pelagian theologians such as Augustine, who proclaimed salvation by grace alone; and the same synergy earned Wesley the antagonism of traditional reformers for the same reason.

You refer to Symeon's teaching of the "gift of tears," which, as the process of perfection continued, transformed from tears of repentance to tears of enthusiasm to tears of joy. This was a part of a larger meditative discipline in which the

Christian ascended to union with God. The discipline relied on the guidance of a spiritual mentor and the use of the "prayer rope" (akin to the Western "rosary"). The meditative technique included a prolonged posture of prayer (head and shoulders bowed, eyes open and fixed on heart or prayer rope); slowed and controlled breathing; and mentally imaging the descent of the intellect into the heart, lungs, and other psychosomatic centers of the body. Throughout the process, the Christian simply meditated or repeated the name of Jesus—a meditative "mantra," if you will, the practice of which began as early as the seventh or eighth centuries.

I mention this detail because the meditative technique is a micro-imitation of the larger process of sanctification. The Christian proceeds from the "prayer of the lips" (sincere repentance and promises for alternative behavior), to the "prayer of the intellect" (radical surrender to God and contemplation on the fruits of the Spirit), to the "prayer of the heart" (prayer that is "not I, but Christ within me," as Paul says in Galatians). Such prayer is union with God, through which individual consciousness is infused with the presence of God and individual lifestyle is infused with the mission of God.

There is no question that charismatic experience, taken to this extreme, blends easily with both the contemplative and monastic rivers of Christian spirituality. Wesley's genius, I think, lay in his ability to translate the process of sanctification into social action.

One of the great values of your story is that you are able to speak knowledgeably and experientially of all the great streams of Christian spirituality, appreciate their uniqueness, and accept them as all equally relevant to the greater Christian movement. You speak of having discovered a new "incarnational river." The image that comes to my mind is that you have been exploring a network of rivers, thinking each to be separate and distinct, only to discover that you have really just been exploring a large and complicated delta through which various branches of water have split from a single river of grace and eventually empty into a single ocean of life. It is this "river-beyond-rivers," or this all-encompassing movement of Christ, that has been shaped and institutionalized by culture, history, and the idiosyncrasies of individual minds.

You wisely call this an incarnational river because it really is an experience of intimate companionship with Jesus Christ. It is a movement because it is not only a knowledge of Christ, but a walking with Christ on his journey of mission. The postmodern quest is really just this search for both the headwaters of grace and the destination of life. In the postmodern view, all the various rivers that you have described have become so laden with silt and the weighty, dirty particles of institutionalization that they are hardly moving at all. Instead, these rivers are meandering across the delta so slowly that postmodern people think they will *never* reach the sea! Moreover, these ever-meandering, increasingly slow-moving rivers attract more crocodiles, snakes, and mosquitoes than they do real fish. In postmodern experience, rafting down these denominational rivers is a painfully slow and dangerous proposition. Their experience with church life is one of increasing bureaucracy that blocks creativity and increasing conflict that devours healthy people.

Postmodern people long for another river. Denominational orthodoxies of any brand do not satisfy. In many ways, the contemporary situation resembles that of the church in the third century. Constantine had not yet risen to power, but the Christian movement had multiplied dramatically, survived various persecutions, and was rapidly settling into liturgical and organizational patterns. Already Origen would complain that deacons and bishops were abusing power, that decision-making bureaucracies were becoming more focused on money management and cemetery maintenance, and that powerful sees were becoming more competitive for power than zealous for mission (sure signs of institutionalization). It was precisely this context that motivated spiritually-minded Christians to explore two options to orthodoxy.

Gnostics opted out of orthodoxy to escape an inherently evil world through elite knowledge. They were convinced that the divine spark within them could achieve unity with the divine, a human achievement requiring only access to "secret" sayings of Jesus unavailable to ordinary Christians. The option is remarkably similar to contemporary spiritualities that ignore the necessity of the cross, complain of ecclesiastical conspiracies that hide the truth, and encourage a therapeutic/mystical ascendance to salvation. The gurus often seem to be movie stars, journalists, scientists, artists, and the literati of contemporary culture.

Montanists opted out of orthodoxy to embrace an apocalyptic eschatology. They were convinced that the Spirit revealed to select prophets and prophetesses the timing and location of the judgment day and the nature of the New Jerusalem. Rigorous in behavioral expectations and exclusive in dogmatic formulas, they denounced any accommodation to culture. The option is remarkably similar to contemporary fundamentalists (conservative and liberal alike) driven by particular ideologies. The gurus often seem to be activists, university mavericks, politicians, middle managers, and the "illiterati" of contemporary culture.

It may come as a surprise to the various rivers of Christian spirituality, Dwayne, that you can value them all equally for making a contribution to a larger experience of Christ. But it will come as an even greater surprise to the institutional advocates of each of these denominational rivers that the postmodern public lumps them all together into an institutional orthodoxy that they equally do *not* value and reject. We see in the emerging twenty-first century the kind of theological confusion and chaos of the third century, with similar destructive implications for the peace of society and the welfare of the state.

This is not the place to speculate whether it is even possible for another Constantine to draw together councils of wise Christian leaders from all the rivers of spirituality to build a new consensus. Yet it is true that there is another option: the revitalization of orthodoxy that returns the church to its original roots. This is a life movement that is simply an intimate companionship with Jesus, fully divine, fully human, an infinite paradoxical mystery, but crucial for abundant life (to paraphrase the ancient Chalcedonian Confession). It is a mystical participation not only in Jesus, but in the mission of Jesus, for the person of Jesus and the ongoing work of Jesus are inseparable.

I find it fascinating that your personal story returns to the unsettling issue of "obedience." As you explore the thought of Thomas Merton (a great synthesizer of Christian movements), you react instinctively against his notion of "solemn obligation" to the Christian vocation of holiness:

"Obedience is the heart stroke of holiness. Impossible!"

The rejection of what postmodern people perceive as orthodoxy is really just an extension of the willfulness and pride implicit in the competition among denominations and rivers of Christian thought over the past several centuries. Indeed, much of your own story has been focused on yourself—*your* failures, *your* experiences, *your* needs, *your* life. The real key to holiness is that *it is not about you at all!* It is about God in Christ, Christ's mission on earth, and how that mission is relevant *to everybody else.*

By the end of your story, obedience has come to mean something very different than at the beginning of your story. Now, it means obedience to a larger biblical vision, to an experience of Christ, to credible spiritual mentors, and to a process of relentless and sometimes painful sanctification. Previously, it meant obedience to a denominational polity, to an experience of institutional loyalty, to certified church officers, and to a process of confusing and sometimes contradictory accountability. The passage from one to the other is willful and personal, but in the end it comes back to obedience. To remain forever willful ultimately leads to despair and alienation. Merton (and the monastic movement that preceded him) was right: Obedience is the heart stroke of holiness.

CHAPTER 4

River-running the Rapids of Spirit
Level 1 Teamwork

	A Disaster Plan for a Compulsive Spirit	Spirituality for the Depths	A Confused Spirit Finding Center
CLERGY	Confront the speed demons	Find spirituality for desperate times	Rediscover shepherding
CONGREGATION	Prepare to maneuver over chaos	Embrace and proclaim jubilee	Organize "Seekers Anonymous"
DENOMINATION	Develop a plan for disaster	Speak openly about passions	Nurture clergy self-care

The Team Concept

I have experienced both rafting in solitude and group rafting within the church. I have learned that we can never fulfill our mission outside of a commitment to group rafting. But to our commitment we must add expertise. The church was created as the dream team. Clergy, congregations, and denominations raft in sync with the multiform mission of the church. In sync should be true for our darkest defeats as well as our brightest victories. We are inseparable. We succeed as a team, and we fail as a team. The church is a team concept. The levels of teamwork indicate increasing complexity of white water.

Clergy

I live with a real sense that I am unworthy to coach the servants who have been faithful to their calling from first to last. I have great respect for the countless clergy who practice "effective guiding"[1] day in and day out. Knowing clergy are stronger paddling together as teams in sync rather than as individuals out of sync, I share the insights earned from chaos through moral failure with the passionate hope that these insights will reinforce wisdom, promote servant leadership, enhance clergy effectiveness, and deepen faithfulness to the mission of Jesus Christ.

The relationship between paddle captain and crew is not dissimilar to the relationship between clergyperson and congregation.

> Team rafting straddles a line between shared elation and communal frustration. When a paddle crew perfectly executes difficult maneuvers in intense whitewater, the feeling is incomparable. But when the team falls out of sync and lets the raft ricochet off of rocks and hydraulics, paddle rafting can be a nerve-wracking endeavor. The paddle captain provides the critical link between the raft and its engine–the paddlers. Equal parts coach, choreographer, cheerleader, and drill sergeant, the paddle captain strives to balance paddlers' strokes, translate maneuvers into understandable commands, and provide the necessary inspiration to complete a successful descent. All the while, the paddle captain picks the course through rapids and executes turning and rudder strokes to keep the raft moving along a safe course.[2]

The lessons will keep clergypersons moving down a safe course by executing difficult maneuvers even in rapid descents, in pursuit of their vision.

Congregations

Congregations are ill-prepared to prevent or respond to the devastation of clergy sexual misconduct. Their responses impact the clergyperson and family, the member-victim and family, the church as a family system, and the judicatory as the disciplinary body. The mission of the church is a team thing. Words and actions must be in sync if the team is to maneuver down the rapids safely. The team depends on the clarity and the integrity of the captain's commands to achieve the desired destination.

Effective group rafting requires mutual trust. Disaster looms when the paddle captain breaks the confidence of the team. The same is true for the clergy-congregational team. Congregations must be able to count on the harmony of words and actions among all in positions of accountable leadership. All fallen clergy would dismiss any notion that sexual misconduct was the intended outcome of their sacred vows. Congregations play a vital role in the employment and empowerment of clergy and should learn lessons from the dismissed clergy. Clergy faithfulness and failure occur within the context of congregations. We rise and fall together.

Denominations

Judicatories are the governing structures of denominations that surround every congregation. These structures are "designed to support and strengthen the total mission of the church."[3] When rafters capsize over raging waters, judicatories come to the rescue. Judicatories have the difficult duty to mete out discipline and enact restoration. The challenge is to execute faithful care to all concerned. I offer lessons earned from chaos to these empowered groups of governing leaders.

White-water rafting is a risky venture. The more exciting and difficult the white water, the greater is the risk. It is dangerous for veteran rafters to mock danger. Jeff Bennett warns, "[U]ncontrolled risk invites calamity. Accordingly, safety should be the primary concern on any river outing."[4] Bennett's words parallel the daring adventure of ordained ministry. A vision-driven life thrives on the challenge. Risk is a constant companion of mission. Danger lurks within uncontrolled risk. Downstream, uncontrolled risk can become out-of-control chaos. Denominational judicatories have a vital role in the guiding of risk. The paddle strokes of denominational leaders facilitate the risk management of clergy and laity on any river-running mission.

Team Paddle Strokes—A Disaster Plan for a Compulsive Spirit
Clergy...Confront the Speed Demons

Confront the speed demons of compulsive living before they overpower you. The desert streams demand that we break through the shallow compulsions of life and return to the core of being. The process is painful, but the benefits are beyond price. The desert movement began as a protest against the intrusion of evil into the church, embodied as worldliness. The lesson these pilgrims learned in the desert is that evil lurks within us. This evil came to be identified as the seven deadly sins, all manifestations of the false self. These explorers of the spirit discovered that death to the false self did not come without struggle. These mothers and fathers of the desert became inner resistance fighters. Their stories helped me face down the inner enemies of pride, lust, and anger. The hard lessons of the desert streams channeled me to the end of self-rescue. I entrusted myself to the Christ-Friend all over again. This spiritual warfare led me to commit to orient my life and service around "being" rather than "doing." Inner addictions are powerful opponents. I call them "speed demons" because they create an inner drivenness. The desert streams invite us into the depths to confront them. The fathers and mothers of solitude teach us ways to break through to the re-creating voice of God. Go deep enough, and discover another presence more powerful yet–the gentle voice of divine love. It is an amazing thing to hear a gentle voice in the midst of the clash of inner warfare. The speaking voice tames the passions. They called it "apatheia." The passions are brought to calm by the mercy of Christ.

Attention to sacred scripture is central among the ways to "*apatheia*." The desert streams birthed a unique approach to sacred reading called *lectio divina*. The desert teachers tell us that the discipline of listening to scripture carries over into the active life. I recall a defining moment in a movie theater watching a scene in the Disney movie *The Lion King* in which the young lion Simba, running from his destiny, looks into the water and sees the reflection of his dead father. Simba hears his father say that Simba has forgotten who he is. The inner voice took those words and touched the core of my being. I was running from my destiny. I had forgotten who I was. I was a child of God. I was called to live and act as a God-child. The compulsion to run away from my calling, now inseparable from my humiliation, was brought to calm.

Attention to sacred scripture, more than any other means of grace, ushered me into "apatheia" (abiding calm) of the passions. As scripture is read slowly–with a listening ear–a word, phrase, thought, feeling or image becomes invitation into the presence of transforming love and is transformed into a prayer of the heart. We speak our deepest longings to the God who withholds no good thing from us. We listen for the response of love beyond our best imaginations. We enter the realm of silent intimacy embraced by unconditional love. The inner compulsions are vanquished or, at the least, are put in their place to minimize their power. We leave the presence filled with the desire to live out the word that has provided the nourishment of spiritual milk. Downstream, the desert streams formed the contemplative river, with its unique approach to scripture. The missional movement of Ignatius of Loyola invited retreatants into an imaginative contemplation of the life of Jesus. As you move deeper with Jesus into the gospel narratives, the compassionate Jesus comes to free you from the false self and to invite you to live out of your being as a child of God through Jesus Christ. Jesus the Christ becomes mentor in all our encounters with God. Christ is more forgiving, more accepting, more understanding, more compassionate, more patient, more liberating, and more shepherding than we could have imagined. The Divine Lover changes hearts, heals open wounds, and supplies transforming love that makes us feel secure enough to face the enemies within.

Scripture exposes these inner enemies, defeats them, and creates wholeness out of brokenness. The words of M. Robert Mulholland, Jr., resonate with my odyssey.

> [T]he Word of God is portrayed in scripture as doing at least three things. (1) When that Word of God intrudes, encounters, or breaks in, it addresses human beings in their brokenness. That is part of the Good News: we don't have to measure up to some level of wholeness before the Word addresses us. (2) The Word calls us to wholeness right at the point of our brokenness!…In Revelation 3:19, Jesus says, "Those whom I love I reprove and nurture. Here God's encounter with human brokenness and God's offer of nurture into wholeness are conjoined. The scripture is a revelation of the Word addressing our brokenness and calling us to wholeness. (3) Scripture is the revelation of the Word as the agent of transformation.[5]

As I listened through the Scriptures I recognized the sound of that speaking Voice as patient, gentle, yet persistent in the direction of healing and wholeness.

We dare not underestimate the deceptions of these inner foes even with the resources of Spirit and Word. Some discernment issues are complex and require careful scrutiny. We need all available resources when we face down the speed demons. I could encounter and overcome any challenge alone, so I thought. Success had led me to this confidence. Then a convergence of internal and external situations coalesced against me and proved me wrong. The care of another discerning person is necessary to aid in the movement toward spiritual and psychological health.

A codiscerner fills a strategic role as we face the speed demons of compulsive living. Reginald S. Ward (1881–1962), English Anglican priest, presents the role of director as "physician."

> The task of the physician of souls is twofold. His first duty is that of diagnosis, by which he must endeavour to discover the poison which is doing most to hinder the soul's contact with God and the shaping of his life to carry out the purpose of God. His second duty is to find out how the contact with God through prayer, which is the source of health and strength in the spiritual life of the individual, can be increased and trained.[6]

A "physician of souls" can be a codiscerner for the interrelationship between spiritual and psychological health. The enemies of wholeness may lurk in the unconscious, abiding their time, until the right set of circumstances releases them from their den.

Congregations...Prepare to Maneuver over Chaos

A prudent church anticipates. Congregations must prepare for the eventuality of chaos. When we live in denial, we fail to prepare adequately for clergy and congregant disaster and rescue operations. Emotional systems are complex. The human heart is convoluted. Congregations can expect to maneuver over chaotic waters. The internal and external dangers are real and nearer than we think. Are congregations ready for the chaos that ensues when clergy emotional and ethical systems break down? Are congregations trained to employ rescue teams to all persons wounded by the fallout?

Harrison Owen, the creator of Open Space Technology, claims that chaos is a natural part of life. It represents a growth point in any human system, religious or otherwise. He reasons,

> [C]haos creates the Open Space in which the new can emerge. Obviously, there are no guarantees here, for chaos can equally mark the end, in fact it always does. The central question is not about ending, but rather the possibility of new beginning. Chaos may therefore be the essential precondition for all that is truly new. No chaos, nothing new.[7]

Owen proposes that "chaos creates the differences that make a difference, through which we learn."[8] The point is not to minimize or justify the devastating aftermath of intrapersonal, interpersonal, or moral breakdown, but to maximize the learning outcome of chaos for clergy and congregations. The "ultimate gift" of chaos is that it forces us to the depths where transformation can begin. We learn what is important again. A new vision emerges from the depths.[9]

The wounds that penetrate the church as a result of clergy sexual misconduct cannot be overstated. Only a church that has endured it can speak to the depth of the hurt, the sense of betrayal, and the long journey to healing. The abrupt end of my relationship with the offended congregation was pure emotional chaos. Formal access to the church leaders and people ended. I was given the opportunity to make a public confession the Sunday after my resignation. I was in no frame of mind to accept. An amputee tells about feeling a missing limb long after it is gone. The end of my relationship with the betrayed congregation feels like an amputation to this day. The work of reconciliation by means of letters and second-person representatives feels incomplete.

Is it fanciful thinking to expect that clergy and congregation can share experiences of chaos together in some form as offender and offended, at least to connect face-to-face during reconciliation time? I wonder if transformation might have occurred sooner if we could have engaged in some form of grief work together. It would have been a struggle. Another complicating factor is that I was not responding as one who was ready to change course.

Kenneth Leech believes it is the role of the local church to facilitate the process of "Christ-ening," of sharing in Christ's nature. This is the way we become biblical people in our response to the world. The local church provides a setting for maturing in Christ by helping us grapple with the scriptures in today's world. The local church provides an encounter with the Word in the world through a threefold pattern of "confrontation, exploration and struggle."[10] The local church is

- **a wrestling center**, a forum in which there can be open debate and struggle on the crises of the day in the light of biblical insights;
- **a still point** in which individuals can find the space and the solitude for the necessary inner creative brooding and prayerful reading;
- **facilities** for continual weeding, purging, clarifying of the truths of the Gospel message.

Only

> in this way can Scripture come to live in us, to unsettle us, to grow within us, to unify our vision. The aim of this process is that we become a biblical people: a people formed and nourished by the Word, a people of contradiction and of authentic nonconformity.[11]

It is self-evident that the relationship of clergy and congregation has to account for moral sin and the profound rupture of trust as well as the clergyperson's subsequent responses to the betrayal of trust. Church discipline is essential for healing and restoration. Discipline cannot and should not be dismissed or delayed. Nevertheless, the immediate amputation of the relationship turned my personal chaos into a dangerous and alien world. I believe it set back the process of "Christ-ening" on my spiritual odyssey. Congregations can create a better way to maneuver over the chaotic waters of clergy fault. Healing can be advanced when the fault is addressed within the congregational context in which it occurs. The sin cannot be isolated from the emotional systems that reared it. It is worth the struggle for both fallen pastor and people to enter the depths of chaos together, because it is from out of the depths that transformation begins. It can begin with a reconciliation team composed of minister, congregation, and denominational leaders to discern the way forward.

Denominations...Develop a Plan for Disaster

Assessing the models of prevention and intervention in the wider church can be instructive for denominational leaders charged with the mission of disaster prevention and rescue. A denomination will craft a position statement on sexual ethics consistent with its biblical and theological agenda. Any statement will be inclusive of the multiple terms used to classify the breakdown of sexual ethics within pastoral relationships: moral fault, adultery, sexual misconduct, sexual abuse, sexual harassment, sexualized behavior, sexual assault, and child sexual abuse.

I cite the United Methodist Church (UMC) as a bold model for addressing the issue of sexual ethics. Denominational leaders acknowledge openly:

> There is little doubt that sexual misconduct in church and society is a significant and troubling topic for our communities and congregations worldwide. We are aware that this unwanted behavior damages the moral environment where people worship, work and learn. In 1996, the General Conference made a commitment to focus on sexual misconduct within the church and take action to address this brokenness and pain within the United Methodist Church.[12]

To begin, the United Methodist Church (UMC) provides a thorough treatment of the terms of sexual ethics for its constituents, including the meaning of sexual misconduct and sexual abuse.

> Sexual misconduct within a ministerial relationship can be defined as a betrayal of sacred trust, a violation of the ministerial role, and the exploitation of those who are vulnerable in that relationship. Sexual abuse within the ministerial relationship occurs when a person within a ministerial role of leadership (lay or clergy, pastor, educator, counselor, youth leader, or other position of leadership) engages in sexual contact or sexualized behavior with a congregant, client, employee, student, staff member, coworker, or volunteer.[13]

In 1996 the UMC confronted the issue of sexual abuse. It called for the development of programs and practices that would prevent and eradicate sexual misconduct and abuse in the church. In 1998 a survey of annual conferences assessed progress in four key areas: prevention, education, intervention, and healing. The outcome of the survey enhanced prevention and intervention in five critical areas:

1. resources for various constituencies within the church addressing prevention, education, intervention, and healing after lay or clergy sexual misconduct
2. more training (entry-level, follow-up, and advanced) for the various constituencies within the church addressing prevention, education, intervention, and healing
3. discovery, development, and implementation of models for intervention and healing in order to provide a consistent and thorough response when complaints of lay or clergy sexual misconduct are initiated
4. development of a model for ongoing assessment of policies, practices, and responses of conferences in addressing clergy and lay sexual misconduct
5. opportunities for annual conferences to share their resources and experiences in responding to complaints of clergy and lay misconduct of a sexual nature[14]

Unequivocally, the UMC stands in opposition to the "sin of sexual misconduct and abuse within the church" and is committed to the "eradication of sexual misconduct in all ministerial relationships."[15]

Discipline is an essential expectation within the life of the church. Accountability to the community of faith is fundamental to the church as a hospitable, healing community. The lessons I earned from chaos resonate with these umbrella words:

> Support without accountability promotes moral weakness; accountability without support is a form of cruelty.
>
> A church that rushes to punishment is not open to God's mercy, but a church lacking the courage to act decisively on personal and social issues loses its claim to moral authority. The church exercises its discipline as a community through which God continues to "reconcile the world to himself."[16]

If the practice of the UMC is consistent with its statements, the constituents appear ready to manage the polarities around sexual ethics: accountability with support, discipline with mercy, and patience with decisiveness. All polarities seek to achieve reconciliation as the dream of God for the world.

I was unaware of the position statements of my denomination of origin on the prevention, consequences, and intervention of sexual misconduct. I understood the ethic of sexual purity, fidelity in marriage, covenant-keeping, the sin of adultery, and the absolute unacceptability of any form of sexual misconduct in the pastoral relationship. Nevertheless, I received no preemptive education on sexuality in pastoral relationships at any point in my seminary training or continuing education. The first training session on the topic of sexual ethics came as a requirement for ministerial service in my adopted denomination. It was presented as a video session on real-life ministerial encounters. The actors role-played pastoral situations. The instructor used professional role-playing as a springboard to class discussion about appropriate and inappropriate responses. I wondered why it took so long to receive sensitivity training on a topic so vital to ministerial faithfulness. Every denomination could require sensitivity training around issues of sexual ethics.

Team Paddle Strokes—Spirituality for the Depths
Clergy...Find Spirituality for Desperate Times

Clergy can venture into the flow, energies, and life-power that are at the fountainhead of Christian spirituality. "Just enough" spirituality will not do when confronted with monsters. If clergy can find spirituality for desperate times, it will be more than sufficient for the good times. There is explosive interest in all forms of spirituality all around us and a growing desire for something more among clergy also. Converging rivers lead to powerful encounters. Consider how each Christian river made a unique and indispensable contribution to my reclamation.

At the core, the heart yearns for what physicist-theologian John Polkinghorne calls the "central Christian experience."

> The central Christian experience of encounter with Christ is that in him is found a redeeming and transforming power so great that it can only be described in terms of metaphors of a new creation (2 Cor. 5:17) or a new birth (Jn. 3:3–8) or life from the dead (Rom. 6:5–11).[17]

The experience of Christ is breathtaking in its many expressions throughout history.

It is simplistic to divide the varied Christian traditions into the two categories of traditional and charismatic. I do so to express a valid point made by Loren B. Mead, founder of The Alban Institute. He said that one of five challenges facing the future church is to "discover a passionate, even charismatic, spirituality." Mead explains the challenge:

> Contrary to the behavior of the traditional mainliners and traditional charismatics, the challenge is not for one group to eliminate the other, but that the gifts of the ordered, structured approach to faith may be integrated into the vital, enthusiastic, Spirit-filled approach. The challenge is to move beyond the war between religious sensibilities and experiences to discover a new expression of faith that incorporates the gifts of both traditions...
>
> To face the future, the church must find ways to bring the gifts of charismatic spirituality to the heart of the church life without denying the gifts and contributions of traditional spirituality. My hunch is that the presence of both, living in tension but not in opposition, will increase the vitality of both kinds of spirituality. Can we do that? Can

we learn not only to tolerate each other (that's hard enough for many of us), but also to affirm and even sometimes love each other?[18]

Charismatic spirituality has been effective for desperate people during desperate times. Charismatic spirituality has taken root among people in emotional and socioeconomic distress. Some situations call for a "primal spirituality" that reaches down to the core of human experience. I could not find relief from deep emotional hurt, nor could I find resolute confidence that God possessed a plan for me, until the Spirit healed the broken places and dissolved the doubts with an undeniable touch of the Spirit. Harvey Cox explains:

> When you ask Pentecostals why they think their movement grew so rapidly and why it continues to expand at such speed, they have an answer: because the Spirit is in it. They may be right. But as I have pondered these questions from a more pedestrian perspective, it has occurred to me that there is also another way to think about why the movement has had such a widespread appeal. It has succeeded because it has spoken to the spiritual emptiness of our time by reaching beyond the levels of creed and ceremony into the core of human religiousness, into what might be called "primal spirituality," that largely unprocessed nucleus of the psyche in which the unending struggle for a sense of purpose and significance goes on.[19]

I learned that a convergence of the rivers of Christian spirituality releases a dynamic flow of the Spirit, sufficient for the deepest of human experience. I witness to the all-sufficiency of the rivers to shape a spirituality for desperate times. From the

- **Evangelical,** a transforming friendship with Jesus Christ
- **Contemplative,** a conversational relationship with God
- **Desert,** a return to being as the axis of life
- **Social Justice,** compassion in action out of which a new future can come into being;
- **Charismatic,** Spirit-energy zones of healing
- **Holiness,** obedience as loving response to the moral character of God
- **Incarnational,** the church as the material embodiment of the life, death, resurrection, and reign of Jesus Christ

Congregations...Embrace and Proclaim Jubilee

Words Jesus read to inaugurate and announce his mission (Lk. 4:18–19; Isa. 61:1–3) are the rudder passages that guide my personal vision. Insights into them have changed dramatically. I have learned that each expression of the church has an indispensable gift to offer the other. Congregants are drinking from the springs of living water beyond their church denominations and are returning home transformed by the encounters. A hopeful convergence is moving downstream and gaining momentum.

100 Christian OptiMystics

The history of the church provides multiple illustrations of this widening effect in the lives of leaders, congregations, and movements. E. Stanley Jones (1884–1973), the famous missionary to India, provides a case in point. Jones served during the period of the "fundamentalist-modernist split" and overlapped the life of Walter Rauschenbusch (1861–1918), the father of the social gospel in America. Jones, a conservative Protestant, chose another course. Influenced by his exposure to world cultures including the challenges posed by Communism in the 1930s, Jones, like Rauschenbusch, came to view God's reign as both a theological and practical design for the transformation of individuals and society. The challenge to Communism was Christ's alternative.

Howard A. Snyder outlines the rethinking of E. Stanley Jones on the Isaiah 61 and Luke 4 passages.

1. Good news to the poor–the economically disinherited.
2. Release to the captives–the socially and politically disinherited.
3. The opening of the eyes of the blind–the physically disinherited.
4. The setting at liberty the bruised–the morally and spiritually disinherited.
5. The Lord's Year of Jubilee–a new beginning on a world scale.
6. The Spirit of the Lord upon me–the dynamic behind it all.[20]

Jones soared above the "fundamentalist-modernist" controversy and set a course of convergence. He saw in Luke 4 a program that called for "a fresh application of the gospel of the kingdom in society."[21]

Can congregations affirm, regain, and maintain this convergence? Congregations as deep and as wide as Jesus' vision for humanity will be the difference-makers in society. These churches refuse to engage in the river-rivalries of former eras. As mission-driven churches, embracing and proclaiming jubilee, they affirm and encourage a diversity of passions and gifts. The walls of their church structures are open, fluid, and welcoming; not closed, petrified, and clique-ish.

Denominations…Speak Openly about Passions

I make no claim to grandeur when I report that I was one of a group of persons who mediated a passionate spirituality to theological students and pastors within my denomination of origin. I researched, taught, and sought to live the dynamics of relationship with Jesus Christ inspired by the rivers of Christian spirituality. I sought and taught the model of pastor as spiritual guide. It is a statement about my emotional intelligence that I gave spiritual direction to the one with whom I had forged an emotional bond, the outcome of mutual grief. I sought to channel the emotional energy, along with a lot of chemistry, into spiritual expression. She is my partner in marriage and ministry today. An unknown and unforgettable association was about to be unleashed within me. I was unaware of a powerful connection.

I direct this paddle stroke to denominational leaders charged with the risk management of clergy and congregations. Clergy and laity share a great interest in passionate spirituality– an essential component of vital ministers and thriving congregations. We set ourselves up for painful surprises if we do not acknowledge the common energy source of "erotic sexuality and passionate spirituality." The link is not underscored to excuse the inexcusable. On the contrary, the lesson is given to avoid the avoidable. Sometimes moral breakdown comes in the context of profound spiritual yearnings. Research on the history of revival unearths a surprising finding: Sexual misconduct increased among pastors and laity touched by revival. Gerald May addresses the human or psychological side of the Divine-human relationship. May claims:

> The experience of emotions as manifestations of raw energy can shed considerable light on the relationship between sexuality and spirituality. If the energy that fires both sexual and spiritual feelings is indeed a common "root" force, the distortions of sexuality and spirituality… can be seen as resulting not only from confusions about the nature of the longing but also from primary misdirections in the processing of emotional energy. Any great stimulus may become connected with either spiritual or sexual associations and thus acquire a sexual or spiritual label and feeling-tone…
>
> From the standpoint of human contemplative experience, sexual and spiritual phenomena do indeed seem to originate from the common energy source of all experience–the basic life-force that we have chosen to call spirit. Spirit, then, comprises all energy and its manifestations at the most fundamental level and in the purest form. Sexuality, as we experience it, is constituted of all those expressions of spirit that are directed toward creating.[22]

Some will consider the suggestion outrageous that erotic sexuality and passionate spirituality are manifestations of a common source within the human person. Even if we agree that erotic sexuality and passionate spirituality derive from spirit, the unifying force within, there is an important distinction between erotic love and agapic love. Erotic love strengthens self-importance, whereas agapic love diminishes self-importance and, if permitted, increases humility.[23]

What if spiritual encounters result in the convergence of "multiple energy paths," the experience of which is awesome? May describes the challenge:

> Erotic sexuality and passionate spirituality not only represent the "two big highs" of human experience, they also constitute the two most dramatic ways in which energy convergence and release can take place. The magnitude of either of these forces alone is awesome, but when the two come together the energy potential is beyond comprehension. It is not at all surprising then that we almost invariably become confused as to what is going on when romance stimulates spiritual longing or spiritual experience stimulates romantic passion. It is also easy to understand how one can become extremely frustrated in trying to find some way to express or otherwise deal with such strong energies.[24]

A compelling question is, What do I do with all this passion? The channeling of this surging energy that has come into awareness, and dramatically so, requires "refraining" and "wide-awake waiting in the midst of impulse." Simply stated, "[I]t is critical to stay awake and aware." Coping with these powerful energies is a necessary part of our spiritual discipline and essential for spiritual growth.[25]

It is critical for denominational leaders to speak openly to clergy and laity about these powerful energies that flow within our spiritual yearnings. Without excuse, encounters with these converging energies swept me over a fearsome waterfall with incredible and awesome force. All self-efforts to channel all the passion into spiritual expression ended in confusion, despair, and futility. The point is necessary—people with deep spiritual yearnings and profound spiritual encounters may be pointedly vulnerable to the "unthinkable."

Team Paddle Strokes—A Confused Spirit Finding Center
Clergy...Rediscover Shepherding

While an instructor of Christian spirituality and an avid river-runner, I devoted time to exploring images of God as they pertain to faith journey. I had a felt sense of God as compassionate Shepherd during the most conflicted period of my life. I acknowledged my sin, knew I was conflicted, and I had many unresolved issues. Even so, I felt the intimate shepherding of God, not as justification for my problems but as presence and promise. The Shepherd was with me as compassionate presence in the present and promise for the future.

I returned to pastoral ministry to explore a model of ministry that sought a synthesis of old and new. Thomas C. Oden advocates the reclamation of classic pastoral resources for contemporary ministry.

> The task that lies ahead is the development of a postmodern, post-Freudian, neoclassic approach to Christian pastoral care that takes seriously the resources of modernity while also penetrating its illusions and, having found the best of modern psychotherapies still problematic, has turned again to the classical tradition for its bearings, yet without disowning what it has learned from modern clinical experience.
>
> ...We must define for ourselves again what pastoral care is and in what sense pastoral theology is and remains theology, and in order to do that we must be carefully instructed by the tradition out of which that understanding can emerge. Otherwise there can be nothing but continued and expanded confusion about professional identity.[26]

Ironically, I lost my own identity in the process of recovering the lost identity of pastoral care. Yet I recognize that it was the classic shepherding analogy that was instrumental in the recasting of my self-identity.

Calling shepherding the "central paradigm" of ministry, Oden contends that the rejection of the shepherding image as premodern was premature:

Listen intently to the contemporaneity of the shepherding analogy in John 10:1–18.
- The intimacy of the shepherd's knowledge of the flock. He holds them in his arms.
- The way the shepherd calls each one by its own name.
- The shepherd does not, like the thief or robber, climb in the pen by some unusual means, but enters properly by the gate, being fully authorized to do so.
- The flock listen to the shepherd's voice. They distinguish it from all other voices.
- The shepherd leads them out of the protected area into pastures known to be most fitting–feeding them, leading them "out and back in."
- The shepherd characteristically is "out ahead" of them, not only guiding them, but looking out, by way of anticipation, for their welfare.
- Trusting the shepherd, the sheep are wary of an unproven stranger who might try to lead them abruptly away from the one they have learned to trust, through a history of fidelity.
- Jesus is recalled as the incomparably good shepherd who is willing to lay down his life for the sheep.
- The good shepherd is contrasted with the hireling or temporary worker who, having little at stake, may be prone to run away when danger approaches.
- All members of the flock of which Jesus is the shepherd are one, united by listening to his voice.

Who is to say that ordinary modern people cannot grasp such powerful, moving, straightforward images?[27]

The authority of the shepherd is of a special type: "authority is based on competence...covenant fidelity, caring, mutuality, and the expectation of empathic understanding."[28] I am indebted to the classic shepherding analogy as an integral part of my reclamation and present practice. Rediscover it.

Congregations...Organize "Seekers Anonymous"

Karl Rahner said that the Christian of the future will be a mystic or no Christian at all.[29] Robert K. Greenleaf makes a similar point in his classic work, *Servant Leadership*. He looks to George Fox, founder of the Quakers, for a way to be mystics in the modern world. The Quaker movement was conceived, birthed, and nurtured by a group of unrelenting seekers. Similarly, Greenleaf calls for a group of people in the present that will form "Seekers Anonymous." Seekers can turn a barren period into a fruitful one. A sustained seeking prepares the way for a new vision and new leadership. Greenleaf explains:

> The variable that marks some periods as barren and some as rich in prophetic vision is in the interest, the level of seeking, the responsiveness

of the hearers. The variable is *not* in the presence or absence or the relative quality and force of the prophetic voices. Prophets grow in stature as people respond to their message. If their early attempts are ignored or spurned, their talent may wither away.

It is *seekers,* then, who make the prophets, and the initiative of any one of us in searching for and responding to the voices of contemporary prophets may mark the turning point in their growth and service...

This thesis seems to be supported by the record of the times of George Fox, the first leader of the Quaker movement. For many years before the start of his mission there had been *an unusual stirring of seekers who were expectantly watching for a new vision with new leadership.* Without that sustained readiness, Fox might not have found the response to his initiative that was necessary for his mission to become strong.[30]

When new vision and leadership break out, birthed by stirred seekers, a sustained listening will propel the vision, leadership, and congregation forward. About "seekers anonymous," Greenleaf says:

Those who see themselves as part of "*Seekers Anonymous*" will learn to listen attentively and respond to that faint flutter of wings, that gentle stirring of life and hope. *By their intense and sustained listening they will make the new prophet who will help them find that wholeness that is only achieved by serving.* And out of that wholeness will come the singleness of aim and the capacity to bear suffering that a confrontation with the basic malaise of our time, the failure of our many institutions to serve, may demand.[31]

Greenleaf claims that stirred seekers create great leaders—men and women who are self-defined by the passions that possess them. Corporate seeking propels pastor and congregation downstream into a powerful convergence of personal and social wholeness.

Congregations need to organize chapters of "seekers anonymous." Get people stirred. Congregations can create great pastors through mutual sustained listening and response. Congregational readiness to vision and to action is a preferable future over pastor-do-everything busyness and emotional burnout. Carrying the vision together will prevent strain on a few. Mutual listening and readiness will produce prophetic pastors and servant leaders.

Denominations...Nurture Clergy Self-care

I loved the clergy role so passionately that I did not differentiate my self-identity from my service. I was consumed with pastoring. I did not cultivate a life or identity beyond the church. So when the caricatures of what I had done and what I had become reached my ears, I felt reduced to my sin. I was once a respected pastor, but now a disdained adulterer who longed to be treated as one who was more than the sin committed. Alan Jones provided some respite from the deep emotional pain and helped restore a measure of self-respect.

> I am a sinner who believes that love and goodness are at the heart of things. I am neither proud of being a sinner nor crippled by the knowledge of my failure to love. I have a profound respect for psychotherapy and have been through various forms of counselling that were life-bearing and healing. But I have been hurt by the way my own sinning and that of my fellow pastors has been caricatured by psychological reductionisms, by such things as the codependency movement (which has much to teach us but is not the last word). A human being is deeply hurt when he or she is seen as only a set of problems and not as an unfathomable mystery. The overriding metaphor for the sickness of society is that of addiction. But the metaphor is overdone. We are an addicted people, but that is not all we are.
>
> We love explanations, but human beings...cannot be explained away. We reduce and diminish each other with partial and distorted descriptions masquerading as explanations. We say such things as, "She's neurotic," and "He's compulsive." We think we've solved a problem by naming a person an alcoholic or an adult child of one. Naming things is important, but damage is done when we presume to name a part for the whole. We label people and problems with such conviction that we really begin to believe that we have explained someone away.
>
> To be ordained is to rage against these reductions and diminishments. Our longing and our sinning are often reduced by cheap psychologizing to images of maladjustment. It's not that there aren't issues of addiction and co-dependence for all of us. But there is more to us than these. And it is to this "more" that I wish to speak. I call that "more" the romance of ministry. What then of my own romance?[32]

There was so much more to me than the sins I had committed and the deep wounds my actions had inflicted. Yes, I sinned. Yes, I refused to end the relationship and follow the path to restoration that denominational leaders put before me. There were complicated consequences to consider beyond the spiritual and emotional issues. I felt outraged by the isolation and reductionism. I am an "unfathomable mystery," and I am more than my sin. I was disillusioned. I thought, "I gave everything I had to give; and now that I am wounded on the battlefield, I am being thrown on the ash heap of has-beens." What should be done with wounded ministers?

Chaos taught me a life-changing lesson about loving the role without letting the role take me over. Denominational leaders have it within their influence to nurture clergy self-care, to encourage balance over burnout, and to reinforce the role of each congregation in facilitating clergy care. Roy M. Oswald proposes a reevaluation of the "call" to ministry.

> I must reinterpret my call to a parish as primarily a call to serve God, not necessarily to serve people. My first call is to be a liberated, whole human being. My first responsibility to my congregation is to be a joyful, redeemed human being. This works only if ministry is viewed as a communal activity with people in mission. We are who we are related to. We cannot maintain our health and wholeness unless there is support for this among our people.
>
> Parishioners need to have a stake in us and our health and well-being. What we offer in return is assistance and support for them to live healthy, whole, and forgiven lives. This gets us out of an adversarial relationship with our people and enables us to join them in living in the light of God's grace. Then the minister is not the savior, but the one who offers guidance and leadership through his/her own health and wholeness, and in turn is invited to greater wholeness through the health and wholeness of persons in the congregation.[33]

Denominational leaders would do well to advance a reevaluation of "call" among clergy and congregations. Today I engage service with a radically new mind-set. I love and pursue God above all. I enjoy the roles of ordained ministry even more than before. I am as passionate about what I do as ever before. But from that day on the ash heap to this day, I have never confused the distinction between my person and my callings. I will never forget the lessons of burnout. I have never had more joy in living out my calling than I do this day. And I seek to live my life in sync with a rule of life that birthed out of the lessons earned from chaos.

River-running the Rapids of Spirit—Level 1 Teamwork

MEMO: January 2005
TO: Dwayne Ratzlaff
FROM: Tom Bandy

Dwayne:

Now that you have shared your personal experience of being capsized…and subsequently swimming, paddling, floundering, drowning, and generally being swept along in various "rivers" of Christian spirituality…it makes sense that the first lesson you would share from the experience is that *you can't do it alone!*

In all of my traveling, teaching, and consulting I have met all too many former pastors who did not survive being capsized. You are a rarity. Most never explore the rivers of grace so thoroughly nor have the courage or sheer stubbornness to endure the pain, guilt, and rejection. They are now in other professions. Some are in related work in social services or non-profit organizations. Most have gone to work in other sectors, such as business, education, health care, or politics. Some still look upon the church with affection and may even be active in a Christian congregation. Most are angry at the church and have retreated to more personal and less corporate spiritual disciplines (if they remain spiritual at all).

It is worthwhile to explore their anger. No doubt some of that anger is a projection of their personal disappointment on the institution. Honesty with oneself is one of the hardest things to achieve, and it is easier to reshape history and live in illusions that church authorities were unjust or unfaithful. Yet much of their anger toward the church is understandable. Ordained clergy entered a covenant with the church and assumed they were part of a "team." When the *church* was in trouble (having made bad public policy decisions, or mismanaged funds, or changed liturgies, or forgotten some micro-culture), they stood by the church. They defended the church, worked hard to correct church errors, accepted salary caps for the sake of church finances and mission budgets, tolerated abuses to their families as the public became more hostile to the church, invested enormous amounts of time maintaining church procedures and missions, and frankly forgave the church of many imperfections and mistakes. But when *they* got into trouble, the church seemed all too ready to chastise without dialogue, punish without mercy, and distance themselves from the sinner. Clergy have a right to feel betrayed. It is not that they want to excuse themselves of wrongdoing, or even avoid discipline; but they thought they were part of a *team* and discovered they were part of a *task group.*

In a task group, leaders do a professional job with high quality; and if they fail to do it, they get fired. That's how most of the world operates. In a team, leaders still do high-quality work; but they do it in a partnership that accepts mistakes, negotiates solutions, and seeks both the well-being of the teammate and the success of the team. In the early days of their mission movement, most denominations did function as a team with their clergy. Each helped improve and reprove the other; each made sacrifices for the well-being of the other; each recognized that their health and the health of their shared mission depended on the wholeness of the team. In these latter days of denominational institutionalization, the church has behaved more and more like any other worldly corporation. Clergy are employees, and if they make a mistake, they're out.

It reminds me of the crisis of the church over forgiveness in the second to third centuries. This was a period of some anarchy in the Roman Empire, and circumstances made the church extremely vulnerable to persecution. Christians were considered weird compared to the rest of society; other more personal and selfish religions were hostile; the safety and prosperity of the public was eroding; and it was pretty easy for an emperor or regional governor to blame it on underprivileged Christians, who had little political clout. In the midst of the persecutions, many Christians denied Christ or sacrificed to the emperor's "genius." Many clergy fled their parishes or made some accommodation with the government to avoid martyrdom. Once peace and stability were restored at the end of the third century, however, these Christians and clergy naturally wanted to return to the fold. A huge controversy erupted over whether they should be "forgiven" and received back again. Orthodoxy finally prevailed; negotiations were opened; compassion was extended; and they were restored to the fellowship. The *team* prevailed.

I realize that this historic controversy was about doctrine whereas your controversy has more to do with morality, but I think the two situations are more alike than denominations today think. It's just that contemporary people identify the "breaking point" of inclusion in the body of Christ differently. In ancient times it was seen as a doctrinal issue, and the church was remarkably flexible in shaping the responses to moral transgression. Today it is seen as a moral issue, and the church is remarkably flexible in shaping the responses to doctrinal variations. The "breaking point" may be differently defined, but the issue of forgiveness and the willingness to negotiate and dialogue is still at stake. The ancient church decided to work toward forgiveness; modern denominations seem to have decided to work toward judgment.

Maybe this is because the boundary lines between clergy and laity in ancient times were not as clear-cut as they are today. Clergy and laity, professional and amateur, certified and uncertified, salaried and unsalaried—all distinctions were less clear in ancient times than today. Laity essentially faced the same doctrinal and moral expectations as clergy. Conscious of their own temptation and sin (but for the grace of God, there go I), they were more likely to be benevolent. Today, both community and church culture have placed the clergy on a pedestal. Clergy face a different and more rigorous (perhaps even impossible) standard of belief and behavior than laity. It is easier for a committee of the church to condemn the clergy because they do not hold themselves to the same standard of expectation.

Whatever the reason, the idea of "team" has dimmed as the church has become more institutionalized. Clergy were ordained in ancient liturgy, and the rhetoric led them to believe that they had a covenant that would work with them and not just reward or condemn them. Once again, Christians are considered weird compared to the rest of society; other more personal and selfish religions are hostile; the safety and prosperity of the public is eroding; and it is pretty easy for a corporate official or legal authority to blame it on underprivileged Christians, who have little political clout. The temptations for clergy to "cut a deal" with worldliness are acute, and more than a few will succumb. The question is, Is there forgiveness? Is the church willing to provide preventative support, ongoing negotiation and dialogue, and mentored methodologies to reinstate fallen clergy to the fellowship?

Let me restate your framework of Level 1 teamwork, which seeks to "river-run the rapids of spirit." This level, in particular, has a lot to learn from the second and third centuries.

Fundamentally, for this team to work, each partner must contribute a vital element. The clergy must provide *leadership;* the congregation must provide *trust;* and the denomination must provide *resources.*

Clergy *leadership* is only partly a matter of professional skills. Fundamentally, it is a matter of modeling a spiritual life...literally showing the people how to aggressively and painfully align one's lifestyle with the person and work of Jesus Christ. I know that your terminology sounds negative, but I think this is actually a more productive and insightful way of visualizing leadership.

	Create a Disaster Plan	Develop Deep Spirituality	Find "the Center"
CLERGY	Confront the speed demons	Find spirituality for desperate times	Rediscover shepherding
CONGREGATION	Prepare to maneuver over chaos	Embrace and proclaim jubilee	Organize "Seekers Anonymous"
DENOMINATION	Develop a plan for disaster	Speak openly about passions	Nurture clergy self-care

You describe such leadership as "creating a disaster plan" to deal with inevitable chaos and crisis in ministry. Most clergy today would prefer to focus on "developing a strategic plan" for their career. That would make sense if clergy still lived in the Christendom world that developed from the early fourth century after Constantine. The cultural pressure was off. It didn't take much risk or sacrifice to advance the church. Success was pretty much guaranteed if you just followed the rules and kept your head down. Today, our world is more like that of the pre-Christendom turmoil of the second and third centuries, when risk was the order of the day, martyrdom was just one slip of the tongue away, and failures were almost inevitable. You have to have a "disaster plan."

You not only abstractly describe the disaster plan, but you modeled it in your life. The plan involves a deep, earnest, determined, persistent, stubborn, constant spiritual life. I talk about this to some extent in my books *Moving Off the Map* and *Mission Mover*.[34] As I read it, these are the components:

Face your personal weaknesses: compulsions, addictions, temptations, and self-destructive behavior patterns and desires. Tame them, deny them, confess them, whip them into submission, and wrestle with the devil. I laughed at your metaphor: "speed demons." I am not sure whether you intended the double meaning or not. The first meaning is that leaders confront their own egotistical compulsion to succeed, accelerate into a career, rocket their way up the ladder of authority and influence. "Speed," however, is not just a measure of motion, but a drug. Many clergy allow themselves to be "drugged" by the financial security, public prestige, ecclesiastical authority, and ego rush of modern church leadership. Indeed, I find too many seminarians have been attracted from other careers to the church because they love the experience of telling others what to think, watching everybody sitting still while they talk, and having the last word in the Bible study. These seminarians are headed for a fall. They will become the "problem" of some future congregation and middle judicatory.

Deepen your spiritual discipline: merge your lifestyle with Christ's mission, pray constantly, meditate on scripture, sit at the feet of the apostles and their disciples, invest enormous time and energy on your spiritual (mental, emotional, physical, and relational) health. Clergy self-identity has largely been reshaped in the latter half of the twentieth century by the cultural value of professionalism. The result is that clergy talk about spiritual discipline very articulately, but are in fact not very spiritually disciplined. The same thing has happened to the medical profession. Doctors talk about holistic health very articulately, but in fact lead remarkably unhealthy lifestyles. As teachers, they are all very insightful…as models, they are next to useless. It was not always so. Clergy (and doctors, for that matter) need to return to an older, more spiritual standard of expectation.

Find your Christ center: unite with Christ, experience his grace and acceptance, and reawaken your original experience of call. All of the rivers of Christian spirituality you have described have lost their Christ center through the twentieth century. The evangelical movement has replaced it with dogma and formula; the holiness movement has replaced it with behavioral rigidity; the social action movement has replaced it with ideology; the contemplative movement has replaced it with ritual and abstraction; the established church as a whole has replaced it with institutional loyalty. You are calling clergy to rediscover Christ as an experience that is at once mysterious and crystal clear, crucial for abundant life, and the one enduring reason for hope.

It may be that calling this a "disaster plan" is misleading. It really is not a program or curriculum to be applied universally to all clergy. It is more like a lifejacket, so that when they are capsized into the river, they are more likely to float.

I think the congregational role in the teamwork you describe is perhaps the most problematic, so I will skip that for the moment and talk about the denominational role. The problem, as I consult with denominations from many "rivers" of spirituality, is not that they have failed to do what you have recommended, but that they have only done it in half measures.

Many denominations have developed policies and guidelines that provide a model for disaster intervention. Churches recognize their vulnerability to litigation in a culture hostile to organized religion and have taken steps to rectify any hint of abuse. The problem is that these measures are primarily reactive rather than proactive. The processes through which clergy are chastised or disciplined is getting more rigorous, but the processes through which people are trained and selected to become clergy are still remarkably lax. All kinds of people become "clergy" who, frankly, shouldn't ever become "clergy," and they inevitably bring trouble to the church down the road. Seminaries keep concentrating on cranking out preachers, liturgists, and theologians, but not role models, missionaries, and Christ companions. This is why there is a growing rift between denominations and their own seminaries, but the denominations still are not diligent enough to screen prospective church leaders. The solution seems clear: If denominations pay more attention to who becomes clergy, they will have fewer crises with those who are clergy.

Many denominations have also begun talking more about "passion." They have recognized that motivational focus, zeal, or sheer enthusiasm has been a missing component in church leadership that has become far too cerebral and passive. The problem is that denominations limit their talk about passion to *programs* and do not adequately talk about *lifestyles.* In their view, clergy should become passionate about this or that program or activity but somehow separate the adrenaline rush and emotional arousal from the rest of their life and relationships. Denominations talk a great deal about *agape* and *phileos,* but are remarkably silent about *eros.* I tend to blame the post-war neoorthodox movement for this. Rather than see eros as another legitimate and spiritual form of love, the neoorthodox movement saw this only as a threat to absolute dependence on revealed grace for salvation. Eros was too human, too creative, too individually expressive, too relational, and far too difficult to control. So by ignoring it, they lost control of it altogether. The solution seems clear: Denominations need to see sexual behavior as connected to, not contradictory of, spiritual life.

Many denominations have invested considerable attention to nurturing clergy self-care. They offer more and more opportunities to learn time management and relaxation techniques, and are more aggressive about defending weekly days off, vacation, and study leave. And they provide more and more personal and family counseling support. But do all these strategies help clergy "find their 'Christ center'?" That is certainly more questionable. I think one of the important insights from your personal journey is that all of the sabbatical time and counseling opportunities in the world cannot really nurture the soul if the clergy fail to find this "centered self." My perception is that despite all the denominational opportunities for continuing education, vacation, and counseling, clergy still feel increasingly isolated and alone. They need peer group mentoring, and the middle judicatory no longer can provide that. The solution seems clear: Denominations need to broker higher quality, cross-judicatory, and even cross-denominational networks that clergy can select for themselves for personal health and mission growth.

The congregational role in this teamwork is perhaps more crucial, and also more problematic. I suppose I have become famous for my graphic contrasts between the systemic reasons why churches decline or thrive. The sad truth is that well over two-thirds of the congregations in North America today live within, and are remarkably satisfied with being, a declining system. Declining systems magnetically attract dysfunctional people. These are the people in contemporary culture who have a deep need to shape the church around their personal and family needs (little caring about everyone else!). These are the same needy people who have a deep need to develop codependent relationships with clergy who have a need to be needed.

For this reason I find your first two suggestions for the congregation's role in the team to be worthy but unrealistic. Congregations *should* expect inevitable chaos and prepare themselves to maneuver responsibly within it—but the reality is that dysfunctional congregations and dysfunctional people demand "harmony" in the same way a child demands candy: They *will not* be flexible. Similarly, congregations *should* embrace and proclaim jubilee to free clergy from overwhelming burdens and constant demands in order to deepen their spiritual lives and mental health—but the reality is that dysfunctional congregations and dysfunctional people demand "membership privileges" in the same way a child demands attention.

I admire and support your ruthless self-examination of the root causes for your moral or spiritual failure as a pastor. I meet all too many pastors who simply blame everything on somebody else. On the other hand, the spiritual and moral failures of pastors do not happen in a vacuum. They happen in a congregational context. The principle of teamwork cuts both ways: if it takes two or more to succeed, it also takes two or more to fail. The congregation should commit to as rigorous a self-examination as you have done as a pastor. However, most congregations *will not* do so. This is not a matter of education; It is a matter of willpower.

This is why I do find your last point about congregational teamwork so significant. I like the metaphor of "seekers anonymous." The addictions that clergy have only flourish in communities that have matching or reinforcing addictions of their own. Addiction calls to addiction. The congregation *prefers* pastors who have certain weaknesses; and the pastor *chooses* congregations who have certain weaknesses. We are all in it together. We really do need to simultaneously bring the clergy down from their pedestal—and raise the laity up from their laziness. The one is not going to happen without the other.

I would like to take your metaphor of shepherding further—and I think that is your real intention. Too many pastors may read your story and recommendations and simply conclude they must once again shoulder the heavy burden of "being the shepherd" to the congregation. However, you are saying something more profound that needs to be highlighted. The pastor and congregation are called into an experience of "mutual shepherding." There are times when the pastor shepherds the congregation, but there are times when the congregation shepherds the pastor. Indeed, there are times when both the congregation and the pastor need to realize that they are not shepherds at all—but sheep. Christ is the only real "shepherd" in the Christian faith.

Thriving church systems are environments in which this has begun to happen. Clergy and laity perceive themselves together as fellow seekers helping one another draw closer to Christ. This does not really happen because the congregation initiates some kind of program for "jubilee" or because the congregation develops a policy for personnel oversight and support. This happens because the basic system of church life—the flow of discipleship and the expectations for both clergy leadership and lay membership—have been clearly shaped in current members and intentionally communicated to newcomers.

It is important to see that traditional denominational oversight cannot create the environment of "seekers anonymous." The annual visit from the judicatory officer, or the annual statistical report to the head office, will not accomplish this.

Self-critique from within the denominational circle is akin to children asking their friends on the playground if they have a problem. Today, there is no substitute for a comprehensive review of congregational life and mission every five years by a competent outsider.

Finally, it appears to me that you may want to expand your notion of who belongs on the team in the postmodern world. (I write about this in *Mission Mover*.) The old Christendom team consisted of the clergy, the congregation, and the pastor—with a nod to the seminary. But it becomes clear that the teams of the future will be configured differently. The denomination may or may not have an important role, and the seminary may well not have the same influence as it once did. Instead, clergy and congregations will be searching for peer mentors and coaches among outside consultants, parachurches, other congregations beyond their normal polity or geographic boundaries, and educational or health institutions far and wide.

CHAPTER 5

River-running the Rapids of Morality
Level 2 Teamwork

	Supporting Moral Integrity	Responding to Moral Breakdown	Recovering Moral Integrity
CLERGY	Get help for difficult places	Check for emotional IQ	Fall into grace
CONGREGATION	Explore motives for selecting clergy	Avoid the flip side of holiness	Be a community of compassion
DENOMINATION	Contextualize misconduct	Manage broken humanity	Structure support clear through

Conflicted Teamwork

Level 2 teamwork requires a higher level of commitment to the team concept. Stress points increase for clergy, congregation, and denomination. A higher probability of team dissension occurs with the deep emotional stresses around moral breakdown. The team is dealing with its own disappointments at the failure of a colleague minister. Emotional stress points include the competing commitments to provide appropriate support to all involved in the misconduct: the victim and family, the congregation as family, the minister and family. Polarization sets in rapidly. It is vital for the team to manage its own inner conflicts. Conflict is part of church life. The direction of conflict is what matters most. Conflict moves in constructive and destructive ways, so it must be channeled constructively. This is dangerous white water. A breakdown of teamwork can carry lifelong consequences for all affected by the disintegration of moral integrity.

Paddle Strokes for Supporting Moral Integrity
Clergy...Get Help for Difficult Places

Difficult places may vary among clergy, but the need to seek help is constant. Help came to me in various ways: through therapy, assigned readings, support people, processes of discernment, vital expressions of Christian spirituality, an inclusive denomination, and a willing congregation.

My troubles became overt in my violation of our marriage covenant. I have come to view marriage as a place for growing wholeness. Candace R. Benyei has helped me in this regard. She calls marriage a place where we resolve the issues of our family of origin and grow into wholeness. Benyei's point is compelling:

> One of the most demanding relationships that we can enter into is marriage It is hard to maintain a façade when one is face-to-face with another on a daily basis. As a result, marriage is one of the most powerful tools that exists for personal development, individuation, or self-actualization. It is also a powerful instrument for self-destruction when entered without awareness and with a great deal of emotional baggage from one's family of origin.
>
> Marriage is one of the primary places where we are challenged to become conscious of our strengths and weaknesses and grow into wholeness by finishing our "old business."[1]

Marriage is very hard work, because the flip side of the coin is that we will inevitably choose partners who will constantly confront us with our difficult places, *so that the opportunity to grow will always be in front of us.*[2]

I should have addressed the difficult places in my first marriage. I was forced to face these issues over the rapids of restoration. Only the setting of the "hard work...to grow" shifted. The "old business" still had to be resolved. River-running in the direction of wholeness is ongoing work. The lesson earned from chaos is clear: Get help before the difficult places turn into an altar of self-ruin. Choose to use the wound as an opening for wholeness.

Congregations...Explore Motives for Selecting Clergy

A similar point can be made for "clergy-congregational couples." Congregations and clergy participate in discerning processes before extending and accepting a call. Are the real issues behind the call and acceptance hidden from our mutual awareness? Could the subconscious issues touch our shadow side or unresolved wounds from our family of origin? I recall the candidate process that led to my call and acceptance. The decision to change rafts from teaching in theological education to a pastoral charge was a difficult one. I struggled with a choice and engaged in an extensive discernment process. Both options appealed to me for different reasons. I opted for taking my vision back into a local church. I relished the opportunity to explore the metaphor of pastor as spiritual guide. The experiment was all I hoped for it to be. It was a consuming passion, but the never-anticipated end came.

Always there is the insight of hindsight. I did engage in a spiritual process of discernment, but I did not assess other factors in the discernment process: strong ego needs for challenge and risk-taking, a subtle ambition to climb the ladder of success, a desire for reputation, and a willingness to sacrifice almost everything to get there. Lurking in the shadows was a craving for affirmation, admiration, and advancement. The call came from a pastoral charge that appealed to this hidden agenda. Add marital stress as an emotional system to these issues. Then the church itself as a family system had its own unresolved issues brought by the family units within it. Clearly, the congregation and candidate selected each other for a variety of underlying motives. One can argue that the hidden reasons had the greatest potential for growing wholeness. Benyei explains:

> What we have known for a long time about marriages, however, and for a shorter time have realized about clergy-congregational couples, is that the most important reasons for our getting together are out of our conscious awareness. Instead, God seems to bring us together to work out issues that are unresolved in our families of origin. We pair up to resolve difficulties that somehow hamper us from becoming whole…
>
> In *committed* relationships we can risk the task of pushing against our partner and trying out new behaviors that we were afraid to chance as children. And in so doing we grow up and we grow into God. We can do this because we have *covenanted* with our partner *not to abandon us in the process.*[3]

The key to a committed relationship is faithfulness to covenant. A covenant is a promise that we will not abandon each other in the process of growing. The congregational context did push my unresolved issues to the surface, where a coalescing of circumstances brought them to a crisis. I broke covenant with marriage and congregation. I abandoned the process of growth. Often these issues do not present themselves until the clergy-congregational couple are living and serving together. The surprises come after the honeymoon period has ended. Then, the hidden motivations of clergy and congregation impel to the top. Only then can the real work of growing to wholeness begin for the clergy-congregational couple.

The mission of the pastoral relations team is vital and critical–to process the presenting issues for minister and congregation. The hidden motives underneath the call and acceptance can become the containers of wholeness. Circumstances that impel the motives to the surface vary. If the motives remain hidden and active, the covenant between clergy and congregation will be at risk. It would be preferable to deal with the hidden motives at the outset. Expect to work through them together as they rise to the surface. A change of charge may serve only to delay the call to wholeness for both pastor and people. Frequent changes by pastoral charges and/or ministers may reflect an unwillingness to grow.

Denominations...Contextualize Misconduct

Disaster prevention and rescue is the judicial responsibility of the denomination. I challenge the wisdom of isolating the sexual misconduct from the context in which the misconduct occurs. I endorse the essential need to protect the victims, victim-families, minister's family, and victim-congregation from further harm beyond the betrayal of sacred trust. Therapeutic support for all is fundamental. I acknowledge the need for appropriate discipline also. I walked into the office of my denominational leader, where I confessed and resigned. I assumed that resignation was automatic as a consequence of the sin of adultery. I was invited to confess before the congregation the next Sunday, but I declined. I was in no state of mind to accept. I never received another chance to meet with the congregation, in part or in whole, or with the representative elders of the congregation. I assume that denominational leaders made a decision to suspend any and all formal contact between me and the congregation throughout the period of discipline. All formal contact with the denomination came through denominational representatives.

The moral failure occurred within the context of a congregation. I was working with various emotional subsystems that made up the larger emotional system of the congregation. The betrayal of trust affected many subsystems: my family system, the family of the participant church member, all other family units within the church, people related by family of origin, the original congregation as family that relocated to the new site, and the growing congregation as family that formed at the new location.

Congregational issues, unresolved from the past, continued to influence the present. All efforts to influence the subsystems contributed to burnout. These factors are not an excuse or a sufficient reason for sexual misconduct– no reason can be sufficient. However, multiple emotional factors did come against me simultaneously and pursued me relentlessly.

A process of discipline that included representatives from the offended congregation could have been healing for both a fallen pastor and a wounded people. Such a scenario would have called for unconditional love on the part of the congregational representatives. Sharing the emotional chaos together would have been risky for many reasons. I was angry, disillusioned, and blaming others. I faced complex real-life issues as an outcome of the adultery. I did not respond as expected. I felt isolated and rejected. I believe the participation of the congregation in the process of discipline would have been a healing intervention. This could have been achieved through a few willing elders on a team with denominational participants charged with the role of discipline.

The reductionist statement, "At mid-life he couldn't keep his zipper closed," does not capture all that is active in clergy sexual misconduct. I appeal to the seminal work of Edwin H. Friedman for understanding.

> It is the thesis of this book that all clergymen and clergywomen, irrespective of faith, are simultaneously involved in three distinct families whose emotional forces interlock: the families within the congregation, our congregations, and our own. Because the emotional process in all of these systems is identical, unresolved issues in any one of them can produce symptoms in the other, and increased understanding of any one creates more effective functioning in all three.[4]

The concepts of family process can increase understanding and solve problems within the church. Friedman claims that the "family model" is more instructive than the "individual model." The family model locates the problem in the "structure" of the system rather than in the "nature of the symptomatic member."[5]

Family systems theory posits five basic interrelated concepts that distinguish the two models: the "identified patient," "homeostasis (balance)," "differentiation of self," "the extended family field," and "emotional triangles."[6] The concept of the "identified patient" is of particular relevance. Friedman explains:

> The concept of the identified patient…is that the family member with the obvious symptom is to be seen not as the "sick one" but as the one in whom the family's stress or pathology has surfaced. In a child it could take the form of excessive bedwetting, hyperactivity, school failures, drugs, obesity, or juvenile diabetes; in a spouse its form could be excessive drinking, depression, chronic ailments, a heart condition or perhaps even cancer; in an aged member of the family it could show up as confusion, senility, or agitated and random behavior. In a congregational family it could surface as the drinking, burnout, or sexual acting out of the "family leader."[7]

Friedman says the "identified patient" should not be treated outside of the context of the "problemed" family member's interconnections.

> And so it is, says family theory, with the organism known as the human family. When one part of that organism is treated in isolation from its interconnections with another, as though the problem were solely its own, fundamental change is not likely. The symptom is apt to recycle, in the same or different form, in the same or a different member. Trying to "cure" a person in isolation from his or her family, says family theory, is as misdirected, and ultimately ineffective, as transplanting a healthy organ into a body whose imbalanced chemistry will destroy the new one as it did the old. It is easy to forget that the

same "family" of organs that rejects a transplant contributed to the originally diseased part becoming "foreign."[8]

I have accepted full responsibility for my sexual misconduct and subsequent divorce. I have portaged upstream through the waters of reconciliation. So I dare to make this point: I believe many factors were at work in my sexual misconduct beyond my personal sinful actions. I felt that no one was really caring about the wider context that eventually gave rise to the adultery. I was the "sick one," and the emotional systems that reared it seemed exonerated.

I appeal to denominational leaders to contextualize clergy sexual misconduct. Too much is at stake to choose the easy path. To isolate the patient and the treatment from the context is self-defeating for both pastor and people. I cannot speak on behalf of the victimized. However, I can say from observation that a pastor who follows the fallen in a wounded congregation could end up as another "sick one," albeit with a very different symptom than clergy sexual misconduct. Even a different symptom has the potential to capsize another ministry. When a church gains a reputation for capsized ministers, although the symptoms in the ministers may vary significantly, more is at work in the hydraulics of a congregation than meets the surface view. Alan Jones may be on to something when he claims,

> The maturity of a congregation is tested when its minister falls apart. Some congregations have a reputation for chewing up their pastors and then spitting them out. Others seem able to cope with ministerial failure with humility and grace. Too few congregations know *how* to help their ministers even when they know that their ministers need nurturing.[9]

Paddle Strokes for Responding to Moral Breakdown
Clergy...Check for Emotional IQ

On the portage upstream to seek reconciliation with my denomination of origin, I learned that they felt a strong sense of betrayal from me. Colleagues felt betrayed by my adultery and subsequent refusal to submit to the disciplinary guidelines for restoration of marriage and ministry. Betrayal is consistent with the alienation I felt. Marcus J. Borg supports the idea of sin as "betrayal of relationship." In his "Spirit model," Borg opts for a "Christian life that stresses relationship, intimacy, and belonging." Such change requires a new view of sin and repentance. Borg clarifies:

> *Thus sin remains.* Only now the emphasis is not on sin as a violation of God's laws but on sin as betrayal of relationship and absence of compassion. Repentance also remains, only now it does not mean primarily sincere contrition of sins committed but a turning and returning to that to which we belong, God as Spirit.[10]

The adultery and subsequent choices were a betrayal of relationship: toward God, marriage, children, family, church, and denomination. It caused the deepest pain possible. I was forgiven for this profound rupture of relationships in a letter of release from my denomination of origin.

Clergy misconduct wounds so many people: from the primary victim (the person abused) to the secondary victims (family of the clergyperson, family of the victim) to the families of the congregation, and to the congregation as a religious system. The consequences of clergy sexual misconduct are ravaging of these relationships. The outcome of marriage with the one who participated in the extramarital relationship did not minimize the seriousness of the misconduct. The choice to continue the relationship and eventually marry hurt the spousal victims and congregational families even more. It deepened their sense of betrayal and woundedness.

The new openness to confront the serious problem of clergy sexual misconduct is a positive development. Contributions from authors such as Candace R. Benyei are essential reading for all "clergy-congregational partners." Benyei writes from a systemic perspective. Her insights enabled me to appreciate the many factors at play when clergy misconduct occurs and to identify the root of my own sexual misconduct as a clergy-practitioner. It began as "transference/countertransference love" in the service of bereavement. Benyei explains:

> When a counselee (or congregant in this case) comes to the clergyperson for help, he or she already perceives the pastor, by nature of the clerical position, to be kind, sympathetic, caring, affirming, longsuffering, strong and godlike. This benevolent picture is called *transference* and may or may not be characteristic of the counselor in question. The clergy-person, as recipient of this rosy projection, feels competent, affirmed, and valued whether or not he or she is indeed capable of performing usefully as a counselor in an objective sense. This is called *countertransference*. Because caring and valuing are two of the most sexually arousing activities that can happen between people, this sort of transference/countertransference quickly develops into what is called *transference love*–the warm, gooey, filled-up, no-longer-lonely, safe, embraced, exhilarating, *sexually powerful* feeling that our culture has co-opted us into believing is *true love*...The power, in fact the sheer force of the sexual attraction that arouses from transference love, cannot be emphasized enough. The feelings might be compared to a tidal wave on the desert or the sight of a banquet to a starving person...It is a well-known statistic that of the various persons suspended as members from the American Association of Marriage and Family Therapists every year for sexual ethical violations, clergy comprise by far the largest group.[11]

I hope that this story will prompt ministers to check their emotional IQ. I serve as an illustration of both the subtle movement into clergy sexual misconduct and the high cost of personal reclamation. Along the way many persons were left wounded on my battlefield. And I offer my story as an example of God's grace-filled restoration of life and calling.

Congregations...Avoid the Flip Side of Holiness

Moral misconduct caused a rethink of the issues around personal holiness. I was raised in a denomination with roots in the holiness movement. I taught a clear theological paradigm of sanctification as crisis and process. I continue to believe in experiential sanctification. I received a lesson in spiritual relapse as well as one about the flip side of holiness.

Douglas John Hall has a message to all rafters running the river of holiness. In *The Future of the Church,* Hall envisions a "cruciform model" that encompasses an authentic expression of holiness. A "cruciform church" or "disestablished church," in contrast to a Christendom church, will have to overcome the temptations of self-righteousness, mediocrity, and ghettoization. As a child growing up in the church, Hall learned,

> more moral meant, in an almost exclusive sense, personal morality; and personal morality meant, in an almost exclusive sense, refraining from various temptations which constituted strange obsessions for those who harangued us on them. Already the child in me wondered whether personal morality ought not to include doing something about the pride, the self-righteousness, the obvious lack of compassion demonstrated so consistently by the *most moral people.*[12]

Hall warns that the temptation to "self-righteousness" is close at hand. It is near to all who aspire to be "truly Christian!" Motive is something I have struggled with throughout the white-water odyssey and will continue to do so. We ignore to our peril the insight of Jeremiah: "The heart is devious above all else; it is perverse—who can understand it?" (Jer. 17:9). Hall identifies the thing so "deadly to the faith of the Christ":

> There is first the temptation to self-righteousness. All those throughout the history of the Christian movement who have come near to... *authenticity...*; all those from Stephen to Dietrich Bonhoeffer who have had to follow dramatically and all the way "the way of the cross"—they have all known this temptation. It is a heady thing to think oneself... *truly Christian!* Paul understood how attractive this ideal was...and therefore he spoke about "the thorn" (2 Cor. 12:7), undoubtedly—whatever its *physical* aspect—a spiritual antidote to his own spiritual pride.[13]

Christian introspection opens the door to inner truth: I am a mixture of motives. Even the most self-effacing choices have been mixed with self-approving desires. On those occasions when I do manage to do the right thing, both selfless and selfish motives stand behind it. Such inner knowledge is an antidote to self-righteousness as the flip side of holiness.

Congregations might benefit from a rethinking of the source meaning of holiness. Holiness refers to that which is set apart for God. Hall distinguishes the popular thinking of holiness as "otherworldliness" from its classic meaning as "prophetic justice" and "profound awareness."

> Moralistic "separateness" ("holier than thou") and church pomposity, whether of the formal or allegedly informal variety, are no substitutes for prophetic justice and the profound awareness that our lives are more than they appear to be.[14]

Denominations...Manage Broken Humanity

Clergy seek to experience and mediate the "ecstasy" of God. God uses broken humanity to that great end. Alan Jones speaks to the daring job description of clergy.

> Clergy aren't cures for anything either. They are the willing and unwilling carriers of a deep need in human beings, the need for the "madness of God"–ecstasy. They are those chosen to affirm that humanity is related to the infinite...Who would dare to be someone set apart to serve, heal, and enlighten? Who would dare to claim to be a sign of the untapped power of God in everyone?[15]

It is a daring vocation. So what do we do when ordained men and women end up requiring the "humiliation" of grace? Alan Jones appeals for a better way to care for one another.

> The Church is notoriously bad about handling the weaknesses and sins of its ordained ministers. One hears of congregations missing opportunities to confront, forgive, and restore many a pastor. No one is to blame for this failure to heal and to reconcile. We are all at fault. We all resist the promise of the gospel. We are deaf to the Word. We also do not know how to look after ourselves and to minister to one another.[16]

I made a major advance in personal healing when I accepted unconditional responsibility for my actions: I began to take care of myself.

Paddle strokes for denominational leaders are not intended to shift the responsibility for my moral breakdown and subsequent choices. The blaming game ended long ago. I do seek a sincere appraisal of the way the sins and weaknesses of ordained ministers are handled. I sought and celebrated reconciliation with my denomination of origin. At the same time, I continue to think and feel that the leaders who had constituted authority over me never knew how to rescue me. Some thought that I did not want to be rescued because I did not follow the guidelines for rescue. Truth is, I longed for people to be near me with the gift of open space.

I wonder, with so much expertise and skill available in the church, does anything prevent judicatories from applying the same skill and expertise to handling the sins and weaknesses of ordained ministers? Whether for confession of sin or for reconciliation, I appeal to judicatories to manage broken humanity with restoration ministries and liturgies of reconciliation.

Paddle Strokes for Recovering Moral Integrity
Clergy...Fall into Grace

River-running chaos lets you earn countless lessons, but no greater lesson than the sheer amazement of God's grace. Grace is not a quality within our control. Grace is a gift. Neither earned nor deserved, it is given as outflow of God's love. Gerald G. May, mentor of spiritual directors, explains the constancy of God's love even in response to human failure.

> The freedom that God preserves in us has a double edge. On the one hand, it means God's love and empowerment are always with us. On the other, it means there is no authentic escape from the truth of our own choices.
>
> But even when our choices are destructive and their consequences hurtful, God's love remains unwavering. Thus, regardless of our own insulation and defensiveness, God is constantly open and vulnerable to us. God is joyful when we are joyful and when we bring joy to others. God hurts when we are hurting and when we hurt others. Such is the constancy of God's love. God's Spirit is the vibrant essence of creation and transformation, and grace flowers in constantly surprising ways, but in the root of love that bears this Spirit and grace, God is changeless.[17]

Two factors kept me from a crisis of faith in God. First, the images of God as Intimate Friend and Compassionate Shepherd preserved me throughout the darkest period of my life. Second, the accumulative power of scripture and the ongoing struggle to attend to the inner Guide through the dangerous rapids kept a flicker of hope alive. I rafted through the chaos into a new world sustained by God's presence and promise. At every moment I am aware that the gospel of the second chance is created by the awesome grace of God. I resonate deeply with May's description of grace:

> Grace is much more than a static possibility of love. It is an outpouring, a boundless burning offering of God's self to us, suffering with us, overflowing with tenderness. Grace is God's passion...Living into the mystery of grace requires encountering grace as a real gift. Grace is not earned. It is not accomplished or achieved. It is not extracted through manipulation or seduction. It is just given. Nothing in our conditioning prepares us for this radical reality.[18]

Add my name to the list of clergypersons who have come to know, live, and serve in the radical dimension of God's amazing grace. The best of all possible responses to failure is to fall into grace. Resist the blame game. Calm the passions. Own up. It is better to hit bottom sooner. Allow God to immerse you in grace. Soak in its "radical reality." You will discover the truth about pride and humility (1 Pet. 5:5–7).

Congregations...Be a Community of Compassion

A congregation's compassion quotient is put to a major test in response to sexual misconduct. Polarization sets in quickly as people gravitate to sides and positions. Compassion can become selective, and dysfunctions in the emotional system of a congregation can override compassionate responses. People respond differently to crisis. Responses to the betrayal can range from anger and contempt to sadness, hurt, and deep disappointment. Surprise encounters with members ranged from questions, compassion, understanding, and angry confrontation. Letters from well-intentioned colleagues admonished me to make things right.

Jesus Christ revealed the fullness of God's compassion in specific, concrete ways: "He has embraced everything human with the infinite tenderness of his compassion."[19] Nouwen, McNeill, and Morrison, on the call to compassion, breathe hope into the hearts of all people who cry out for help.

> To us, who cry out from the depth of our brokenness for a hand that will touch us, an arm that can embrace us, lips that will kiss us, a word that speaks to us here and now, and a heart that is not afraid of our fears and trembling; to us, who feel our own pain as no other human being feels it, has felt it, or ever will feel it and who are always waiting for someone who dares to come close–to us a man has come who can truly say, "I am with you." Jesus Christ, who is God-with-us, has come to us in the freedom of love, not needing to experience our human condition but freely choosing to do so out of love. (Phil. 2:6–8).[20]

Clergy failure is a severe test for a congregation in crisis. Where do tough love and compassion meet? What would Jesus do? Maybe these questions can be answered through soul-searching prayer alone. One answer may include the gift of compassion to all affected by the fallout.

Denominations...Structure Support Clear Through

Each person affected by sexual misconduct is wounded in a variety of ways and has immediate, short-term, and long-term needs. I dare not presume to speak for the wounded others. I can account for my own wound only. To associate the words *gift* and *wound* would be deeply offensive to the wounded victims.

Sin marked the end of a calling, a vision, a home, a vocation, a salary, and the basics of life. How long does it take for a deep wound to become a gift?

Where do I live? Where do I work? Where do I find a support group? I focused on the lower end of Maslow's hierarchy of needs for the longest time. It was over a year before I could begin to invest emotionally in attending to the wound. The two-year period of discipline was winding down before I could dip my finger in the wound for the first time. It would take many dippings before the wound became a gift.

The gifts of immediate needs came through friends who provided a room to sleep in, a church that provided groceries, another church that offered spiritual and emotional support, my family of origin sending financial support, a group of mainline ministers who invited me to their study group, and an adopted denomination that gave me monetary gifts at Christmas season and a bursary to enroll in qualifying courses. Many of these gifts came from a denomination that both adopted me and gifted me with the gospel of the second chance even before I had served within it.

How long does it take for a wound to become a gift? Does a certain period of time transform wound into gift? Or is it a strong structure of support that empowers one to dip a finger into the wound again and again until the wound becomes gift? Robert Bly explains:

> I think we can regard therapy, when it is good, as a waiting by the pond. Each time we dip our wound into that water, we get nourishment, and the strength to go on further in the process. Initiation, then, does not mean ascending above the wound, nor remaining numbly inside it; but the process lies in knowing how or when, in the presence of the mentor, to dip it in the water.
>
> The wound that hurts us so much we "involuntarily" dip it in water, we have to regard as gift...Those with no wounds are the unluckiest of all. (Of course one can't think that, because no such person has ever been found.)
>
> ...[W]here a man's wound is, that is where his genius will be. Wherever the wound appears in our psyches...that is precisely the place for which we will give our major gift to the community.[21]

I appeal to denominational leaders to provide a strong structure of support clear through to the genius that lays hidden within the wound. If disciplinary bodies can give the gift of presence, patience, and support each time the fallen dip into the wound, a "genius" will grow out of the wound that can become gift to the entire denomination. Dipping the wound into the water can neither be legislated by church constituencies nor placed on timelines. It is a process of labor and birthing. Can a commitment of caring alongside a strong structure of support, time, and resources be enacted to heal the wounded-in-battle back to health and gift? I hope so. If so, a blessing awaits the faithful community. God takes the wound and transforms it into mission. Listen to the voice that leads to the gift.

River-running the Rapids of Morality—Level 2 Teamwork

MEMO: May 2005
TO: Dwayne Ratzlaff
FROM: Tom Bandy

Dwayne:

Although the crisis of morality is what precipitated falling overboard, I affirm and emphasize the fact that you look first to the crisis of *spirituality* that lies behind both success and failure. It is the shallowness in the spirituality of contemporary society that has also given rise the moralistic judgmentalism of contemporary society. The less clear people become about God, the meaning and purpose of life, sin and grace, the more legalistic they become about behavior, human relationships, right and wrong. The much vaunted "relativism" of contemporary life is not an absence of absolutes. It is the relocation of "absolutism" away from God and toward the personal preferences and ideologies of individuals, factions, and subcultures.

Fundamentalism, whether conservative or liberal, actually reveals the absence of spiritual depth. Wherever one finds spiritual depth, one finds recognition of essential ambiguities about God and humanity that political advocacy or moralistic rules cannot resolve. Ultimately, God is beyond human reason; grace is beyond human rules; sin is beyond human control; and life is beyond human organizational efforts.

You are seeking to sort out responsibilities for teamwork among clergy, congregations, and denominations. I think it is worth noting at the outset that if any one of these "partners" in the team fails to pursue deep spirituality, that person will inevitably experience crisis in morality and quite probably involve the other members of the team. If we imagine these three partners with their legs tied together in a kind of "three-person relay race," it is not difficult to see how the shallowness of any one partner will trip the other two as well. Paradoxically, the more moralistic any one partner becomes, the more vulnerable that person and the team also become to moral failure. Moralism and moral failure go hand in hand.

If the clergy lack spiritual depth, they are more likely to be both judgmental toward the colleagues and prone to moral transgression themselves.

If the congregations lack spiritual depth, they are more likely to be intolerant of lifestyle diversity and clergy misdemeanors, and also more likely to fracture and remain self-righteously small.

If the denominations lack spiritual depth, they are more likely to fall into acrimonious debates about ethical issues, and also more likely to abuse public trust.

I am not seeking to excuse your own moral failure (or that of any leader), nor minimize the importance of your own moral growth (or that of any leader). The larger context, however, is that if one partner fails, they all fail together. The failure of one leads to an incredibly complex, frustrating, and deadly tangle of bureaucracy that lowers the credibility of the church as a whole in the eyes of the public. Once lost, that credibility is hard to regain. If it is to be regained, it must start with deep spirituality, and not with new laws and regulations.

As I did in the previous chapter, let me restate your framework of Level 2 teamwork, which seeks to "river-run the rapids of morality." This level, in particular, has much to learn from biblical history and the teachings of wise leaders from the Talmud to Jesus.

	Confront Temptations	Develop Accountability	Find the Grace
CLERGY	Get help for difficult places	Check for emotional IQ	Fall into grace
CONGREGATION	Explore motives for selecting clergy	Avoid the flip side of holiness	Be a community of compassion
DENOMINATION	Contextualize misconduct	Manage broken humanity	Structure support clear through

Fundamentally, for this team to work, each partner must contribute a vital element. The clergy must *model* the positive behavioral expectations of faith; the congregation must *moderate* the pressures for leadership perfection; and the denomination must *manage* sound personnel policies and human rights guidelines.

I think we need to explore more deeply the source of temptation that confronts the clergy. Certainly our entire society is experiencing a breakdown in covenant loyalty and family integrity. Pressures from the media, the mobility of our society, and the great potential for anonymity in evil acts accelerate the process. There is no reason to believe that clergy are any more immune to these pressures than anyone else. As the incidents of extramarital affairs, spousal abuse, divorce, and any number of intimacy breakdowns increase in society, so also it increases among the clergy. Are clergy less or more vulnerable than others?

On the one hand, one would expect clergy to be less vulnerable to temptation than others. One would expect that they were more deeply grounded in the spiritual life, trained in professional ethics, sensitive and compassionate to the lives of their parishioners, dedicated to model biblical values that honor covenants of intimacy, and disciplined to monitor their emotions and practice self-denial. This may be why it seems worse for clergy to be guilty of sexual misconduct than it is for anyone else. It also seems worse for congregations to be guilty of exclusivity and judgmentalism than it is for anyone else, and worse for denominations to be guilty of ambiguity about ethical issues and public policy than it is for anyone else. These expectations may be extreme, but they are understandable.

On the other hand, the history of all spiritual movements suggests that clergy may well be *more* vulnerable to temptation than others. These are people who, more than any others, put themselves in the way of God. God is the "uncontrollable Holy," the "apocalyptic one," who turns life upside down and inside out. No single set of moral rules can ultimately constrain God, and no rational definitions can ultimately contain God. God impacts the whole life of the individual—including the emotions. The "desire" for God among all spiritual movements is a function of *eros* as much as *agape*. It is a desire for union with God, merger with the Spirit, oneness with the Creator. It is no accident that the language of many mystics, from many religions, is singularly erotic. Sexuality has never been far from the experience of the divine.

It would seem, then, that clergy (or let us say "spiritual leaders") throughout history have been known as defenders of rules and as breakers of rules. They have been known for reasonableness and also for ecstasy. Our society is so broken, idolatrous, sexually active, prone to disloyalty, and sinful that it needs to idolize a social strata of "religiously perfect people" in order to rescue them from their own shame. By idolizing the one to be morally perfect, they tacitly give themselves permission to be morally promiscuous. Little do they know that spiritually active people have put themselves in a flow of nonrational, highly emotional experience that makes them even more vulnerable to temptation.

So Dwayne, when you say, "Get help for difficult places," it sounds awfully glib even for your own experience. You are in a "difficult place." The very moment you connected with God—the very moment you were ordained to be clergy—you put yourself in a "difficult place." The difficulty is not that your profession will throw you into therapeutic situations with emotionally vulnerable people, but that your calling has thrown you into ecstatic situations with an emotionally uncontainable God. The latter makes clergy more vulnerable to the former. Clergy do, indeed, need help. Of course, they need the help of accountability to standards of professional conduct—and they need help to avoid projecting onto therapeutic professional relationships the shortcomings and disappointments of their own marriages, families, and careers. They also need help from pilgrim companions and spiritual mentors who can help them survive an ongoing relationship with an emotionally draining, uncontrollable God.

I think you are quite right that in the interests of accountability, clergy need to measure their emotional IQ. The trouble is that, unlike intellectual IQ, the emotional IQ tends to go up and down according to circumstance. One moment clergy can be a paragon of virtue, and the next dissolve into emotional jelly. And ironically, *that is just the way congregations love the clergy to be*. Let them have iron in their souls when preaching against the heathen, but let them have jelly in their hearts when counseling the beloved members. There is a "feverish" quality to the lifestyles of many clergy today: obsessive, immersed in the bubbling emotions of parishioners and communities, burning with desires to rescue people and grow churches and change society and defend the helpless and rise in their career and, and, and…!

My greatest fear is for the clergy who come after you. You are now a rare breed of clergy—called at an early age, a lifelong pastor and Christian leader. Most clergy today are entering a second career. They are not grounded as you have been in a life of biblical teaching and spiritual growth. They often have little actual church experience, and indeed experience an approach/avoidance, love/hate, attraction/aversion attitude to church life and church people. If *you* were vulnerable to temptation, imagine how vulnerable *they* are! When Marcus Borg speaks of sin as "betrayal," imagine how vulnerable this new breed of clergy is today. Many are as much on a quest to find God themselves as to help others find God. Their ambiguous feelings toward the church are already edging upon betrayal. They already smile kindly to parishioners at the church door, and then complain bitterlyabout parishioners among their colleagues.

When it comes to betrayals of covenant relationships, it seems to me that sexual misconduct is really the gnat we are obsessively trying to strain out of our church experience, while in the meantime we are swallowing camel-sized betrayals of trust in so many other aspects of congregational life. If you really study why churches are declining and dying, it is *not* really because the public thinks clergy have betrayed marriage covenants. It is because they think the church as a whole has "betrayed" its original calling to reach and rescue the lost.

This leads me to comment on the expectations of the congregation as part of the team that river-rafts the rapids of morality. I have always discouraged using the metaphor of "marriage" to describe the relationship between a pastor and a congregation. For one thing, it is not biblical. The church is the "bride" of Christ, not the pastor, and to apply the metaphor to the pastor suggests that the pastor and Christ are the same person. That leads to all kinds of problems, not the least of which is the unrealistic sense of betrayal a congregation feels when the pastor misbehaves. Certainly the pastor betrays a promise to model biblical morals and congregational values, but any guilt here is no different from the guilt any congregational board member or core leader should feel as well.

Negotiating a call, therefore, has nothing to do with negotiating a dowry or making a prenuptial agreement. Many clergy and congregations seek to do exactly that. The "dowry" the church offers is a guaranteed income, adequate housing, and a support package—not to mention various perks related to golf memberships and community profile. The "dowry" the clergyperson offers is a mixture of skills that can address the needs of the members and perhaps a second income from the spouse that can add financial stability to the congregational budget. Whether or not the bride and groom come to *love* each other is a secondary blessing that we hope will result from an otherwise "arranged" marriage. These days, an additional prenuptial agreement (guaranteed by the regional denomination) adds further protections for the career of the clergy and the survival of the congregation should anything go amiss.

What's wrong with that picture? It is not difficult to see how the "marriage" metaphor has left behind the one component most essential to the body of Christ: call. The call is not to each other, but to the bigger, broader mission of Christ to multiply disciples from Jerusalem to Cleveland. (I was born in Cleveland and believe me, like most American cities, it needs all of Christ it can get).

When it comes to river-running the rapids of morality, you identify key strategic moves: Confront temptations, develop accountability, and find the grace. Clergy, congregation, and denomination all have a role in each strategic move. However, even though three is a tidy number, I feel compelled to add a decisive fourth strategic move: *Focus the Mission!*

Our water metaphors cause me to remember a grade-B movie I saw long ago with a scene of a ship becalmed. All sails were set, the sea was a flat calm, and the ship "boxed the compass" as it moved hither and thither without direction. Because no storms were in sight, no crises loomed, and the ship was clearly not going anywhere, the crew had nothing to do but look to themselves. Sailors and church people being what they are, they began sinning. They drank too much, fought among one another, raped the passengers, and generally created mayhem.

The lesson is that immorality is the natural result of purposelessness. Take away mission and confuse vision, and clergy and congregation become self-absorbed. It's not only that they have too much time on their hands, but that they are spending their time in frantic pursuit of the wrong things. The more passionate clergy or congregations become trying to grow a megachurch, expand a television audience, renovate a building, implement the perfect program, write an award-winning sermon, reduce the operating deficit, achieve an ideological agenda, or ensure a legacy that will last forever…the more likely it is that the church will split, the treasury will be embezzled, a child will be abused, or the senior pastor will have an affair. One and all have forsaken the true mission of the church, and clergy and/or laity have lacked the courage to align their life and lifestyle to that mission.

If a fourth strategic move for river-running the rapids of morality is to *focus mission,* then surely the clergy, congregation, and denomination all have a role to play.

First, the clergy have got to have courage. Mission and courage go together. If the mission does not demand courage, it probably isn't a mission at all—it's just a strategic plan. I find that far too many North American clergy are simply unprepared to *stake* much on ministry. They talk a good line about "surrendering to the Spirit," but draw the line at upsetting their spouse, relocating their children, or destabilizing their financial security. The real problem today is not the "comfortable pew." It is the "comfortable pulpit."

In my view, courage means shaping one's lifestyle around a mission. It is about daring to dig deep to uncover the one good reason not to commit suicide—and sharing it with the world regardless of whose addiction you break. It is about elevating "growth" over "love," so that you consistently destabilize the harmony of the church to learn something new about God, the world, and yourself. It is less about doing everything for everybody, and more about deliberately *not* doing some things for some people. Time management is one of the most cowardly ways clergy face mission. Timely intervention is far more risky.

Second, the congregation has got to own a vision. This is an old song, and many (including me) have sung it often. When there is no vision, the people perish—but before they perish, first they play. Most congregations persist in the belief that a vision is nothing more than a "desired destination." In my metaphor of a becalmed ship, there was no landfall visible from the highest lookout. As long as there was no desired destination, the crew misbehaved. A real vision is not a desired destination, but a song in the heart. It is a rhythm that beats unceasingly, or a recollection that elicits incredible joy. If the becalmed ship had a courageous captain, she would turf the crew into the long boat, beat a rhythm to stroke the oars, and tow the ship forward.

I am not saying, of course, that strategic planning encourages moral misconduct in the congregation. Yet in the absence of vision, strategic planning redistributes the energy of a church away from lifestyle alignment to God's mission toward program implementation. The more programs become more important than spiritual life, the more opportunity there is for moral breakdown in the congregation. I cannot help but think this was the great flaw Jesus identified with the synagogue and temple of his time. They knew exactly what to do and how to do it, but they had no deeper vision about the real point of life and mission.

Third, the denomination must get out of the way. One thing that strikes me most profoundly is that denominations have spent extraordinary time, money, and leadership-deployment energy to enforce moral standards on the clergy. At the same time, moral indiscretions have continued to multiply exponentially in all denominations. Denominations pass motions, establish procedures, enforce regulations, and take innumerable *actions* to ensure moral behavior. Perhaps that is part of the problem. Perhaps what is needed is for denominations to stop trying to manage morality. Instead, help the clergy find courage and the congregation discern mission, and then get out of the way.

My reading of church history is that, when it comes to denominational leadership, less is more. Neither congregations nor clergy are stupid. If they once find a clear mission and a passion to pursue it, they can regulate themselves. They really do not need supervisors, regulations, management meetings, and psychological examinations. There will be fewer moral breakdowns and better accountability if congregations are clear about their core values, beliefs, vision, and mission—and if clergy courageously model what it means to shape their lifestyles around that mission—than there would be if the denomination had five times the number of policies and regulations.

CHAPTER 6

River-running the Rapids of Calling
Level 3 Teamwork

	A New Birth	A New Beginning	A New Future	A New Community
CLERGY	Submit to womb-work	Hear the word of absolution	Lead by self-definition	Cultivate the art of knowing
CONGREGATION	Live up to faith, hope, and love	Reconcile with arms wide open	Manage polarities	Serve as a community of discernment
DENOMINATION	Prepare to give birth	Reinforce restoration	Start at the source	Advance the lesson of the butterfly

Prevailing Teams

Level 3 teamwork represents the greatest degree of difficulty. Restoring the fallen to their calling requires prevailing teamwork. When denominational judicatories, congregations, and clergy commit to a full restoration, they invest spiritual and emotional resources, time, and money. Prevailing teams even put their integrity on the line by sustaining the gospel of the second chance. And they put Paul's curious claim to the test about God's irrevocable call (Rom. 11:29). God did not revoke the calling on my life. God turned me around and reclaimed me to ordained service, albeit in an adopted denomination. Many fallen pastors never return to their calling. A dangerous rescue requires prevailing teamwork on the part of all.

Paddle Strokes for a New Birth
Clergy...Submit to Womb-Work

Things may happen to the unborn in the womb of a mother that shape the unborn for life. I have no memory of any event or emotion during the nine months of development in my mother's womb. I will never forget the experience of God's womb-work. Jeremiah said that God's futures are filled with hope (Jer. 29:11). In the womb of God I received the gift of compassion. New hope was born. Nouwen, McNeill, and Morrison describe the shape of God's womb-work.

> Simply being with someone is difficult because it asks of us that we share in the other's vulnerability, enter with him or her into the experience of weakness and powerlessness, become part of uncertainty, and give up control and self-determination. And still, whenever this happens, new strength and new hope is being born. Those who offer us comfort and consolation by being and staying with us in moments of illness, mental anguish, or spiritual darkness often grow as close to us as those with whom we have biological ties. They show their solidarity with us by willingly entering the dark, unchartered spaces of our lives. For this reason, they are the ones who bring new hope and help us discover new directions.[1]

Clergy can attest to personal moments of crisis that invite us to submit to the womb-work of God. The crises we face are as varied as our unique persons and situations. The experiences of God's womb are multiform. The womb may take the shape of a congregation, a support group, a therapist, a spiritual guide, a prayer ministry, a discernment committee, a Bible study group, family members, or longstanding or newfound friends. They are the people who rally around us, give us a shoulder to rest on, embrace us, say a timely word of courage, provide a supportive presence, and grant us unconditional love. Many clergy are called into the womb of God sooner or later. There, God embraces us with the gift of compassion. Seeds of new hope and new directions are born. We are never the same again.

The seeds of my personal failure were planted in the womb of compassion. This I sought to provide as a caring clergy. I had invited hurting people into that womb on many occasions. I pursued with passion a vision to invite people into the womb-work of God: to find God, to heal hurts, and to build dreams. I did not expect the day to come when I would be asked to submit to the womb-work out of my own brokenness. I did not find the womb easily because it was not where I expected it. The womb found me. I am grateful to those who rescued me and carried me into the womb. I chose to yield to the divine design at last. I went into the womb a deeply wounded, burnt-out minister. By the grace of God alone I came out a wounded healer reclaimed to ordained ministry.

Scripture reveals a God who chooses freely to be so connected with creation that this God takes on a deep wound and becomes the suffering God, the One who fearlessly enters into the chaos of life and carries our wounds. This suffering God becomes so intimate as to indwell and abide with us even through the contradictions. God does not draw back from the chaos or the primal mess of life. God does not give up on the broken, even those whose wounds are most uncomforting and whose responses are most nonconforming. This One is a wounded Healer who reserves the right of judgment. The God who is over the primal chaos never abandons. God loves stubbornly, persistently, unconditionally.

God became wounded healer in Jesus the Christ. Nouwen developed the concept of "the wounded healer" as one who proclaims liberation by turning personal wounds into a major source of healing power. Nouwen shows the way.

> Making one's own wounds a source of healing, therefore, does not call for a sharing of superficial personal pains but for a constant willingness to see one's own pain and suffering as rising from the depth of the human condition which all men share.[2]

Congregations...Live Up to Faith, Hope, and Love

After disgrace, a new set of issues confronted me: loss of self-esteem, self-doubts, fear of risk-taking, cloudiness of vision, struggle with motivation, and fear of rejection. Backdrop issues became forefront issues. Before, the adrenaline rush of white-water adventures was addicting. After, the pendulum swung to the opposite pole. I faced fears of adventuring, particularly the interconnected fears of risk-taking and rejection. The new struggle was to confront the issues of self-esteem. These issues were the residue of the odyssey. I found Norman Vincent Peale at a time when I needed his message. Norman Vincent Peale and Robert H. Schuller are the embodiments of the river of positive power.

Congregations are releasers of faith, hope, and love. Two twentieth-century congregations that propelled their ministries around these biblical values are Marble Collegiate Church in New York City and Garden Grove Community Church in Garden Grove, California. I have yet to find the acceptance of the "positive thinking" or "possibility thinking" movements as authentic streams of Christian spirituality. In *The Story of Christian Spirituality,* reference is made to the theme of "positive thinking and self-esteem" along with the names of Norman Vincent Peale and Robert H. Schuller. Within "Spiritualities of the Twentieth Century," Bradley Holt gives an overview of the names and movements that shaped the Christian spiritual landscape of the twentieth century.

Holt assesses the contribution of Norman Vincent Peale.

> One of the more controversial movements in American spirituality has been the "positive thinking" school of thought first named by Dr. Norman Vincent Peale. As pastor of an influential New York congregation, he wrote a number of books to promote the idea that

our thoughts need to be positive if we are to be able to accomplish our goals. Later he was a founder of *Guideposts* magazine. Part of the criticism of this school of thought is due to the similar approach taken in much "success" oriented literature available on the bookstands. It does not seem to be distinctly Christian, and its main focus may directly contradict the idea of grace and focus on the commercial and material rewards that so many seek who are not yet spiritually awakened. But the Christian promoters of this idea have had success themselves in reaching and influencing the American population.[3]

Holt is less critical of Robert H. Schuller, pastor of the Crystal Cathedral and a minister of the Reformed Church in America. Whereas Peale popularized the idea of "positive thinking," Schuller popularized the related idea of "possibility thinking." Schuller calls for a new reformation founded on "self-esteem...the single greatest need facing the human race today."[4]

> For decades now we have watched the church in western Europe and in America decline in power, membership and influence. I believe that this decline is the result of our placing theocentric communications above the meeting of the deeper emotional and spiritual needs of humanity...
>
> I call upon the church to make a commitment to remodel itself until it becomes the best thing that has ever happened to the human race. The church becomes the best friend for all people when we proclaim the gospel of Faith–Hope–and Love which truly stimulates and sustains human self-esteem.[5]

Peale and Schuller claim to have caught their positive faith from Jesus Christ. Peale calls the three commands of faith, hope, and love "powerful Life Lifters."

> The top three-point formula for living is in this immortal verse: 1 Corinthians 13:13. Here are three powerful Life Lifters: Faith, the greatest power in this world; Hope, the attitude of expectancy–the best is yet to be; and Love, one of the greatest qualities of all–a heart of compassion and understanding. Christian love gives deep joy. Let these three shine like stars in your life, and your spirit will be uplifted always.[6]

I despaired over any future at all. Faith, hope, and love confronted my despair. These three life lifters took hold of the promise of Romans 8:28. This promise became the secret to a brighter future. I clung to the hope of its actuality. The secret requires a divine-human synergy. Peale explains:

> [E]verything that happens in your life–harsh, painful, hard though it be–combines with all the rest of your experience for your good, if your life is dedicated to God. This is one of the deepest philosophies

> ever declared. We are to take all things—what we think is good and what we think is bad—and draw them all together into a symphony of creativity and make it work for good. And that's the way it is, if we are in harmony with God's will and mindful of His love. So I submit that this is the secret of having a bright future in this chaotic world. If enough people were to take hold of this idea and live attuned to it, moving out from the churches into the world outside, we could make all things work together for good in the world too.[7]

I commit to take the good and the bad and work them into a "symphony of creativity" in harmony with God's design. I could redeem the past in the present by sharing the lessons earned from chaos.

The river of positive power never did catch the imagination of the wider church. The message of faith, hope, and love continues to have great appeal among secular people who do not see the church as relevant to their spiritual yearnings. I paddled through a period of life when I needed the strokes of faith, hope, and love. I still do. The three-point formula for uplift came to me through various people, in different settings, and from diverse theological agendas. Faith, hope, and love carried me over the chaos. Congregations remain relevant for people in chaos as long as members live up to the potent power of faith, hope, and love.

Denominations...Prepare to Give Birth

Despair touched me at many levels. I was river-running through deep hopelessness over many losses. The emotional aftermath was like capsizing headlong into dangerous white water with no apparent hope of rescue.

I have no practice as a mother in labor except as a deeply affected father-participant in the birthing of my children. I knew intuitively that an old existence had ended and a new existence had to be born. I did not know what was needed at the time. I do now. I needed a structure of support throughout the period of birthing: discipline, repentance, reconciliation, restitution, and restoration.

A midwife in the birthing process is a metaphor for the structure of support vital for wounded clergy. I was in a passageway from one form of existence to another. I had never been through the passage before. I had no prior memory to guide me. I felt totally helpless. Actions had been unleashed, the consequences of which were out of the parameters of my control. I was confused, angry, and playing the blaming game. The old world was gone, physically and emotionally; and the new world was refusing to be born. I needed others to help me to birth again.

Having experienced the grace of rebirth, I now ask denominational leaders to dispatch a team of "spiritual midwives"[8] for the purpose of discipline, reconciliation, and restoration. We need leaders to go on pilgrimage throughout the birthing process. Call them prevailing teams who travail together for a new future. William M. Easum and Thomas G. Bandy explain the role of "spiritual midwives" in the birthing process.

> They do whatever is necessary to facilitate the potential for birth that lies within others. Birth is the most profound and dynamic experience of "synergy" possible. Synergy means *the combined or cooperative action of two or more agents that together increases each other's effectiveness.* The results of synergy will always be more than merely the sum of the parts. In the experience of birth, mother and father, doctor and nurse, all combine and cooperate in a way that increases one another's effectiveness. The outcome–the newborn child–will be far more than the sum of all the personalities and talents involved in the birth. In fact, the synergy that allows birth to happen will include many other agents beyond the parents, doctors, and nurses. The administrators who maintain the hospital, the researchers who create new techniques and medicines, the custodial staff who cleanse the delivery room, and even the unknown taxi driver who rushed the expectant mother to the hospital all play their part. The complexity of the synergy of birth involves practical and emotional, physical and spiritual elements. The midwife is the leader who gathers all the elements together, and guides the combinations of energies, in order for life to be born. If birth is a profound synergy, then the midwife is a capable "synergist." The "synergist" enhances the synergy of life.[9]

Coming to birth again is a complex matter. God served as my midwife-synergist, calling people from a wide variety of Christian spiritual traditions to rescue, heal, reconcile, and restore. May denominational leaders do the same for a host of others.

Paddle Strokes for a New Beginning
Clergy...Hear the Word of Absolution

To invoke the presence of God is an awesome thing. Each river designs rivercrafts for the express purpose of calling God's presence into the material world. The common element in all this is belief in the power of a spoken word. This is the age of multisensory experience. We are shaped by images, and we wonder if words still have power to change reality.

From the beginning of recorded history, until about five hundred years ago, the primary conveyor of communication was the oral tradition. The oral tradition, a personal and powerful form of communication, gave birth to Christianity and transformed the Western world.[10] Central to the oral tradition is the awesome power of a spoken word. In *Future Worship,* Lamar Boschman speaks to the power of oral words.

> Oral words had power–not the power of the heroic ego, but a spiritual power greater than the speaker. And the speaker fully expected

something awesome to happen. Each moment was charged with raw reality, immediate possibility, and manifest presence. The Hebrews... knew from experience that the word they spoke...moved with raw creative power, fulfilled its own prophecy, and manifested its own meaning...their words *intervened* in life–they actually changed life.

Spoken words incarnated power.[11]

I learned that words continue to have the power to bless or to curse.

In the act of blessing, the one requesting blessing and the one pronouncing blessing are "co-participants in the acknowledgement of God's presence."[12] W. V. Arnold describes the singular purpose of blessing in its many forms.

> The forms of blessing and benediction are many...Their intention is to convey the promise of strength to be found, not in the one who speaks, but in the God for whom that word is being spoken.[13]

Along my white-water odyssey, spoken words incarnated awesome power to shape: the words and images of the still, small voice that propel me forward and shape my destiny, the liturgy of ordination, the word of absolution in the first prophetic presbytery, the prophetic symbolism within the three prophecy sessions, the laying on of hands and prayers that invoked God's presence, the words of praise and worship, words of repentance, and words of reconciliation to and from my denomination of origin. These spoken invocations of God's presence transformed everything.

Scripture readings, prayers, spiritual conversations, prophetic images, and extravagant worship that invoke the presence of God are words incarnate with power. When absorbed into consciousness, words change everything! I have learned to employ the awesome power of spoken words to invoke the presence of God. Paddle commands spoken by God's paddle team can change futures. May clergy learn the power of their words of absolution for all members of the congregation, but especially for fellow clergy capsized in the rapids of chaos.

Congregations...Reconcile with Arms Wide Open

I was moved by the Truth and Reconciliation Commission of South Africa. Dullah Omar, a former Minister of Justice, claimed that "a commission is a necessary exercise to enable South Africans to come to terms with their past on a morally accepted basis and to advance the cause of reconciliation."[14] I saw video clips of national reconciliation hearings on television. A nation chose to heal the wounds. I wonder about the potential of reconciliation within the wider church.

The cessation of relationship with my former denomination resulted in a spirit of orphaning. This was another residual issue from my odyssey. I needed a sense of belonging. I had to renounce the spirit of orphaning and claim the spirit of adoption. In dialogue, God assured me that I was a son, not an orphan, and that God's house had no room in which I was not welcome.

Exchanging a spirit of orphaning for a spirit of adoption is vital for people who have passed through the alienation of relationships. I was grateful to be adopted. But I had to deal with the residue of the orphaning experience. One does not foreclose on years of relationships without hurting deeply. The people and places that shaped me are part of me to this day. God led me full circle to a place of reconciliation with the betrayed people. With the exception of one meeting with a representative group of district leaders and another meeting with a district leader, the formal procedure of reconciliation with church and denomination transpired through written communication. I am left to wonder if an opportunity was missed. The reconciliation process will always have an incomplete feel to it. Part of me dismisses the sense of incompleteness as the best one can hope for in a complex case. On the other hand, the reconciliation meetings of a nation suggest otherwise.

I wonder if face-to-face reconciliation with the offended congregation might have been possible. Reconciliation occurred through a district representative to a church board. Is it ever too late to reconcile with arms wide open? A larger reason transcends my personal need for healing. It goes to the heart of the relationship between the history of a church and its present life. When a pastor engages in sexual misconduct, that accountable person destroys trust and introduces a wound into the emotional system of a congregation that can have a residual effect for years. Nothing can change that reality unless a genuine repentance and reconciliation can introduce healing into the wound. Wounds may recede into the basement, but that does not mean they are inactive. We know that an emotional wound can shape a child throughout a lifetime. Can emotional wounds within congregations carry that longevity? Pastoral experience in a variety of churches has confirmed it. Ministers know that every day in every way we work with the emotional histories of congregations.

In a simple and insightful manual on church revitalization, Robert D. Dale claims that every church has a script.

> Your church has been scripted to behave by its dream, history, and decisions. Past patterns may be more deeply entrenched than you have seen or believed before. Persons and churches quickly become creatures of habit...Discovering your church's script will help you understand and minister better–even if you find some ruts that run almost from coast to coast.[15]

Many factors shape a script: founding minister, founding dream, subsequent pastors, greatest growth periods, issues and problems, people conflicts, prevailing spirit, traditionalizing forces, crisis moments, magic moments, special projects, and special celebrations.[16] We are not powerless. Churches have three choices about their scripts. Dale explains:

> (1) They can *live* their scripts, whether healthy or unhealthy. (2) They can try to *avoid* their scripts, if they are unhealthy. (3) They can rewrite

their scripts, *changing* from unhealthy to healthy. Rewriting demands an awareness of the destructive pattern of the old script and a congregational choice to end the old and commit themselves to a new script reflecting a kingdom dream. A new vision of the ministry your church can develop is the surest route to a healthy ministry and a story worth telling.[17]

Reconciliation goes a long way toward writing a new script for a congregation. It is never too late to reconcile with arms wide open. Reconciliation is a central way for a congregation to care about its spiritual health and vital future.

The parable of the prodigal son is a revolutionary story (Lk. 15:1-2, 11-32). Tom Wright claims that stories "create worlds." This story created a new world for me. It served as a paradigm of reconciliation. In its cultural context the story contains shocking features. It has an explosive message. The prodigal returned to say, "I was wrong" and to confess, "I have sinned." Is it easier to dismiss the hurtful event as an aberration better left buried in historical forgetfulness? Is reconciliation with the past an undignified intrusion into the church's present life? If acknowledged, should the reconciliation be private or public? Only congregations can answer these questions. The work of reconciliation is a threat to dignity. Wright explains:

> But why does Jesus tell it this way, with these characters? At the heart of the story *is the reason for the party.* Jesus was being heavily criticized by the guardians of the ancestral traditions because he was celebrating the kingdom, not with the righteous and the religious elite, but with all and sundry—with the riff raff, the no-goods, the down-and-outs. And, in the process, he wasn't just throwing his own dignity to the winds; he was threatening God's dignity, and, with it, the hope of the whole nation. Yes, says Jesus: Just like a father who...The story explains why Jesus has been acting in the shameless way he has. He is bringing in the kingdom of God; he is bringing about the real homecoming, the real return from exile; so of course there has to be a party. Of course you have to celebrate. Who cares about dignity when the kingdom of God is arriving?[18]

When will our congregations open wide their arms, inviting their prodigals to reconciliation?

Denominations...Reinforce Restoration

I could not envision a recovery from the awful devastation. Capsized by my choices, all I could see was the chaos. I fought against the undertow daily, but without hope. I saw myself as an utter failure. I had committed the unthinkable sin. No church would ever want me again. It was over. That sums up my state of mind. Colleagues hoped for restoration, even speaking and writing to me with that great end in view. Their good intentions did not convince me. Devoid of hope, I did not believe them. I needed to hear the vision of restoration repeatedly from the people and leaders who could speak the vision into my life and who had the power to make it so. I cannot make claim to a different outcome. All I know is that I was filled with anger, guilt, and shame and emptied of hope. I had no vision for anything.

Disillusionment is a child of burnout. I do not know if there is a correlation between burnout and sexual misconduct. I am certain that burnout removed the final barrier to adultery. The bearers of hope could not penetrate my disillusionment. Even call to ministry came into question. Roy M. Oswald describes the "over-committed person":

> These people are so focused on their mission that they continually press on, ignoring the admonitions of friends and family and their body's increasing exhaustion. This is not commitment. In fact, we may need to question whether we are really serving idols or ego rather than the Kingdom. I do not believe God calls us to be physically and emotionally exhausted, cynical, disillusioned, and self-deprecating.[19]

The passageway from overcommitment to burnout leads through the deep dark valley of disillusionment. Oswald employs the words of Robert Sabath (*Sojourners* magazine) to describe the redemption on the other side.

> Burnout is a refining fire that can detach us from an excessive identity with the results of our work and the impact we make in the world. It can teach us a deeper trust in God by forcing us to withdraw all hope, ideals, visions and expectations from every other object, situation, thing or person–except God...
>
> So burnout becomes not just stages of disillusionment, but if persisted in faithfully, it can become a maturing process of faith. Burnout de-establishes our illusions and establishes true faith...
>
> Burnout holds the potential for making us either cynics or saints. In the midst of burnout, we have a choice. We can swing from the heights of all our unmet expectations to the detached withdrawal of no expectations at all. Or we can learn to grow in faith and transfer our misplaced expectations to the proper focus in God alone.[20]

As judicatories charged with the enactment of discipline and as carriers of the vision of restoration, do not be surprised or discouraged when an offending pastor appears unresponsive to the overtures of God's grace manifest in your invitations to repentance, confession, and reconciliation. The mind is disillusioned, and the heart is disconnected. The process of de-establishing illusions has begun.

Find the redemptive side to burnout. The virtues will be restored to supreme value over time. The vision of restoration will return to the heart. God alone knows when, where, and how it will happen. For some, the time will be sooner; for others, later. Never cease to speak the vision of restoration into a fallen heart. The vision actualized may look different from the vision idealized. God will grant a harvest of hope. God reigns.

Paddle Strokes for a New Future
Clergy...Lead by Self-definition

The minister as CEO is an aberration not to be recycled. I came to leadership by self-definition only after riding the waves of charisma and consensus. I paid dues at both extremes.

Leadership styles fall along the charisma-consensus continuum. Leadership by charisma seeks to make the most of one's magnetic personality, positive energy, and personally attractive qualities. Contagious enthusiasm can go a long way toward galvanizing a church in the pursuit of mission. The problem is that the charismatic leader tends to be forced to overfunction. Clergy who rely on charisma tend to the never-ending work of keeping emotional triangles in balance. They serve in a chronic state of stress.

At the other end of the continuum is consensus, a leadership style that seeks to avoid the dilemmas of the opposite extreme. It tends to value peace above progress and turns the leader into a resource person. With no voice willing to say, "Here I stand," the goals of the community can be thrown overboard by those least willing to cooperate. Both the charismatic and consensus leadership styles tend to diminish the health of the organism in the long run.[21]

Neither style tends to empower the congregation to reach its potential over time. I employed the charismatic style to some degree of effectiveness. I sought to move the church by the force of vision, personality, skill, motivation, and enthusiasm. After my restoration, and given a second chance at leadership, I found myself employing the consensus style. I worked at both ends of the continuum. For me, the consensus style was less effective than the charismatic style, although consensus was less destructive on relationships and less prone to producing burnout.

Neither charisma nor consensus held the key to the health and vitality of the church. I lost the sense of self in both styles, albeit for different reasons. With the charismatic style I lost the sense of self through burnout. With the consensus style I sacrificed the sense of self for peace. Although both styles can be important accessories, there is a better way. The alternate style is leadership by self-definition.

Edwin Friedman provides the guidelines for leadership by "self-differentiation."

> The key to successful spiritual leadership...with success understood as not only moving people toward a goal, but also in terms of the survival of the family (and its leader), has more to do with the leader's capacity for self-definition than with the ability to motivate others...

> The basic concept of leadership through self-differentiation is this: If the leader will take primary responsibility for his or her own position as "head" and work to define his or her own goals and self, while *staying in touch* with the rest of the organism, there is a more than reasonable chance that the body will follow. There may be initial resistance but, if the leader can stay in touch with the resisters, the body will usually go along...
>
> There are three distinct but interrelated components to leadership through self-differentiation...First and foremost, the leader must stay in touch...
>
> The second central component is the capacity and willingness of the leader to take nonreactive, clearly conceived, and clearly defined positions...*Define self and continue to stay in touch*...The triangle-potentiating approaches of motivating their "minds," or overcoming their resistance are thus bypassed; *it is their need for a head that will move them*...
>
> Crucial here is the leader's capacity to distinguish process from content, and the ability to be playful, that is, not serious or anxiously helpful.[22]

Friedman helped me gain clarity on my chaos: overriding of values, loss of identity, burnout, and vocational self-ruin. Self-definition promotes spiritual and emotional wisdom.

At the core is a simple paddle stroke: "Define self and continue to stay in touch."[23] The formula will move a church in the direction of its goals. The stroke maximizes a leader's ability to function in healthy ways. So I challenge clergy to lead by self-definition.

Congregations...Manage Polarities

My story, as well as those of many others, overflows with polarities. People call them contradictions. I choose to live with their tensions. I accept the mysteries of faith. The mission of the church is to embody the mystery of God's reign. Howard A. Snyder aided me with an instructive discussion on the "key tensions or polarities" of God's reign. Snyder identifies eight models of the "kingdom" based on six polarities:

> Models: future hope, inner spiritual experience, mystical communion, institutional church, countersystem, political state, Christianized culture, and earthly utopia.
>
> Polarities: present versus future, individual versus social, spirit versus matter, gradual versus climactic, Divine action versus human action, the Church's relation to the kingdom as essentially the same or as clearly different.[24]

These models and polarities embody the good news of Jesus Christ in the world. As carriers of the mission of Jesus, congregations will be called on to manage these polarities or tension points, not to dissolve them. To dissolve them is to deny vital elements of the good news. It is to engage in ongoing river rivalries that serve no constructive purpose for the mission of Jesus Christ in the world.

My denomination of origin locates its comfort zone at the individual pole of personal salvation. My adopted denomination finds its comfort zone at the social pole of social salvation. Each has a vital gift to offer the other. I have come to be at ease with these tension points. I encourage congregations to be at ease with these polarities also. I believe the polarities are carriers of transformation within the church. So rather than ignore, deny, or reject the tension points, choose to welcome and manage[25] them in wise ways.

Denominations...Start at the Source

I did not receive instruction about intimacy in ministry or sexual ethics in my theological education. I received no sensitivity training about sexuality in clergy-member relationships in any of my continuing education. I facilitated courses in college and seminary on spiritual direction and pastoral methods without addressing sexual ethics. I never deemed the topic of sexuality and ministry a matter of priority need. A life-altering lesson lay in waiting for an unsuspecting pastor.

An emotional bond had formed as an outcome of mutual grief. I made a decision to manage the friendship rather than sever it. A personal issue that surfaced in doctor of ministry assessment and case study analysis was fear of intimacy in relationships. Should I run from the emotional bond or channel it? I sought perspective through spiritual direction. I sought impersonal counsel from readings on sexuality and ministry when the direction came to an end. Evelyn Eaton Whitehead and James D. Whitehead identify personal strengths for intimacy:

> Friendship, love, collaboration, negotiation, compromise, conflict—these are the arenas of intimacy. Our embraces range from the erotic to the competitive, from the friendly to the antagonistic. These differing experiences raise the questions: Are we sure enough of our self to risk drawing close to someone else? Are we open to the new information that may arise as we come together? In these questions we face what frightens us most about intimacy—not what we learn from others, but what we learn about ourself...
>
> Intimacy, then, carries costs. If its rewards are great, so are its requirements. To meet these demands requires a robust range of personal resources—strengths that we develop in the give-and-take of the relationships of our life.
>
> As a strength of adult maturity, intimacy is the capacity to commit ourself to particular people in relationships that last over time and to

meet the accompanying demands for change in ways that do not compromise personal integrity.[26]

I did not carry the capacities for intimacy. I did not seek professional help. Believing I could manage the matter, I sought a historical model of spiritual friendship from Christian spirituality. I found a model in Francis de Sales and Jane Chantal. Henri J. M. Nouwen describes their Jesus-centered friendship.

> In a time in which there is so much concern about the right professional distance within a helping relationship and in which there is so much preoccupation with transference and counter-transference, Jane de Chantal and Francis de Sales offer us a fresh perspective on a healing relationship. They dare to take risks with each other and those they care for. Mutuality is the word here. It is the mutuality of the ministry of Jesus the Good Shepherd who says: "I know my own and my own know me" (Jn. 10:14). A mutual openness, a mutual sharing, a mutual confession of needs, a mutual confession and forgiveness, a mutual knowing and being known–that is the source of a community where God's strength is made manifest among weak people. The Jesus-centered affectionate friendship between Francis de Sales and Jane de Chantal, generously shared with the many who came to them for spiritual comfort and consolation, is a great gift to our century.[27]

I was in denial about the direction of the friendship and its influence on my marriage. At the confluence of many rapids, I succumbed to the undertow. It is pointless to suggest that this or that would have changed the outcome. I do believe that sensitivity training about sexuality in ministry would have reduced the personal naïveté with which I engaged the issue. I was afraid to admit the emotional bond to the people who could really help me. I thought I could nurture my marriage and continue the friendship. I feared that admitting the presence of the bond would jeopardize my ministry, even though no sexual acting out had occurred. I put myself into a mental and emotional box.

I lacked the sensitivity training that asked, "What does a pastor do if/when…?" It might have prepared me to seek the help required at the outset, to ask, "What do I do now?" I missed the self-evident answer. I lacked emotional intelligence. I was far too confident about what I could manage. I brought a flagrant naïveté to the management of the issue.

Prevention and intervention should begin at the seminary level with an open treatment of the issues of sexual ethics and sexual misconduct in the church. Denominational leaders would do well to continue to address sexuality and ministry issues through continuing education. I found the use of professional materials (including visuals, role-playing, and discussion) to be very instructive for exploring sexual themes. I do not blame theological education, nor can I claim that sensitivity training would have changed the outcome, but I do believe that the inclusion of this component into the curriculum would have confronted an emotional naïveté about intimacy in ministry. I challenge the denominations to start at the source of the problem and offer the educational tools future and present ministers need.

Paddle Strokes for a New Community
Clergy...Cultivate the Art of Knowing

River-running requires the art of discernment. Maneuvers have consequences. Ethical leadership anticipates the outcome of a decision for good or evil. Chaos taught me the indissoluble link between direct guidance and ethical behavior. The inner guide never failed me, though I failed to follow the direct guidance. The clarity of the counsel that came through dialogues with the inner voice amazed me. It was the only light in my darkness through to resignation. I was invited to follow the path of faithfulness in all my callings. The call to nurture my marriage was ever-present. I failed. I was warned to act decisively. I failed. I was counseled to honor covenants and be faithful to my callings. I was warned about not retaining or persevering in the words God was speaking to me. I was even given the reason for the special attack against me. In the failure of the messenger, the message would be damaged. The speaking voice reached out to me with the gift of compassion even to the end. The divine whisper told me I would test God's love. God would not abandon me. I received a promise two days before my resignation: "We will start new." God has kept the promise.

The pursuit of direct guidance from God is not the problem. The Quaker tradition points clergy to the true art of knowing: to cultivate a powerful and indivisible union between direct guidance and ethical behavior. In his classic work *Servant Leadership,* Robert K. Greenleaf reprinted an article he wrote for the *Friends Journal–Quaker Thought and Life Today,* October 15, 1974. Greenleaf writes about the article.

> It deals with what I believe to be the central element in the leadership of George Fox in founding the religious Society of Friends in England in the Seventeenth Century. Fox, an earnest seeker after truth when quite young, records the early event in his Journal: "I had forsaken all priests...And those called the most experienced people; for I saw that there was none among them all that could speak to my condition. And when all my hopes in them and in all men were gone, so that I had nothing outwardly to help me, or could tell what to do, then, oh then, I heard a voice which said, 'There is one, even Christ Jesus, that can speak to thy condition.' And when I heard it my heart did leap for joy...And this I knew experimentally." The principal impact of Fox, in my judgment, was upon ethical practice, immediately and permanently, in all walks of life. The impact was impressive: a new commercial ethic, equal status of women, education for all; and, in America, the Quakers were the first religious society to denounce slavery and forbid the holding of slaves among members–one hundred years before the Civil War. While my article was addressed to "those

working out of the Quaker tradition," it may serve any who sense power in the words "This I knew experimentally."[28]

"This I knew experimentally"–these words express Fox's greatest insight. He expected direct guidance from God through his own reading of scripture. These words may capture the core of the Quaker tradition. It is possible that this gift of knowing experimentally gave Fox his "extraordinary leadership." He guided his followers "to a sharp return to the spirit and substance of early Christianity."[29] Greenleaf says about Fox's leadership:

> Leadership, as demonstrated by Fox, is knowing experimentally what is superior wisdom–**now**...Superior wisdom might be defined as competence and expertise plus the experimental knowledge that tells one what to do with these **now**. And with such superior wisdom one is empowered to go out ahead and show the way–to lead. One is given this power by others who believe that that particular individual knows better where to go and what to do now. And those who bestow the power to lead can take it away if they change their minds.[30]

Dangers are present in an approach to leadership that positions commitment to one's inner guidance at the forefront. Fully in tune with the hazards, Greenleaf sounds the note of urgency for present leaders to know experimentally and to lead in a way that is "appropriate and effective for our times."[31] The lesson earned from chaos is that the preeminent character quality of servant-leaders who seek to lead by their commitment to inner guidance is the virtue of ethical behavior. Greenleaf concludes,

> What makes the tradition from Fox so terribly relevant today is the urgent need around the world, for **leadership by strong ethical persons**–those who by nature are disposed to be servants (in the sense of helping others to become healthier, wiser, freer, more autonomous and more likely themselves to be servants) and who therefore can help others to move in constructive directions. Servant-leaders are ***healers*** in the sense of ***making whole*** by helping others to a larger and nobler vision and purpose than they would be likely to attain for themselves. This, in essence, is how Fox served–***as a healer***.[32]

The church today calls for such servant leaders who know by personal experiment, are ethical persons, and heal the congregations.

Congregations...Serve as a Community of Discernment

I learned on occasion that the apparent voice of God turned out to be more oneself than God. My journal includes statements of guidance that seemed to be the wisdom of God at the time. The outcome revealed it to be otherwise.

The outcome on other occasions revealed clearly that God was at the center of the guidance. The calls to seek reconciliation with the offended parties were God's divine whispers to my heart. I thought the inner voice to be out of tune with reality. The persistence of the promptings led me to seek the counsel of others. The fruit of that discernment exceeded all expectations. Reconciliation became a gift beyond price.

I am committed to the wisdom of communal discernment. Co-discerners are essential for paddling through the changing currents caused by the hydraulics hidden beneath the surface waters. With the exception of spiritual direction through Ignatius's *Spiritual Exercises in Daily Life*, I sought discernment alone through scripture, meditation, journal writing, and prayer. The complex emotional issues that caught me unawares required co-discerners to keep me in the raft of covenant-keeping. Jules J. Toner speaks to the complex nature of listening.

> The direct promptings of the Holy Spirit as Paraclete arise within our complex, flowing, conscious life that is hidden from all but God and self; and they have to be distinguished from our own spontaneous impulses (egoistic or generous), and from the promptings of our environment (good or bad) or of the evil spirit.[33]

Learning to listen and respond is fundamental to a complete Christian life in spite of the innate problems of listening. The listening-responding dynamic opens us to making our "singular gift" to the church in the world. Toner explains:

> To recognize, by the power of the Holy Spirit given to me, when he is inspiring my thoughts and feelings and urging me to action; and to interpret these rightly, so that I can freely open myself to receive them and respond truthfully to his inspirations, this is essential to living a full Christian life. Only in this way can I fully answer God's call to me to enter into a unique union with him and make my singular gift to the whole body of Christ.[34]

Community might have kept me accountable to live up to the private discernment of covenant-keeping, but I was afraid to ask for help. I did not want to reveal a vulnerable persona. I sought self-counsel only, though severely conflicted. I was closed to help at the end. I would not accept the pathway of discipline for restoration of marriage and ministry. I was confused, exhausted, and angry.

In contrast, communal discernment was a central feature of my restoration to ordained service. Private and communal discernment served in harmony. After being received into church membership, the first step was to work alongside a discernment team. Communal discernment was a function of the church all the way to reordination and beyond. I am not in a formal relationship of discernment at present, but I serve alongside a leadership team of co-discerners. Danny Morris and Charles Olsen give the proper balance between private and communal:

Discernment is personal, but never entirely private. It engages the person in the depths of his or her soul and therefore in a profound relationship with the Spirit of God. Discernment also involves the person in the community of faith and brings the community to decisions that order its life and ministry. Spiritual discernment draws both the individual and the community into the world.[35]

Communal discernment is the calling of the community of faith. It serves as safety equipment for both paddle captain and rafting team. Paddle commands are in sync with paddle strokes on a rafting expedition. On church mission, private discernment is in sync with communal discernment.

Denominations...Advance the Lesson of the Butterfly

Rafters are ever aware of God's beautiful creation while river-running the rapids. One cannot overlook the presence of a beautiful butterfly flapping its delicate wings above the white water. The "butterfly effect" cannot be underestimated.

Guiding a risk-taking, mission-driven congregation is an adventure in controlled chaos. The insights that arise from uncontrolled chaos are never outlived. There is no take-out from the consequences. Breath-taking is the innocence of the beginning. Chaos theory and congregational life appear worlds apart, but a lesson lurks within. The theory of chaos claims that "randomness operating through the deterministic laws of physics on a microscopic level– may actually be necessary for larger scale physical patterns to arise."[36] Chaos theory reveals that "randomness" lurks at the core of any deterministic model of the universe.

The "butterfly effect" illustrates chaos theory. Scientists say that the atmosphere is chaotic. Meteorologists study the atmosphere to predict weather patterns. We listen to weather forecasts and plan our expeditions accordingly. The "butterfly effect" refers to the astonishing possibility that a butterfly flapping its wings in a certain part of the world can incite a storm on the other side of the world one year later. Because of the "butterfly effect," meteorologists accept that only short-term weather forecasts can be accurate, even with the most sophisticated instrumentation.[37] A butterfly flapping its wings, creating a movement of wind, represents the randomness that occurs within the predictable laws of the physical world. So chaos exists where predetermined laws rule. Even the gentle movement of a butterfly can produce a chaotic effect over time.

Clergy and congregants are given guidelines to live and serve by. God has given a rule of life in the written word and a transformer of life in the Living Word. Functioning as judicatories, denominations furnish us further with guidelines for hosting congregations in ways that are faithful and ethical. I engaged ordained ministry with the best of intentions. I never viewed ordained service as a medium for sexual acting out. God's call was preeminent. And then one day a butterfly moved its wings ever so gently. I became aware of an emotional bond as the outcome of deep grief. I openly acknowledged the emotional bond to the one with whom I felt it. So gentle are the beginnings of chaos. A question is, How could he (or she) have fallen into sexual misconduct? There is a sense of disbelief. Ask pastors who succumb to moral sin–it does not begin as a conscious decision, "Today looks like a good day to have an affair." Clergy with honorable intentions succumb to the "butterfly effect."

When the storm arrives, the effect is like a furious relapse into the first week of the *Spiritual Exercises*. The fallen do not need to pray for the grace of shame and confusion. The grace of knowing one's sinfulness is granted beyond expectation. The experience of sin weighs down inner freedom and obscures spiritual insight. The desire for God above every other desire dims dramatically.[38] In my case, a prolonged period of time lapsed before grace could free me from the undertow.

Disciplinary bodies should attend to the unique story of the offender and discern the exact nature of the offense. Most clergy who fall into sexual misconduct are not predators. They wonder, "How could I have…?" Clergy can be so devastated by their moral failure that they sink into deep despair. I hasten to add that this fact does not minimize or justify the sexual misconduct or gloss over the terrible consequences and emotional pain for the victim-member and victim-church that require priority care. The point is that the discipline necessary, added to the self-devastation already felt deeply, can send the offending minister into unimaginable depths of despair.

I did not stay in the place of despair. I am about to reflect on why I am a Christian optimystic.

River-running the Rapids of Calling—Level 3 Teamwork

MEMO: June 2005
TO: Dwayne Ratzlaff
FROM: Tom Bandy

Dwayne:

Your story is an argument for what I call the "purposeful circularity" of life. This chapter is about providence, inevitability and hope, and making a deeper peace with personal failure and God's embrace. In the biblical perspective, there have been strong elements of the prophetic, the priestly, and even the apocalyptic in your story. This is a return to Wisdom. Because scripture refers to God with female metaphors in the Wisdom literature, you rediscover the return to the womb and rebirth.

I think we mistake the conversation between Jesus and Nicodemus (John 3) as a story about sanctification or some other-worldly perfection. If there is any clear break with the holiness movement in which you were involved as participant and pastor, it is here. In the end, life in the Spirit is not outside of actual living, but the deeper purposefulness of real life. The cycle of sin and grace—redemption and fall and redemption again—means that spiritual life is a constant renewal. Each time one returns to the womb, the cycle of pain and joy, failure and forgiveness, is repeated—and moves the person deeper in the experience of God.

Because we have been using water metaphors, I think of the relentless action of ocean waves on the shore. Each wave is a cycle of life. It begins with a hidden gathering of strength and a strong undercurrent of spirit; accelerates momentum, emerges into the light, exuberantly crests, and breaks upon the shore; only to withdraw again, back into the depths, gathering strength for another try. The repetitiveness is not meaningless. Each cycle advances further up the beach, and each crash erodes that much more of the shoreline. So it is with God's purpose. Overall, it is as relentless and purposeful as the ocean. Manifest in any individual's life, however, it comes in waves. Failure follows success, and success can follow failure; saint and sinner are but two aspects of the same wave. We understand our true calling when we discover we are part of a larger motion of grace. Rather than admiring ourselves by the size and sparkle of our splash or hating ourselves with the mud and filth of our undertow, true calling surrenders it all to the cycle of birth and rebirth that is the motion of God's grace against the rocks of existence.

Once again, my responses to your meditations follow your chart for river running the rapids of call. My final thoughts to your previous chapter linked the lack of mission to the emergence of moral confusion. Now I can elaborate my case more positively.

One of the most important insights is that personal calling seldom happens in a vacuum. Most people assume that in order to hear a call one must get lost in the wilderness or isolate themselves in a cave, forsaking friendship, counsel, and culture. It may be that Moses saw the burning bush all alone in the desert and that Amos heard the call all alone in the sycamore trees, but even then they were not isolated events. Moses carried a lot of emotional and spiritual baggage into the desert with him (he was, after all, a murderer), and Amos grew up a child of Israel. Each had kin to help him reflect on the experience, and each sought companions to live out the call.

Still, in our age of individualism and personal spirituality, I can imagine some skepticism about your conviction that congregations and denominations have much to do with call. Indeed, the evidence of the last fifty years suggests that congregations and denominations do more to block, sidetrack, subvert, and confuse call than anything else. In my book *Mission Mover*,[39] I argue that few people feel called to institutional church leadership any more, but many people do feel called to mission immersion. Insofar as congregations and denominations are the epitome of institutionalized Christianity, they are positively counterproductive to the discernment of call for most Christians today. Other partnerships, friendships, counselors, mentors, and organizations have taken the place of the congregation, denomination, and seminary as the primary context for the discernment of call.

Yet this does not *necessarily* have to be true. It is *possible* that the congregation and denomination can become influential in the discernment of call or the rekindling of call. Your journey illustrates not only the conditions under which fallen clergy can regain the integrity of their call but also the conditions under which fallen church institutions can regain the integrity of helping people discover and rediscover their call. The key strategic moves have strong Biblical overtones: *submit, hear, lead,* and *cultivate.*

Submission is first step toward the discernment of call. Such obedience is more radical than most modern people like. We are happy to obey reasonable demands and meet reasonable expectations, and by "reasonable" we usually mean that the requirements for spiritual discipline are not too uncomfortable, daunting, or troublesome. At most, it's the kind of obedience we learned in public school that involves semesters and trimesters of study, occasional cramming, momentary stabs of pain during final exams, and then a few weeks to relax and recuperate. No hair shirts, please! No serious fasting! No vows of poverty, chastity, fidelity, and moderation.

	A New Birth	A New Beginning	A New Future	A New Community
CLERGY	Submit to womb-work	Hear the word of absolution	Lead by self-definition	Cultivate the art of knowing
CONGREGATION	Live up to faith, hope, and love	Reconcile with arms wide open	Manage polarities	Serve as a community of discernment
DENOMINATION	Prepare to give birth	Reinforce restoration	Start at the source	Advance the lesson of the butterfly

Let's face it, the verb *submit* is not a seeker-friendly word. Your personal history prepares you better for submission than mine. I grew up Methodist, and the "Wesleyan Quadrilateral" is second nature to me. This is the conviction that all truth (including, presumably, the truth about personal calling and destiny) is mediated through human reason, history, scripture, and the contemporary or personal experience of the Spirit. Whether or not Wesley intended it, most Methodists in my experience approach such discernment *in that order.* The call had better be reasonable and then point toward clear historical precedents. If that seemed OK, then the scriptures would be searched to interpret it or at least to make sure that nothing biblical directly contradicted it. And if that seemed OK, the individual, congregation, and denomination safely assumed that the Holy Spirit would bless it; and the hearts of the seminary student, ecclesiastical board, and denominational students committee were all strangely and nostalgically "warmed."

Yet your word *submit* turns all of that upside down. It starts, first and foremost, with the heart strangely warmed. There is an intervention of a Higher Power. It may feel less like a warmed heart and more like one's lips are being seared by a hot coal. This is the deepest meaning of submission. It means subjecting oneself to the irrational, uncomfortable, uncontrollable experience of the Holy without flinching, theologizing, or fleeing. Submission does not evoke the response, "Who, me?" It evokes the response, "Oh God, please not me!"

After that comes the search of scripture to figure out who this Higher Power really is who has just swept my life away, changed my career path, and downsized my income expectations. Bible study is approached in a kind of panic-stricken frenzy to understand what is happening, who caused the crisis, and where it is all leading. Last of all, like a rescue team arriving late to the scene of an accident, one turns to reason. I begin to think about how to do it, what I need to learn, and how I will endure it to the end.

One implication of radical submission is that it changes our intimate relationships. In ancient times, men and women left wives and husbands to follow their vocation. In modern times, marriages can fracture. I am not saying this is a "good thing" from the perspective of moral life and family stability. I am saying that it is an "inevitable thing" when we are dealing with the God above gods. One hopes that a husband or wife (and children and parents) will understand and support a person submitting to the call, even though they may be angry or resistant to living that call as a minion of institutional religion. Maybe not.

One of the missing pieces in your story, Dwayne, is that you spend so much time regretting the pain you caused your first wife when you forgot your true calling—but remarkably little time celebrating the support of your wife today when you regained your calling. I think that is little short of miraculous. That is probably a better, more accurate sign of God's forgiveness and blessing upon you than any approval from a denomination or reconciliation with a congregation. Indeed, I think it a miracle that any wife or husband will continue to love, support, and accompany any Christian pastor into ministry today. As postmodern Christianity returns to premodern experience, we are rediscovering the meaning of submission.

How does the congregation help the individual truly submit to God's call, given the original sinfulness of the human heart and the temptations and persecutions of the world? Gone are the days when a congregation could reasonably expect years of calm, unchanging ministry that made everybody happy and nice. Evil is too powerful within the heart and at large in the world, and that is just not going to happen. So what can the congregation do? Practice "positive thinking." You have elevated the advice of Norman Vincent Peale beyond individual optimism to challenge the corporate courage of the church. Although the cultural disciples of Peale have made this into a mantra for personal success, the real insight of Peale and Schuller is that this is a secret of congregational endurance, hope, and victory. The congregation cannot support a pastor in radical submission to the Holy unless they are prepared to unreasonably believe in faith, love, and hope. It is not an ecclesiastical dogma or board policy, but a corporate culture and attitude.

How does the denomination help the individual truly submit to God's call? Here, you resort to another water metaphor: the womb. The denomination can provide a midwife and a birthing environment, as the fallen pastor is "born anew." Here, I find your terminology both paradoxical and profound. You speak of "submitting to the womb" as if the womb were an ordeal rather than a peace, because the goal is not the womb itself but the cleansing pain of labor and the fresh start of birth. Literature is filled with metaphors about people longing "to return to the womb." Psychologists talk about it constantly. The womb, however, is not a place to stay, but an experience necessary for new life. Many long for the womb, but few long to leave the womb to be born yet again. The real role of the midwife is not to comfort or console, but to convince the church to let the baby go and to cajole the baby to enter this sad and ambiguous world.

Denominations today don't really want to let go of their clergy and turn them loose to be creative for God in the real world. They keep them tied by umbilical cords of polities, pensions, and prestige. Clergy today don't want to be cut loose to fend for themselves in the real world of mission, preferring the security of polities, pensions, and prestige. It is up to denominational leaders to act the role of the midwife and cut the cord.

"Hearing" is the second step in the discernment of call, and I believe you are correct in saying that the first words you hear are words of absolution. "Purge me with hyssop, and I shall be clean; wash me, and I shall be whiter than snow" (Ps. 51:7). It is with the hyssop that the doors of Passover are dabbed with blood. It is with the hyssop that the vinegar is lifted to Jesus' lips on the cross. The author of Hebrews makes the connection between cleansing and calling and Christ (Heb. 9:19–28). For all the self-deprecation about never "deserving" the call, the institutional church has never really believed it. Congregations recommend candidates to ordination because they are good church members; denominations ordain candidates because they are knowledgeable, obedient, and (usually) have never committed a felony; and clergy really do believe they deserve that salary, pension, protection, and prestige because they are seminary graduates and in good standing with the church.

The sad truth about calling is that most clergy (and their congregational and denominational partners) really do think they deserve it. Perhaps they were incredulous at first, but they became convinced that they really did have gifts, skills, and inclinations that had just gone unrecognized. Deep in their hearts clergy think they deserve it; and deep in the hearts of congregation and denomination, they want only clergy who are deserving. So it comes as a shock that no clergy deserve it, that the first word of a true calling is a word of absolution.

Therefore, the congregation needs to be ready for reconciliation. I like your phrase, "arms wide open." These days, many clergy find only a hand shaped like a fist, arms folded intimidatingly across the chest, and even the occasional raised finger. I find that your own story, Dwayne, challenges such optimism about the congregational potential for "arms wide open." You articulate your own regret about betraying the congregation and express your longing to bring healthy resolution to your parting. But I hear nothing about the congregation's regret about their failure to be more sensitive to your time of moral ambiguity, nor do I hear that they ever attempted to bring healthy resolution to your parting.

I think you have to see it both ways. If clergy, congregation, and denomination all share a partnership in the call, then clergy, congregation, and denomination all share responsibility in the breakdown of a call. God will hold them accountable on judgment day for your moral lapse, just as God holds you accountable, because the call is indeed heard in the context of partnership. The congregation that *fails* to have a corporate culture of real faith, hope, and love contributes to the breakdown of the clergy and the betrayal of trust. The denomination that *fails* to provide midwife leadership and an environment for birth and rebirth contributes to the breakdown of the clergy and the betrayal of trust.

I think this is implied in your use of family systems theory to interpret the Christian congregation. The dysfunction of any single family member reveals the broader dysfunction of the family as a whole. While it may be true that negative behavior on the part of the one will impact the well-being of all, it is also true that negative habits on the part of all will undermine the mental, emotional, or physical health of every individual. Most denominations live in an illusion that moral transgression must be the fault of the clergy. They do not hold a congregation accountable for the moral transgression of the clergy, even though they insist the congregation be honored for the call of the clergy. Denominations do not hold themselves accountable for increasing the stress on clergy, nor do they accept any blame for the rising tide of clergy going on disability—but surely it is there. Surely God will hold the denomination accountable for its failure to provide the healthy environments that contribute to the trust of a call.

The third step to discernment of call is the act of leadership itself. The best way to learn anything is to teach it, and the best way to figure out where you are going is to start walking. I can also understand your conviction that leadership through self-definition is more effective—and more stable—than leadership through charisma. Whether the congregation *appreciates* leadership by self-definition rather than leadership by charisma, however, is a matter of doubt.

I think you are quite right that congregations should learn how to "manage the polarities" present and future, individual initiative and corporate consensus, spirit and matter, evolution and revolution, grace and works; the kingdom present and the kingdom to come. They can do it. They can be trained and educated to do it. The question is, Do they really want to do it? It is, after all, much easier to pretend that the polarities do not exist, or at least to assume that a charismatic and authoritative leader should be able to resolve those tensions for them.

I think the key here is that you need to expect the congregation to live up to the same standards of spiritual life that you yourself have experienced. In the end, clergy and laity are no different. All Christians are sinners (like you); all Christians require grace that they do not deserve (like you); and the journey from shame to hope requires a submission and disciplined reflection that is as demanding of laity as it is for clergy. So it seems to me that the one thing missing in your advice is that clergy who define themselves must help the congregation to define itself and the various members to define themselves. You are defined in the crucible of those polarities. The charismatic clergy who came before you—and who led the church by their personality, personal authority, and consciousness of status—have done you and the congregation no favors. There is an ingrained habit (or co-dependency, if you wish to follow family systems metaphors) that blocks the congregation from learning how to manage these polarities.

How do we train clergy and congregations to define themselves and manage the polarities? I must say, your suggestion that we start at the source and begin with the seminary strains my imagination. I am not confident that the real goal of seminary education is to equip either clergy or congregation to do this, nor am I confident that this can or should change in the future. The problem is in the pace of change and the expansion of chaos. These polarities are not just sitting there waiting to be investigated, studied, and preached about. They are unfolding at light speed and morphing in a zillion different directions, across sectors, microcultures, economies, and media. By itself, the academic world cannot keep up. By the time tenured seminary professors and curriculum tracks have caught up to a conversation, their contribution is only modestly relevant. This does not mean that the seminary is irrelevant. It's just not primary to the management of these polarities anymore. I talk about his in my book *Mission Mover*.

Denominational leaders are recognizing this more and more. That is why, when it comes to equipping congregations to manage the great polarities you have named, they only secondarily rely on seminaries. Instead, they are developing innovative partnerships with other educational sectors, consultants, and agencies around the globe and inventing new ways for rapidly responsive lay training. Two big revolutions are shaking the denominations today. First, the denomination is finally, fully understanding that the primary mission unit of the Christian movement is *not* a denominational committee, agency, or missionary, but the congregation itself. Second, the denomination is also recognizing that the congregation itself must take responsibility as the primary unity of Christian training and education, not the seminary. The time is coming when seminaries will send their students to the local church to learn to manage these polarities, instead of churches sending their apprentices to the seminaries. The age of dependency on educational institutions is ending, and the age of true parity and partnership in action/reflection is emerging.

The fourth step in the discernment of call is cultivation of the "art of knowing." Despite my criticisms of the academic seminary, it is important to recognize that the "university" emerged from the monastic libraries of the Dark Ages precisely due to the need for "managing the polarities" that beset life, the church, and Christian mission. The last thirty years has witnessed the demise of "liberal arts" education in favor of professional training and practical or theoretical science. With that shift, the most elemental facet of education has been forgotten: humility before the truth. The stress of radical humility has been reduced because we have narrowed the meaning of truth to be so small and inconsequential as to imply simply the ordering of verifiable facts. The manipulation of data is one thing humans can do well; and if truth is reduced to that, then we can take pride in our knowledge. Unfortunately, truth cannot be reduced to that, and humans are left vulnerable in their arrogance.

Knowing is an art, not a science; and the professional clergyperson is no more privileged to "know the truth" than the amateur layperson. This bias in favor of any expert who can memorize and manipulate data permeates Western culture and is one of the most fundamental and tragic ways in which the modern church has accommodated to culture. "Knowing the truth" involves three fundamental steps. In *Mission Mover,* I place these in the context of the spiritual life:

Humility: If we really believe that human reason is tied to our connection with God as the very originator of order (Logos), then we face a perpetual ambiguity about our most logical conclusions and brilliant insights. Certainty escapes us. Questioning never ends. God (and Truth, Beauty, and Goodness) is never within our grasp, controlled by our technologies, or contained in our test tubes. God can never be identified with our institutional rites, controlled by our preaching, or contained in our theologies. If the questions never go away, then the answers always remain partially hidden as a judgment on our lives. Take that implicit judgment upon all our dogmas and structures away, and all that is left is pride.

Intuition: If reasonable analysis can only take us partway in the quest for truth, then our discernment must be guided by a combination of memory and yearning. Learning from the lessons of faithful struggle and imagining how to extrapolate from the past to cope with the future form the stuff of intuition. Some call it "lateral thinking." I prefer to call it "judicious guesswork," or a "sixth sense," or a "memory of God." Whatever you call it, intuition involves risk. It's the difference between sending a mechanical probe to investigate the moon and going there yourself. Take that intuition and risk away, and all that is left is complacency and self-satisfaction.

Compassion: If we really believe that God (and Truth) is more likely "out there" than "in here," then our intuition tells us we are most likely to find traces of the divine in other people. Compassion is the awareness that every person is more than the sum of his parts. She is more than the total of her gifts, skills, relationships, successes. He is more than his tears, illnesses, brokenness, and failures. They are "more"—and this potential is what awakens our love. People are more than objects to cajole, persuade, and manipulate. Take that compassion away, and all that is left is control.

My point is that one reason we have such difficulty today discerning call is that clergy, congregational leaders, and denominational leaders have allowed culture to corrupt them. Humility before the truth has been distorted to become loyalty to the church; intuition of the Holy has been reduced to good theology; compassion has been sidetracked into professional ethics. Such accommodation creates a context for moral failure. You see it in the world, and it is paralleled in the church.

If there is a "butterfly effect" in ecclesiastical culture, in which the smallest change in the church or world can cause ripple effects that grow and multiply and eventually provide that one last push that tips even the well-intentioned pastor overboard into moral failure, its origins are here. It all starts with our culturally acquired arrogance that we know what we know and that what we know is all there is to know.

I agree wholeheartedly, Dwayne, with the vision of the congregation as a community of discernment. Yet the modern church is so far removed from such a vision that it is hard to know where to begin to reform it. There is a reason why vital, mission-driven Christians are avoiding seminary, withdrawing from denominations, and resisting congregational offices. Today, the nonprofit, parachurch, health care unit, volunteer agency, small business, and even corporation are offering better "communities of discernment" than the church. These other organizations are proving to be more humble before the truth; more intuitive about the quest; and even more compassionate toward their volunteers and employees, publics and clients, than the church.

The countercultural wave is not being led by the church, but by other organizations. Some call it "postmodernism." It's a term that can mean almost anything, but in our conversation it means that organizations today are *finally* moving beyond the scientism of "external relations." They no longer see the world as just an assemblage of data to be used and manipulated to create whatever truth the most powerful controller envisions. They see the world as a network or web of "internal relations" in which every individual and thing participates in the internal constitution of every other individual and thing. To value myself necessarily implies valuing others; to devalue others necessarily implies contempt for myself. The "butterfly" metaphor is really not about little things causing chain reactions; it is about being intrinsically connected in a web of relationships so vast and intricate *that in reality I am the butterfly.* That is how small and how puny our theological certainties, dogmatisms, moral indignation can be—and yet it is also how powerful our spiritual quests, intuitions, and compassion can become.

Admittedly, my mentors in this have been people such as Alfred North Whitehead, Henri Bergson, Brand Blanshard, and a whole history of neo-Platonists critical of the culture of scientism and the arrogance of a world interpreted by "external relations." Certainly I could speak of Christian mystics, missionaries, and theologians over history. And your references to Henri Nouwen and Robert Greenleaf support this countercultural shift. In the main, however, there are few voices in the enormous volume of modern Christian writing that go far enough and deep enough to connect the current moral failure of church leaders with the accommodation of the church to modernity's assumptions about knowing the truth. That is my point. More "discernment of call" is happening beyond the church than within it.

Finally, I return to the metaphor of the womb and the possibility that you, me, and other fallen church leaders (such as Nicodemus in the gospel) might actually return to the womb and be born again. Your metaphor makes no sense. You say that you did not really return to the womb, but that "the womb found me." I can imagine many readers scratching their heads, scoffing at the idea, or assuming that you have just mixed up your metaphors. Yet there is something important here that is the real foundation for all hope. It is the one thing that can save even the most despairing and guilty clergyperson from professional or literal suicide.

It is easy to imagine a bruised and hurting person going in search of a womb. It is less easy to believe that there is a womb that is desperately and longingly searching for bruised and hurting people. In a sense, God is that eternal womb, constantly searching for a baby to birth. There is nothing passive about God's desire to gather her brood like chicks under her wing (Mt. 23:37). God's passion is to reclaim prodigal children. God's yearning is to make adults like little children, even returning them once again to the womb of creation, so that they might be born again. Our God is Lord of the second chance.

CHAPTER 7

Why I Am an OptiMystic
A Theological Reflection

Defining Moments

Who can predict where God's mighty river is leading. God has many surprises downstream. The river flows to reclaim creation. The rapids rage with polarities–disruptive and peaceful, mysterious and strategic, alluring and dangerous, providential and creative. The river rages because Spirit cohabits spirit. The comingling of the two opens to the options of chaos and creativity. Both chaos and creativity occur at the point where divine sovereignty converges with free will in the vigorous ferment of spirit, morality, and calling. I came out of the chaos with an unshakeable confidence in the future. My confidence turns on the axis of Christian optimystics.

Optimystic people pass through defining moments. Transforming events change everything. Personal chaos can precede encounters with God. Consider Augustine (354–430). He came to the garden in a crisis of spirit, morality, and calling. As is so often the case, human desperation is God's opportunity.

> And, far off, I heard your voice saying I am the God who IS. I heard your voice, as we hear voices that speak to our hearts, and at once I had no cause to doubt. I might more easily have doubted that I was alive than that Truth had being. For we catch sight of the Truth, as he is known through his creation.
>
> I probed the hidden depths of my soul and wrung its pitiful secrets from it, and when I mustered them all before the eyes of my heart, a great storm broke within me, bringing with it a great deluge of tears. I stood up and left Alypius so that I might weep and cry to my heart's content, for it occurred to me that tears were best shed in solitude…I

had much to say to you, my God, not in these very words but in this strain: *Lord, will you never be content? Must we always taste your vengeance? Forget the long record of our sins.* For I felt that I was still the captive of my sins, and in my misery I kept crying, "How long shall I go on saying 'tomorrow, tomorrow'? Why not now? Why not make an end of my ugly sins at this moment?"

I was asking myself these questions, weeping all the while with the most bitter sorrow in my heart, when all at once I heard the singing voice of a child in a nearby house. Whether it was the voice of a boy or a girl I cannot say, but again and again it repeated the refrain *"Take it and read, take it and read."* At this I looked up, thinking hard whether there was any kind of game in which children used to chant words like these, but I could not remember ever hearing them before. I stemmed my flood of tears and stood up, telling myself that this could only be a *divine command* to open my book of Scripture and read the first passage on which my eyes should fall. For I had heard the story of Antony, and I remembered how he had happened to go into a church while the Gospel was being read and had taken it as a counsel addressed to himself when he heard the words *Go home and sell all that belongs to you. Give it to the poor, and so the treasure you have shall be in heaven; then come back and follow me.* By this divine pronouncement he had at once been converted to you. So I hurried back to the place where Alypius was sitting, for when I stood up to move away I had put down the book containing Paul's Epistles. I seized it and opened it, and in silence I read the first passage on which my eyes fell: *Not in revelling and drunkenness, not in lust and wantonness, not in quarrels and rivalries. Rather, arm yourselves with the Lord Jesus Christ; spend no more thought on nature and nature's appetites.* I had no wish to read more and no need to do so. For in an instant, as I came to the end of the sentence, it was as though the light of confidence flooded into my heart and all the darkness of doubt was dispelled.[1]

The garden produced a revolution. Augustine confessed that God can carry out purposes for us that exceed our hopes and dreams. He possessed an unshakeable confidence in the God of futures. The darkness of doubt was dispelled. That revelatory moment changed Augustine into a Christian optimystic. A transforming event defined a life and shaped a future. A form of dialogue may occur in the moment of revelation. The story of Christian spirituality records conversations with God that overturned paradigms, transformed life, shaped leaders, and birthed mission.

Transforming moments of new birth and Spirit baptism shape the structure of personal faith. Their memory and reality capsize into the chaos of spirit, morality, and calling. Personal chaos intersects the stories of two words downstream: optimism and mysticism. I found hope at the intersections. I scout these words with the help of guides–scripture, tradition, reason, and experience– that enlighten the way.[2]

The stories of the two words began with the shakers and shapers of seventeenth-century France. They created two nouns named optimism and mysticism. The nouns have a unique connection with the intimate listeners and passionate lovers who gave shape to Christian spirituality. The words inspire the creation of a third noun: optimystic. An optimystic is an intimate listener and passionate lover engaging God in a compelling style of dialogue that infuses all aspects of life with faith, hope, and love.

The Story of Optimism
Best of All Possible Worlds

The German philosopher Gottfried Wilhelm Leibniz (1646–1716) claims this world is the "optimum" world–"the best of all possible worlds." In *Théodicée* (*Theodicy*), Leibniz addresses three issues: the existence of God, the problem of evil, and the question of optimism.[3] William Turner explains the reason for Leibniz's optimism:

> [I]n his discussion of the problem of evil he tries to trace out principles that will "justify the ways of God to man" in a manner compatible with God's goodness. It had become the fashion among materialists and freethinkers to draw an over-gloomy picture of the universe as a place of pain, suffering, and sin, and to ask triumphantly: "How can a good God, if He is omnipotent, permit such a state of things?" Leibniz's answer...Evil should be considered in relation not to the parts of reality, but to reality as a whole. Many evils are "in other respects" good. And, when, in the final resort, we cannot see a definite rational solution of a perplexing problem, we should fall back on faith, which, especially in regard to the problem of evil, aids reason.[4]

The World of Grace

Leibniz had infused German idealism and pietism by the time John Wesley (1703–1791) made his trip to Germany. The Enlightenment was underway.[5] Wesley rejected Leibniz's system of metaphysics as fatal optimism, as the misguided outcome of rationalism. The denial did not limit Wesley's personal optimism of grace over evil. Optimism was pivotal to Wesley's practical Christianity. Wesley balances several ideas: the limits of human understanding in this life, the full revelation of knowledge in the life to come, and the "unspeakable blessings" that arise out of evil. Wesley writes:

> This knowledge is therefore denied us on earth because it is an entertainment for heaven. And what an entertainment! To have the curtain drawn at once, and enjoy the full blaze of God's wisdom and goodness! To see clearly how the Author of this visible world fastened

all its parts together—by what chain both the pillars of the earth were upheld, and the armies of the sky! How he effected and maintained that amazing union between the body and the soul of man, that astonishing correspondence between spirit and matter, between perishing dust and immortal flame! How the Holy Ghost, the Author of the world of grace, upheld our soul in mortal life! How, in answer either to our own prayers or to the prayers of others, his blessed influence overshadowing us out of the darkness, storm, and confusion of our unformed natures, called forth light, and peace, and order! To see why he suffered sin and pain to mingle with those works of which he had declared that they were very good. What unspeakable blessings those are which owe their being to this curse; what infinite beauty arises from, and overbalances this deformity; why it was just and right, as well as merciful of God, to deal to every man his distinct measure of faith, "and anoint some whom he chose before the world began with the oil of gladness above their fellows"; why he dealt to every man his distinct measure of suffering; why particular men were prone to particular vices; why the several gifts of his Spirit were distributed as they were with respect to kind, degree, time, and persons. What an entertainment must it be to a reasonable soul to have such a prospect displayed before him![6]

I cannot claim to have lived the best possible life in the best of all possible worlds. I marvel at the interviews that ask, "If you could do anything differently, what would you change?" and then the response, "Nothing." I do not identify with the answer. I would like to do some things differently. My hope does not rest in the belief that I have lived the best possible life in the best possible world, as in Leibniz rationalism. Hope is anchored in the world of grace, as in Wesley. God has brought unspeakable blessing out of personal evil. I realize the claim comes close to Paul's unthinkable reason for "sin...that grace may abound" scenario (Rom. 6:1–2). Also, there is the law of the harvest that applies to all (Gal. 6:7). Choices can last for an eternity. Acts done cannot be undone. Wounds imparted cannot be cancelled. Nevertheless, God's amazing ability to overcome the deformity of choices astounds me. I never anticipated the unearned blessings of God's grace.

A paradox remains unresolved. A segment of the church judges me disqualified for ordained ministry while another part deems me ordained in good standing. Biblical proof texts are exposited to support positions. The prodigal son could return, but not to stay. I cannot resolve the paradox; I live with it. I resonate with Wesley's personal optimism of grace over evil. God is the author of the world of grace.

Sovereign Grace

In America, Jonathan Edwards (1703–1758) changed the shape of Christianity. Edwards left glimpses of his spiritual journey in diaries, personal narrative, and resolutions. Writing his personal narrative in 1739, at the age of thirty-five, Edwards presents a fascinating look into his early childhood, his relationship with his father, and his struggle with sin. The doctrine of God's sovereign grace pervades the encounter with personal evil.

> My wickedness, as I am in myself, has long appeared to me perfectly ineffable, and swallowing up all thought and imagination; like an infinite deluge, or mountain over my head. I know not how to express better what my sins appear to me to be, than by heaping infinite upon infinite, and multiplying infinite by infinite...When I look into my heart, and take a view of my wickedness, it looks like an abyss infinitely deeper than hell. And it appears to me, that were it not for free grace, exalted and raised up to the infinite height of all the fullness and glory of the great Jehovah, and the arm of his power and grace stretched forth in all the majesty of his power, and in all the glory of his sovereignty, I should appear sunk down in my sins below hell itself; far beyond the sight of every thing, but the eye of sovereign grace, that can pierce even down to such a depth.[7]

The picture is a moving one. As infinite as Edward's sin appears to him, "sovereign grace" reaches down "below hell itself" and cancels it. This is Calvinistic optimism rooted in God's sovereign grace. The Calvinist Edwards and the Arminian Wesley found common ground in the amazing world of grace that overcomes evil.

Does sovereign grace infuse our stories? Yes. Could I have faced the issues in my life any other way with a different outcome? Yes, although the latter is a slippery question because the answers are unverifiable. I cannot know the outcome of other choices. As for the past, I lean hard on sovereign grace. I cannot change the past. I can create a future with present choices that are in sync with God's deepest values.

What about children conceived through acts of moral failure? Is sovereign grace present here too? Yes. An influential evangelical pastor agrees:

> You are not an accident.
> Your birth was no mistake or mishap, and your life is no fluke of nature. Your parents may not have planned you, but God did. He was not at all surprised by your birth. In fact, he expected it.
> Long before you were conceived by your parents, you were conceived in the mind of God. He thought of you first. It is not fate, nor chance, nor luck, nor coincidence that you are breathing at this very moment. You are alive because God wanted to create you!...
> Most amazing, God decided *how* you would be born. Regardless of the circumstances of your birth or who your parents are, God had a plan in creating you. It doesn't matter whether your parents were good, bad, or indifferent. God knew that those two individuals

> possessed *exactly* the right genetic makeup to create the custom "you" he had in mind. They had the DNA God wanted to make you. While there are illegitimate parents, there are no illegitimate children. Many children are unplanned by their parents, but they are not unplanned by God. God's purpose took into account human error, and even sin.
>
> God never does anything accidentally, and he never makes mistakes. He has a reason for everything he creates.[8]

I believe this is true for my daughter, who was conceived and born in the chaos. She is a blessing beyond description. God's covenant to overcome evil with good is manifest in the gift.

What about marriage that has its roots in sexual misconduct? Can God's sovereign grace overcome evil with good? Yes. However, God's grace overflows with obedience. God's blessing is upon the marriage covenant–even one with such beginnings. I say this with full knowledge of the divorce clause (Mt. 5:31–32). I appeal to sovereign grace in response. I accept a necessary aspect to the blessing of marriage in these circumstances. God expects a genuine work of reconciliation with the past. Going forward in freedom requires going backward in repentance.

Does sovereign grace require a reckoning with issues? Yes. Divorcing a spouse or leaving a denomination does not change the inner issues that gave rise to a moral crisis. For me, working with the chaos produced necessary changes. The aftermath of sexual misconduct pushed me deeper into self and the heart of God. I went in a Christian mystic but came out a Christian optimystic. The world of grace overcame evil with good. Admittedly, I could not see a good outcome through the in-between time. The good outcome was only a prayer and a hope. God answered the prayer and blessed the hope. It was in God's good time. I wondered if it would ever come. I had to reckon with the issues.

Healthy-mindedness

Up to now, optimism had two classic meanings: (1) the doctrine of Leibniz, understood as "the best of all possible worlds," and (2) the idea that good will ultimately prevail over evil in the universe. The pragmatist William James (1842–1910) put a new face on optimism. James chose to ignore or deny evil. He promoted a healthy-minded religion that exalted the universal good. James displays his sympathies:

> Systematic healthy-mindedness, conceiving good as the essential and universal aspect of being, deliberately excludes evil from its field of vision…
>
> The advance of liberalism, so-called, in Christianity, during the past fifty years, may fairly be called a victory of healthy-mindedness within the church over the morbidness with which the old hell-fire theology was more harmoniously related. We have now whole

congregations whose preachers, far from magnifying our consciousness of sin, seem devoted rather to making little of it. They ignore, or even deny, eternal punishment, and insist on the dignity rather than on the depravity of man. They look at the continual preoccupation of the old-fashioned Christian with the salvation of his soul as something sickly and reprehensible rather than admirable; and a sanguine and "muscular" attitude, which to our forefathers would have seemed purely heathen, has become in their eyes an ideal element of Christian character. I am not asking whether or not they are right, I am only pointing out the change.

The persons to whom I refer have still retained for the most part their nominal connection with Christianity, despite of their discarding of its more pessimistic theological elements.[9]

And yet James describes Luther's "Commentary on Galatians" as a healthy-minded expression of forgiveness and freedom. He classifies Luther's experience of deliverance from the burden of guilt as healthy-minded religion. James admits this in spite of the psychologist's bias against evil as a category of reality.[10]

Two world wars later Reinhold Niebuhr penned a new introduction to the classic in 1961. While affirming the genius of James, Niebuhr provided a mild critique of his thought as the product of late nineteenth-century optimism. That period could not have known all that lay ahead, namely, "the anxieties of two world wars and of a nuclear dilemma."[11] James does justice to the quest for perfection but omits a critical factor in his chapter on "Saintliness." Niebuhr explains:

[James] does not come to terms with the charge of Reformation thought, that the quest for perfection is bound to be abortive, since even the most rigorous human virtue cannot escape the ambiguity of good and evil, with which all human striving is infected.[12]

I have served on both sides of the theological divide. I inherited a conflict of church cultures with my choices. The evangelical side places a strong emphasis on personal evil. The liberal side opts for institutional evil. Both cultures have left their imprint on me. The liberal tendency is to critique the institution as evil and uphold the individual as good. The conservative tendency is to personalize evil and absolve the institution that reared it. I live in the point of tension at the middle. I cannot deny either end of the continuum. I cannot escape the "ambiguity of good and evil" that indwells me. The most altruistic thought or action is infected with egocentricity. To acknowledge the ambiguity does not turn me into a pessimist, as James claims. On the contrary, it turns the world of grace into something all the more amazing.

"Healthy-mindedness" did not come from denying my personal choices as evil or from blaming persons, the church, or the denomination. Peace of mind came from facing up to, accepting responsibility for, expressing genuine repentance of, and seeking reconciliation with all involved. I believe the church and denomination that serve as the context for sexual misconduct have to discern their own responsibility. A denial of any part of the continuum of evil cannot serve the cause of reconciliation. Even for the twenty-first century, David's confession reveals the passage to healthy-mindedness (Ps. 51:1–12).

A Good Outcome

In twentieth-century America, Norman Vincent Peale (1898–1993) became the ambassador of Christian optimism. Peale was convinced of the practical power of Christianity and the optimism it unleashed. He cited the Fulton Street prayer meeting (1859) in New York City as proof of this assertion. The prayer meeting incited one of the greatest spiritual revivals in the history of the United States, birthing a grand period of spiritual and material prosperity. People began to think positively and to believe and work accordingly. Dr. Peale identifies the lesson learned from these small beginnings:

> The lesson learned here is that optimism is a powerful influence. And it can work wonders by setting loose an amazing resurgence of Christianity that affects the whole social order. When optimism and faith go together, a wonderful thing happens in people's lives.
>
> Now what is optimism? Well, before we answer that question, let us ask what pessimism is. Pessimism is a philosophy that holds that the evil in life overbalances the good in life.
>
> Optimism, on the other hand, is a philosophy based on the belief that basically life is good, created and sustained by a good God; and that in the long run the good in life overbalances the evil; also that, in every difficulty, every pain, there is some inherent good. And the optimist means to find that good…
>
> An optimist is a person who believes in a good outcome, even when he can't yet see it. He is a person who believes in a greater day, when there is no evidence of it. He is one who believes in his own future, when he can't see much possibility in it…
>
> An injection of Christian optimism will rejuvenate the entire social order.[13]

The ambassador of optimism inserts the concept of "overbalances" into the dialogue about good and evil, similar to Wesley. Good and evil exist, but the idea of good prevailing over evil ultimately gives way to good overbalancing evil here and now. Peale simply changes the emphasis to victory in the present. This is the power of positive thinking based on the teachings of Jesus. Peale claims real-time optimism as the "essence" of Christianity.

> The reason Christianity survives as a philosophy is because it faces all of life, including all the evil thereof and all the wickedness in man; it paints the whole picture but, nevertheless, affirms that, in the midst of

all this trouble, pain, and confusion, there is a good outcome, there is a lilting something that sings its way out of sorrow…

There had never before been a philosophy of human life like Christianity. It realistically deals with all of the hardships of the human condition, but it comes out with victory. That is because of what is in its essence.

At the heart of Christianity, there is a great, splintery, blood-splattered cross. You can't laugh off the pain and the sorrow and the suffering of life. But the lilting note of victory is never absent. That is why it was said of the early Christians that there was something in them akin to the song of the skylark and the babbling of brooks.

Optimism, hope, freshness, newness…That is Christianity in its essence. Newness.[14]

The cross is the greatest plus sign of history. The cross unites hope and optimism, unleashing both against evil.

I recall my white-water odyssey vividly—the most desperate time of my life. One world had died, and the other world refused to be born. Any kind of spiritual exercise was difficult. Silence was painful beyond description. One prayer came continuously, "Oh, God, please don't let me die like this!" I feared this utter failure would be the last word on my life—that this condemnation would be my last will and testament. Only the humanity and suffering of Jesus was able to touch me emotionally during the in-between time. I was nurtured on the deity of Jesus Christ. In this in-between time I sank deeply into Jesus' humanity. I found compassion at the cross. His passion became my source of hope and optimism.

The Art of Hope

Hope became the "stuff" of optimism in positive psychology. Martin E. P. Seligman, a professor of psychology, stands outside the classic treatment of optimism as a question of good over evil. He asserts that optimism and pessimism are "learned" ways of thinking, ways of looking at life. He claims that "learned pessimism" can become "learned optimism." The crucial factor is one's "explanatory style." The concept of explanatory style is similar to self-talk. What does the word in one's heart say about a personal setback or momentous defeat? Seligman explains:

> Explanatory style is the manner in which you habitually explain to yourself why events happen…An optimistic explanatory style stops helplessness, whereas a pessimistic explanatory style spreads helplessness. Your way of explaining events to yourself determines how helpless you can become, or how energized, when you encounter the everyday setbacks as well as momentous defeats…
>
> Your habitual way of explaining bad events, your explanatory style, is more than just the words you mouth when you fail. It is a

habit of thought, learned in childhood and adolescence. Your explanatory style stems directly from your view of your place in the world–whether you think you are valuable and deserving, or worthless and hopeless. It is the hallmark of whether you are an optimist or a pessimist.[15]

One of Seligman's projects has shown the importance of historical documents in the life of an individual or a denomination.[16] The documents that absorbed into my life prior to my sexual misconduct played a vital role. These spiritual documents did not save me from the misconduct; they saved me after it. This is a disturbing admission. Scripture says there is a way out (1 Cor. 10:12–13). I do not doubt it intellectually. I did not feel it emotionally. That God failed to prepare me to overcome the stronghold of temptation is a discomforting mystery. It is an arguable point (Jas. 1:13–16).

God had more in view for my love of the spiritual classics. That the classics encompassed the varied Christian streams was not a coincidence. I believe God was shaping me for two things in advance of the deepest crisis of my life: first, a spiritual life that when shaken to the core would not be destroyed, and second, service within a broader Christian culture. God employed a broad range of spiritual classics to these ends. The journey into the classics began with Henri Nouwen's spiritual classic *The Wounded Healer*. Nouwen became an influential friend during a painful passage. He describes "the Christian way" in mystic terms.

> [I]n Jesus the mystical and the revolutionary ways are not opposites, but two sides of the same human mode of experiential transcendence… [C]onversion is the individual equivalent of revolution. Therefore every real revolutionary is challenged to be a mystic at heart, and he who walks the mystical way is called to unmask the illusory quality of human society. Mysticism and revolution are two aspects of the same attempt to bring about radical change. No mystic can prevent himself from becoming a social critic, since in self-reflection he will discover the roots of a sick society. Similarly, no revolutionary can avoid facing his own human condition, since in the midst of his struggle for a new world he will find that he is also fighting his own reactionary fears and false ambitions…
>
> For a Christian, Jesus is the man in whom it has indeed become manifest that revolution and conversion cannot be separated in man's search for experiential transcendence. His appearance in our midst has made it undeniably clear that changing the human heart and changing human society are not separate tasks, but are as interconnected as the two beams on the cross.[17]

Nouwen became the transition to the second word that intersects my personal odyssey.

The Story of Mysticism
Christian Mysticism

Christian spirituality proposes a chaos of voices: God, self, reason, wisdom, culture, evil, and more. Christian mystics claim that the inner voice of God and the inner voice of self can engage in interior dialogue. A "pivotal change" occurred in the treatment of mysticism during the seventeenth century, particularly within Western mysticism. So pronounced was this divergence that it fashioned "before" and "after" effects. Before, mysticism had a liturgical and scriptural context as exhibited in patristic and medieval Christianity. After, the criteria of "private illumination" and "unusual psychosomatic experiences" became the center of interest.

The attempt to define mysticism is a complex task. The word is used broadly, and its manifestations are controversial. Mysticism encompasses three themes: an element of religion, a way of life, and an attempt to express a direct/immediate awareness/consciousness of the presence of God. The first theme suggests a mystical element in Christianity from its origins. The second theme claims an encounter between the Spirit of God and the human spirit. The result is an intimate relationship of union. The third theme proposes the word *presence* as a unifying way to express this encounter with God given its varieties. Christian mystics crave a direct consciousness of the presence of God.[18]

Jesus Christ Is Present

Clement of Alexandria (150–215) introduced the adjective *mystical* and the adverb *mystically* into Christian literature.[19] Born in Athens, Clement became a teacher in Alexandria. He converted to Christianity, and fled from Alexandria during a severe persecution by the emperor Severus. Clement used the words *mystical* and *mystically* more than fifty times to describe Christ, a deeper understanding of scripture, and the practice of a gnostic Christian.[20]

Clement is a controversial person for those who think of mysticism as a pagan invasion into gospel Christianity. Themes such as vision, divinization, and union are central to his teachings. These themes become vital elements of Eastern Orthodox Christianity. Clement borrowed Platonic themes and gave them christological focus. Harvey D. Egan defended Clement against the concerns Spener and others expressed over his use of Platonic themes. Louis Bouyer agrees:

> (Christian mysticism)…is always the experience of an objective invisible world: the world whose coming the Scriptures reveal to us in Jesus Christ, the world into which we enter, ontologically, through the liturgy, through this same Jesus Christ ever present in the Church.[21]

In 1675, Spener began the reform of Protestantism by publishing *Pia desiderata* ("Pious desires").[22] Spener argues for the integration of "mysticism" and "mystical theology" into the curriculum alongside the study of "dogmatics."

Spener agrees that some mystics engaged in unhealthy speculation, especially through the claim of "direct divine revelation." Even so, Spener defends mysticism with a proverb:

> But, just as one does not cast aside gold, silver, or precious stones if they are covered with filth, but cleanses them and according to the proverb does not throw out the baby with the bath water, in a like manner according to this principle one ought not to move against mystical theology.[23]

Spener responds to the charge of enthusiasm. An "enthusiast" was known as a "radical" who claimed a divine revelation without the use of means: the word of God, preaching, prayer, the sacraments, and the like. Spener derides what he calls "the fantasy of direct divine revelation." The reformer contrasts enthusiasm with a genuine work of the Spirit:

> But that person is certainly not an enthusiast and will not be one who experiences the working presence of the Holy Spirit, the sealing, the illumination (by virtue of that which the Spirit brings to us from the truth created from the Word), the Spirit's consolation, the loving taste of eternal things. All these things are indicated in the Holy Scripture and are promised to believers and thus are not empty names or fantasies. He is not an enthusiast who rejoices in such experiences, and with all zeal, and by all holy means endeavors to share in them. This is, according to my belief, the goal to which all mysticism is directed, a goal which is placed before all in the Holy Scripture.[24]

Spener promotes Christian mystics who contribute to the practice of piety: Tauler, Kempis, Gerson, the author of *German Theology,* and writers of similar kind.[25]

Strangely Warmed

Seventeenth-century mysticism also built a foundation for the spirituality of John and Charles Wesley. They immersed themselves in scripture and the writings of the Western and Eastern fathers. The Holy Club was the social context for their search. Four students began meeting together at Oxford in November 1729. They explored Orthodox, Roman Catholic, Lutheran, Moravian, Church of England, and Puritan sources. John Wesley's *Christian Library* of 1750–1756 encompassed fifty volumes of Christian classics and synthesized and abridged the works of seventeen continental experts on Christian spirituality. John Wesley created a synthesis of the Protestant stress on faith and the Catholic emphasis on holiness.[26]

Scholars suggest that Wesley adopted the Reformed doctrine of grace and the genius of Luther and combined them with the organizational strength and piety of Ignatius. Loyola's "mysticism of service" appealed to Wesley.[27] Wesley experimented with the classic mystical way: awakening, purgation, illumination, the dark night of the soul, and union with God.[28] Peter Bohler and the Moravians represented a turning point for the Wesley brothers and prepared the way for Aldersgate. John and Charles set sail for Georgia in 1735 to serve as missionaries. They encountered German Moravian Christians on the way.[29] The "Moravian synthesis of mystical piety and Reformed theology" attracted Wesley to Spangenberg and Peter Bohler. The Moravians combine the internal witness of the Holy Spirit, through faith in Jesus Christ, and a mystical piety similar to the Pietists.[30]

In 1735, John Wesley wrote his preface to a translation of Thomas à Kempis's *Imitation of Christ*.[31] Peter Bohler recorded these words in his journal after a meeting with Wesley in 1738: "The art which we have to learn to believe in the Savior is much too easy for the Englishmen, so that they are not able to adjust themselves to it. The best people in England, especially the scholars, talk only of 'imitating Jesus.'"[32]

Upon his return from Savannah to London, January 1738, John Wesley engaged Bohler in conversations about the nature of faith in Christ. Wesley seeks true faith in Christ with two resolutions:

> And, by the grace of God, I resolved to seek it unto the end, (1) by absolutely renouncing all dependence, in whole or in part, upon *my own* works or righteousness, on which I had really grounded my hope of salvation, though I knew it not, from my youth up; (2) by adding to the constant use of all the other 'means of grace', continual prayer for this very thing, justifying, saving faith, a full reliance on the blood of Christ shed for *me*; a trust in him as *my* Christ, as *my* sole justification, sanctification, and redemption.[33]

On Wednesday, May 24, 1738, the resolutions turned to realization. John Wesley testifies:

> In the evening I went very unwillingly to a society in Aldersgate Street, where one was reading Luther's Preface to the Epistle to the Romans. About a quarter before nine, while he was describing the change which God works in the heart through faith in Christ, I felt my heart strangely warmed, I felt I did trust in Christ, Christ alone for salvation, and an assurance was given me that he had taken away *my* sins, even *mine*, and saved *me* from the law of sin and death.[34]

He went to Germany after Aldersgate to engage the Moravian Christians again, inspired by their "intense piety" and "enthusiastic singing."[35]

The Witness of the Spirit

John Wesley engages the issue of God's direct testimony to our hearts in his sermons on the Holy Spirit. He recognizes the mystery present in an encounter between the human spirit and the Spirit of God.

> To require a more minute and philosophical account of the *manner* whereby we distinguish these, and of the *criteria* or intrinsic marks whereby we know the voice of God, is to make a demand which can never be answered; no, not by one who has the deepest knowledge of God. Suppose, when Paul answered before Agrippa, the wise Roman had said: "Thou talkest of hearing the voice of the Son of God. How dost thou know it was his voice? By what *criteria,* what intrinsic marks, dost thou know the voice of God? Explain to me the *manner* of distinguishing this from a human or angelic voice." Can you believe the Apostle himself would have once attempted to answer so idle a demand? And yet doubtless the moment he had heard that voice he knew it was the voice of God. But *how* he knew this who is able to explain? Perhaps neither man nor angel.[36]

The issue of hearing the voice of God is controversial. Claims require careful consideration. Wesley understood the importance of discernment. He continued to teach the direct and inward witness of the Spirit upon the human spirit even after twenty years consideration. Wesley clarifies:

> I do not mean hereby that the Spirit of God testifies this by an outward voice; no, nor always by an inward voice, although he may do this sometimes. Neither do I suppose that he always applies to the heart (though he often may) one or more texts of Scripture. But he so works upon the soul by his immediate influence, and by a strong though inexplicable operation, that the stormy wind and troubled waves subside, and there is a sweet calm; the heart resting as in the arms of Jesus, and the sinner being clearly satisfied that God is reconciled, that all his "iniquities are forgiven, and his sins covered."[37]

I needed a witness of the Spirit at many points. At one point I longed for a sense of belonging. Did I possess a home within the conflict of Christian cultures? Each denomination possesses a distinct culture. God granted the words of belonging. They came through the relational metaphor of "Abba" and child.

> Inner Voice: "You are not an orphan, Dwayne.
> You are My son!"
> Response: Thank you, Daddy.
> I *reject*...I *renounce*...the *spirit of orphaning*!!!

After the voice of belonging came the words of assurance.

> Inner Voice: "You may not qualify for the...and you
> may not be accepted by the...
> as 'one of them' but you are My son!
> Any room in My house is yours! Come,
> My son. Enjoy. Celebrate. Let me hug you.
> Live and serve in your Daddy's love."

My denomination of origin wondered if involvement in the mystical elements of Christianity was a factor that contributed to my slide into moral failure. Colleagues wondered if I had listened to the clear teaching of scripture at the outset rather than attention to the inner voice I might have been spared. A review of my journal throughout the period provides a contrary insight. When I was not faithful, God was.

Most Romantic of Adventures

Evelyn Underhill (1875–1941) brought the dialogue on mysticism to the broad public. Underhill, an English mystic, describes mysticism as the "most romantic of adventures" and the "art of arts."[38] She explains what mysticism is not, then what it is:

> Mysticism, then, is not an opinion: it is not a philosophy. It has nothing in common with the pursuit of occult knowledge. On the one hand it is not merely the power of contemplating Eternity: on the other hand, it is not to be identified with any kind of religious queerness. It is the name of that organic process which involves the perfect consummation of the Love of God: the achievement here and now of the immortal heritage of man. Or, if you like it better—for this means exactly the same thing—it is the art of establishing his conscious relation with the Absolute.[39]

Mysticism is the art of establishing a conscious relationship with God. It is a process and a way of life. It is a conscious and direct encounter with the presence of God. A fruit of this union with God is the transformation of character, creating an optimystic.

The phenomena that attend a conscious relationship with God are controversial at best. Underhill describes the dialogue around this sensitive issue as "that eternal battle-ground."[40] Messages from God come to the open mind and heart. Underhill observed one of the ways as "the distinct interior voice, perfectly articulate, but recognized as speaking only within the mind."[41] She cites Teresa of Avila as a life guided by voices.

> St. Teresa's life was governed by voices; her active life as a foundress was much guided by them. They advised her in small things as in great. Often they interfered with her plans, ran counter to her personal judgment, forbade a foundation on which she was set, or commanded one which appeared imprudent or impossible. They concerned themselves with journeys, with the purchase of houses; they warned her of coming events. As her mystical life matured, Teresa seems to have learned to discriminate those locutions on which action should properly be based. She seldom resisted them, though it constantly happened that the action on which they insisted seemed the height of folly: and though they frequently involved her in hardships and

difficulties, she never had cause to regret this reliance upon decrees which she regarded as coming direct from God, and which certainly did emanate from a life greater than her own.[42]

Teresa proposed two responses to these distinct interior words: (1) that the message should be obeyed after long hesitation, and (2) that the words must be subject to criticism. She hesitated long before obeying the voice calling her to leave the Convent of the Incarnation and begin her work of reform. She was concerned about the direction of the movement within her heart as a result of the speaking voice. Teresa's criteria for discerning the voices encompassed (1) the fruit of certainty, peace, and joy, (2) the manner of their coming, (3) the bringing to the surface-self a new conviction or new material, and (4) the belief that all should add up to "a positive value for life." These messages seem to be "outpourings of the Divine Mind, crystallized into verbal form on their way through the human consciousness."[43]

These "intimate colloquies" between God and the self may take the "form of dialogue." This form of message is prevalent in mystical literature. Underhill explains the inner dynamics of these dialogues,

> The self, wholly absorbed by the intimate sense of divine companionship, receives its messages in the form of "distinct interior words"; as of an alien voice, speaking within the mind with such an accent of validity and spontaneity as to leave no room for doubt as to its character...[The] self–retaining a clear consciousness of its own separateness and recognizing the Voice as personal and distinct from its own soul–naturally enters into a communion which has an almost conversational character, replies to questions or asks others in its turn: and in this dramatic style the content of its intuitions is gradually expressed. We have then an extreme form of that dissociation which we all experience in a slight degree when we "argue with ourselves." But in this case one of the speakers is become the instrument of a power other than itself, and communicates to the mind new wisdom and new life.[44]

I have sought the Spirit's leading throughout my faith journey. The seeking assumes the shape of dialogues, and sometimes the words are accompanied by an inner picture. I cite a turning point. One sentence came as a surprising expectation of hope.

INNER VOICE: "I want the (denomination of origin) to bless you."

RESPONSE: Impossible! (That was my first reaction.)

The words were accompanied with an inner picture.

MENTAL PICTURE: I was back in my home church on the platform. I was being re-commissioned for ministry! What a moving picture.

> RESPONSE: Lord, what is here? What does this inner picture mean? Where do I begin, Lord?
>
> Silence

There was no immediate answer. It was a moving meditation. I dismissed it as an unlikely scenario. It was one thing to return upstream to seek reconciliation with a divorced spouse. It would be something else entirely to expect the denomination of origin to bless me. However, the words resonated within. A seed was planted. About eight months later, in an open time of meditation I had thoughts about rebuilding some bridges to people in my past. I'm not sure why. The possibility of "rebuilding some bridges to people in my past" held sway on my mind.

I decided to test the words and picture that had come eight months earlier. The thought of rebuilding bridges reinforced them. I took action in the direction of the words. Several amazing events were set in motion. The outcome was an act of mutual reconciliation with the denomination of origin. Leaders blessed me through prayer and forgiveness. I was released to serve in another denomination. I felt free emotionally and spiritually. God's desire for reconciliation was fulfilled, in whole or in part.

Optimystic Dialogues

A New Call Emerges

Dialogue releases a flow of meaning. New understandings emerge from the conversation. A new call surfaces out of the dialogues with God. A new sense of forgiveness and acceptance opens to a new sense of call. God transforms chaos into design. Optimystic dialogues reveal the issues around the call.

> FORGIVENESS
>
> MEDITATION: Romans 3
> INNER VOICE: "My forgiveness of you is complete. I look upon you as the apple of my eye, not as a fallen son."
> RESPONSE: Lord, what a marvelous thought.
> CONTEMPLATION:
>   Oh, the thought,
>   That God looks on me as the apple of his eye.
>   Marvelous God.
>   Magnificent God.
>   Wonderful God.
>
> ACCEPTANCE
>
> SCRIPTURE: Romans 9
> GRACE: To be a carrier of God's presence in the world.
> MENTAL PICTURE:
>   Jesus washing my feet
>   in the waters of *mercy*.
>   I sink into the experience.

EMOTIONAL RESPONSE:
I feel accepted, loved, forgiven, and understood.
Deeply affected by the experience.
Gratitude.

CALL

INNER VOICE: "Dwayne, I place a new calling on your life…
to be a *pastor of my presence*."

AFFIRMATION

INNER VOICE: "Wherever you go, you will carry my presence with you–there is no greater destiny. I seek those, like you, who will be *my presence-bearers*. Carry my presence with you, and I will *show myself* to be with you. Live out of this destiny, and you will be blessed."

GUIDANCE

GRACE: To hear and to follow in the present circumstances of my life.
SCRIPTURE: Romans 5
INNER VOICE: "You are prepared for usefulness, Dwayne…
It will be in the ways I have loved you back to life."

PROMISE

SCRIPTURE: Jeremiah 29:11–14
INNER VOICE:
"Possess the land of these verses.
Make them your life passion.
I will fulfill them in you."

EXPLORE

GRACE: To comprehend more fully all that it means to be a "pastor of my presence."
SCRIPTURE: Ephesians 1:3–14
"God…has blessed us in Christ with *every spiritual blessing*." (author's emphasis)
INNER VOICE: "There is the power of my presence.
And the power of the words of my presence.
Explore the invocation of my presence.
Insight awaits you."

ACT

MEDITATION: John 1:1–18; 1 John 1:1–4
INNER VOICE:
"Share your experience of me.
Trust it."

Any wonder why I am a Christian optimystic? God is a Shepherd who speaks in the chaos. God is a Shepherd who guides with intimate love, knowledge, and wisdom. God's futures are in-spirited with faith, hope, and love. God overcame personal evil with good. I awe at sovereign grace.

Top Ten Paradoxes Plus One

The impression that optimystic dialogues have resolved all questions would be false. I live with paradoxes. They are friends, not foes. Below is a list of the top ten, plus one, contradictory qualities that swirl around my white-water odyssey. I acknowledge the controversial nature about them. I invite dialogue.

PARADOX 10: The God of unity and harmony opts for polarity in leadership.
PARADOX 9: The God of order and design prefers chaos and desperation.
PARADOX 8: The God who opposes evil uses it.
PARADOX 7: The God of all grace is powerless to cancel the world of consequences.
PARADOX 6: The moral God disregards immorality when embracing children.
PARADOX 5: The God of all truth applies it circumstantially.
PARADOX 4: The God of holiness cannot escape ambiguity.
PARADOX 3: The God who resists temptation befriends it.
PARADOX 2: The God of the canonical word risks real-time words.
PARADOX 1: The God of warnings and judgments is all heart and compassion.
PLUS 1: The God of providence co-creates new futures through human choices.

Concentric Rings of Dialogue and Discernment

But paradox cannot be our last word. Even amidst these perplexing paradoxes, we continue to seek dialogue and discernment. A dialogue with God can be a defining moment for any person. Transformational moments of Christian leaders have shaped the Christian story across the centuries. Men and women have become the shakers and shapers of Christian mission. I call them Christian optimystics. In dialogue with God, leaders navigate the full diversity of God's white water to transform sin into forgiveness, guilt into grace, hurt into healing, despair into hope, and failure into mission.

Dialogue with God is never isolated from attending to the tradition. The shakers and shapers of the Christian story listen to the tradition without exception. The structure of discernment carries within it the larger axis of the Christian story. Christian optimystics begin with contemplative listening to the voice of scripture as the center to all. The dialogue expands like concentric rings around the axis of scripture to encompass the voices of the Christian tradition. Always there is the convergence of two or more Christian rivers that create a new concentric ring–a movement, so to speak. Christian optimystics dialogue with the voices of the Christian tradition that pursue and apprehend God. In pursuing and apprehending God, the rapids of transformation gain momentum and overpower fortified structures of mind and heart. A new ring or movement emerges out of the chaos. A new spiritual paradigm impels the movement forward.

Dialogue as a template of transformation requires a profound struggle with scripture and tradition. A structure of discernment submits reason and experience to the prism of scripture and tradition. With clarity and eloquence, Jaroslav Pelikan describes the difference between tradition and traditionalism, "Tradition is the living faith of the dead, traditionalism is the dead faith of the living."[45] Pelikan explains the role of tradition in the circle of dialogue.

> [T]he dichotomy between tradition and insight breaks down under the weight of history itself. A "leap of progress" is not a standing broad jump, which begins at the line of where we are now; it is a running broad jump through where we have been to where we go next. The growth of insight–in science, in the arts, in philosophy and theology–has not come through progressively sloughing off more and more tradition, as though insight would be purest and deepest when it has finally freed itself of the dead past. It simply has not worked that way in the history of the tradition, and it does not work that way now. By including the dead in the circle of discourse, we enrich the quality of the conversation. Of course, we do not listen only to the dead, nor are we a tape recording of the tradition. That really would be the dead faith of the living, not the living faith of the dead...Johann Wolfgang von Goethe, saw it all more deeply and said it all more clearly:
>
> > What you have as heritage,
> > Take now as task;
> > For thus you will make it your own![46]

A structure of discernment is not so grandiose as to propose with certitude that reported dialogues with God are from God or otherwise. Encounters with the holy can stand on their own claims and outcomes. Christian movements birthed out of dialogue with God can speak to the issue of source integrity. The purpose is to "process" the raw data of real-time conversation with God in an intelligible way. A structure of discernment that encompasses three factors–the Christian story of optimism, the Christian story of mysticism, and the nature of authentic dialogue–can bring intelligibility to the present spiritual yearning for experience of God. Intelligibility into dialogical encounters can drive mission forward into the future.

Morris and Olsen sum up God's motive for risking real-time conversation.

> God yearns for us to know God's will for the world, for the church, and for ourselves. In fact, the words *yearning* and *will* are interchangeable, though yearning may be less rigid. Think of our yearning to

know God's yearning! God's yearning is what God wants for God's people. The faithful response of God's people satisfies God's yearning.

God wants everyone to know God's will. God doesn't with-hold grace, play games, or tease us to test our faithfulness or our worthiness to be trusted with divine insight. God is far more prone to human revelation than I am to divine encounter. God's will is that you and I, everyone, and our faith communities should discern and act upon God's will.[47]

Augustine's Garden

MEMO: June 2005
TO: Dwayne Ratzlaff
FROM: Tom Bandy

Dwayne:

To reply to *why* you are optimystic, I need to talk about *when* I am optimystic. We share a similar intellectual perspective and faith position toward the journey of life, but an element of timeliness or context needs to be elucidated first. "Optimysm" is not a state of being that one carries about like software in the human CPU. It is not a conclusion about life that, once discerned, banishes worry and restores self-confidence. It is not an attitude of general well-being.

It is more like a flickering candle that grows bright or dim, suddenly igniting a great fire and just as suddenly retreating into inky blackness, reacting to wind and wet, apparently going out and then inexplicably sputtering to life again. Or, using our water metaphors, it is like a spring that is connected to a hidden aquifer, gushing or trickling in response to issues including and beyond any local habitat, disappearing into dust and inexplicably erupting again.

We are apt to translate the Greek notion of *kairos* as simply the kairos *moment.* It is better understood as a kairos environment. Kairos is a convergence of natural and supernatural forces outside the normal sequence of time. It is never passive, always apocalyptic; and the roots of optimysm lie in that environment. These convergences of time and space, with timelessness and relationship, do not occur often because they are only partly (perhaps only slightly) in the control of the individual. Indeed, the kairos environment is an experience of total loss of control to forces beyond oneself. There is an ambiguity in Augustine's question: "Why not make an end of my ugly sins at this moment?" Was Augustine suicidal? Or was Augustine surrendering to a Higher Power? *Or was it both?*

I think we cannot separate Augustine from Augustine's garden. Everything converged. We reread his biographical account and realize that his intense spiritual yearning had intersected with infinite experience. It was not so much that he encountered the incarnate Christ as he was taken inside the experience of incarnation. Notice how the passage of time seems to disappear. The forms of creation (the garden, the plants, the flowers, the bird songs, the Beauty) suddenly become transparent to the Truth. The voice of God is the same as with Moses. It is "I Am" who is speaking. It is the creative Word that started it all, restarted it all, and starts everything forever.

I am struck by the elements of Augustine's garden. There was a companion within it. He apparently comprehended nothing of what was going on. Alypius heard no voice, but the mere presence of a true friend—the feeling of friendship—pervaded the environment. The intensity of Augustine's emotion acted as a kind of filter, eliminating "background noise" yet admitting the distant sound of a child's nonsensical and playful song. It would have been a repetitive, lilting refrain: "Take and read, take and read, take and read…" The world is not absent—but filtered, distorted, or surreal. Was Augustine on drugs? Was the infinite acting on him as a drug?

It is no accident that the convergence in the garden reminds Augustine of Antony. Antony is the faith of monasticism, one not far removed historically from Augustine's own life, whose example of worldly renunciation and radical submission to Christ impressed the entire Roman world. Augustine snatches the Bible from an astonished Alypius and does the one thing modern biblical scholars and seminary professors tell students *not to do!* He reads a single verse of scripture *out of context!* He does not apply higher critical method to it; indeed, he applies no critical method at all. He allows the kairos environment to interpret it for him. He "hears" it for the first time.

The call is akin to that of Antony, but different. Antony was called to the desert; Augustine will be called to the priesthood. Antony will go to the edge of culture; Augustine will live in the midst of culture. Yet the self-discipline and self-renunciation will be the same, and the surrender to Christ and Christ's mission will be the same. Throughout Augustine's life, non-Christian detractors will smirk at the memory of carousing with this supposedly posturing saint. Lifelong church people will despise his colored past and block his career. Yet Augustine changed in that garden. He became "optimystic."

It seems to me that all of your intellectual wanderings and theological reflections have been very valuable for your journey to redemption, but many people I meet are equally serious about their intellectual quest and theological reflections. Your therapeutic counseling and disciplined prayer life have been very valuable also, but many people I meet have also experienced excellent therapy and are involved in serious prayer. Yet you have emerged "optimystic," and so many others are either giving up or settling for lesser goals. The difference is Augustine's garden. There is a kairos environment, or a convergence of finite yearning and infinite Word, that is quite beyond our control but is crucial to the consummation of our redemptive journeys.

What is the difference between "optimysm" and mere "optimism" or "mysticism"?

182   Christian OptiMystics

Mere optimism is the fundamental confidence in human potential. Leibniz set the stage for the Enlightenment and the future of scientific rationalism by attempting to resolve the problem of evil by maximizing the goodness of God at the expense of the power of God. This world is the best it can possibly be under the condition of human freedom. God "makes the best" of a mixed bag of human endeavors, but throughout the course of human development runs an unbroken thread of divine nudging and reasonable development that makes it more probable that tomorrow will be better rather than worse.

Without getting into a lengthy examination of contemporary philosophy and culture, the optimistic view of Leibniz is perpetuated by the pop culture phenomenon of more than nine movies and four long-running television series of *Star Trek*. Jean Luc Picard of the starship "Enterprise" is Leibniz reincarnated. It is the global point of view of European and North American culture.

Of course, you have identified that "optimism" has more profound manifestations. It has been translated into three distinct, powerful, philosophies around which we shape our lifestyles:

1. William James translated optimism into mental health, and this has been expanded to holistic health. If only we maintain emotional balance, mental acuity, dietary disciplines, relational maturity, and reasonable common sense, the world will become a better place; and our lives will be worth living.

2. Reinhold Niebuhr translated optimism into social action. If only we discern true morality, study ethics, leverage the right sociopolitical causes, restrain personal selfishness and global greed, understand the real issues, and appoint the most responsible leaders to political office and corporate board rooms, the world will become a better place; and our lives will be worth living.

3. Norman Vincent Peale and a host of religious and corporate leaders translated optimism into personal success. If only we can maintain a positive attitude, project a confident demeanor, maintain high self-esteem, specialize in important skills, and improve our overall competencies, the world will become a better place; and our lives will be worth living.

The problem with mere optimism is that the problem of evil just won't go away. No matter how well we maintain our health, at any moment we might be run over by a bus. No matter how much we deserve success, dramatic and undeserved failures still seem to reverse our best successes. No matter how many social revolutions reform society, humankind seems to have a peculiar penchant for death and disaster. A point comes when the probability that tomorrow will eventually, necessarily, be *better* defies credibility.

The problem with mere optimism is not just that it can't cope with radical evil. It also can't allow unexplainable grace. Pietism and Methodism have tried to account for radical evil and make room for unexplainable grace; but in the end, despite all the references to devouring fires and hearts strangely warmed, the actual day-to-day *experience* of religion remains remarkably tepid. The fundamental assumption of optimism about the control exercised by the human being over the world for good or ill is really not questioned. We just need to become more methodical, obedient, righteous, structured, or accountable. The truth is that Methodism today doesn't allow much room for hearts strangely warmed, nor is their much room in Calvinism today for divinely devouring fires. God may ultimately be in control, but for the next millennia he has left human beings pretty much in charge. I'm not sure many people share the conviction of Leibniz that this sign of confidence is a good thing.

Mere mysticism is the fundamental confidence in accessible bliss. History really does not matter. The "future" and the "past" are irrelevant. The "now" is all that is important, because unity with the divine only requires crossing a bridge to the infinite. Now, that bridge may be more difficult to cross than expected. It may require the surrender of all possessions or the accumulation of extreme wealth. It may require retreat from the world and intense meditation, or immersion into culture and intense pleasure. It might require abstinence from sex and drugs, or compulsive sex and drugs. One way or another, however, mere mysticism is convinced that we can cross that bridge and merge ourselves eternally with God. We will never change. We will never be interrupted. God and the individual will merge, and we will always, always be content.

I think we both know that your quick summary of the history of mysticism is grossly insufficient, and that there are profound depths to mysticism that I am not even mentioning in my critique of "mere" mysticism. But it is not my purpose or yours to elucidate this history. Our shared purpose is to reflect on how mysticism has been translated into the contemporary experience of culture and the church. If mere optimism is the established global perspective of modernity, then mere mysticism exists at the fringes and in the interstices of that perspective, and is emerging as the global perspective of postmodernity.

The postmodern twist to mystical experience is indeed personal, relational, and "unnatural" (which is to say, it defies scientific explanation and involves psychosomatic experiences of the supernatural). There are more profound manifestations of mysticism:

Clement of Alexandria, Teresa of Avila, and Evelyn Underhill do share a deeper awareness from Plato that the imperfect forms of existence do yearn to return to the perfect Truth, Beauty, and Goodness of the infinite. Existence lies at the outermost rung of the great ladder of being, and it is possible to climb back to the center.

Spener and the later leaders of the pietist, holiness, and charismatic movements do point toward an experience of divine immediacy that elevates human consciousness to another level of relationship with God. Mundane living still connects with a deeper ecstasy that can fill existence with meaning and hope.

The problem with mere mysticism is that the dilemma of human inadequacy just won't go away. No matter how intentionally we empty ourselves of what we think we know or fill ourselves with what we ought to know, our "knowing" doesn't necessarily help us climb the ladder to merge with God. Alienation remains the one constant feature of existence. No matter how ecstatic any given moment might be or how intentionally we align our behavior with momentary glimpses of God, our "rigor" doesn't help us maintain the memory of God. Triviality continues to be the gravitational pull of our world. A point comes when the vision vanishes and the energy required to maintain our sense of expectation is too great to sustain.

The problem with mere mysticism is not just that human inadequacy won't go away. It can't really value radical innovation. If the future and the past are largely irrelevant, engagement with human history in general, or with my history in particular, is difficult to justify. What does it really matter? Why should I be held accountable to imperfectly human standards of justice? What if simply "having faith," or "converting to Christianity," or "speaking in tongues," or "meditating with new age crystals," or "praying about it" don't really have any impact on the complex circumstances that led to my child's drug addiction, the breakdown of my marriage, or another holocaust of ethnic cleansing?

What, then, does it mean to be "optimystic"? Somehow these two streams of optimism and mysticism have merged in your own Augustinian experience of the garden. It seems to me that your experience should give a different kind of hope to others in their quest for redemption. It is not *merely* optimistic hope, because the desired ends of relationship, career, respectability, and inner peace may not be realized in the way that we wish or as completely as we want. It is not *merely* mystical hope, because the desired ends of unity with God, freedom from guilt, personal vindication, and bliss may not be realized either. What, then, is the hope that you have realized and that you hold out for others?

It seems to me that the hope you have found (and offer) is that any earnest seeker can find his Augustinian "garden." She can experience a kairos environment in which (to paraphrase Augustine) "*the light of confidence floods into my heart and the darkness of doubt is dispelled*It is optimism and mysticism all at once. It involves three things.

Acceptance: It is possible that through a peculiar combination of self-disciplined searching and uncontrollable grace any sinner can be acceptable before God. Mistakes and blemishes aside, any sinner, no matter how contemptible, can be received by God like the prodigal son. This acceptance may well be in spite of continued rejection by society, civil law, church polity, and ecclesiastical colleagues; but it implies that both the accused and the accusers will stand equally before a higher court. This acceptance may well be in spite of continued personal regret, impossible psychological closure, and irreparable brokenness; but it implies that both the breaker and the broken have access to a higher power of healing. Acceptance does not erase the past or guarantee the future, but forges a bond of grace for every moment of the "now."

Paradox: You identify eleven fundamental paradoxes with which hopeful people will wrestle all their lives. Despair means that people give up wrestling with these paradoxes. Despair means that they resort to dogmatism, surrender to fundamentalism, collapse into atheism, or flee into hedonism. It is perhaps ironic in our world today to realize that dogmatic religious zealots and dogmatic secular atheists are really just cousins in a larger family of despair. Real hope lies in the constant, prayerful pondering—and perpetual, existential wrestling—with paradoxes such as these. No doubt we could add others to the list. Certainly, there are more than just ten or eleven. What is clear is that these paradoxes are *not eternal.* They are *existential.* They may be resolved in God and revealed at the end time, but in the course of lived history they will remain inexplicable and uncontrollable as long as humanity remains human.

Dialogue: The conversation about these paradoxes will be unending. It will not always be respectful, but will always be passionate. What I like most about your description is that this dialogue is so multifaceted. It is a dialogue between people, and also in spite of people. It unfolds whether you contribute to it or try to remain aloof from it. No matter what, you are a part of it. So get used to it! It is also a dialogue between humanity and God. It will unfold in general as the history of human thought interacts with God's truth. It will unfold in particular as my particular history of pain and mismanagement interacts with God's particular whisper into my heart or God's shout into my eardrums. It's a dialogue. God won't let it go, even if we try to let it go. So get used to it!

Optimism is fundamentally a matter of confidence, not predictability. It is not that the world will get better and better *in spite* of your free involvement in it, but that the world will get better and better *because* of your free involvement in it. Your experience of moral collapse (and for other people it could be an experience of emotional, physical, or mental collapse) signaled a profound collapse of confidence. That confidence you have regained, and it is one born of humility rather than arrogance. Like so many leaders of the "church triumphant," you mistook pride for optimism, and it just about killed you. Now, "the light of confidence floods your heart."

Meanwhile, mysticism is fundamentally a matter of clarity. It is not that you "know" God, but that God "knows" you, and that you-know-that-God-knows-that-you-know. Knowing means you have entered the internal constitution of the divine, and the divine has entered the internal constitution of your soul. Your moral collapse (and again, it could be any collapse) signaled a profound uncertainty about God. You were certain enough about God's existence, but suddenly doubtful about God's nearness. Now, "the darkness of doubt is dispelled."

I have argued often that the *experience* of Christ is the single most important aspect of Christian leadership—and of "being Christian" at all. I always ask, *What is it about your experience with Jesus that this community cannot live without?* It took a long journey through very painful territory, but perhaps for the first time in your professional career you really do have an answer to that question. It cannot be answered in any trite, dogmatic phrases, or even with just a few sentences. This whole book is an answer to that question.

Incarnation is the experience in which acceptance, paradox, and dialogue all happen together. It may not be unity with God, but it is certainly not just walking toward God. Mysticism and optimism, by themselves, cannot help us experience acceptance, paradox, or dialogue, which are the basic building blocks of existence. Incarnation means *companionship* with Christ. It is a mediated unity with God, but unity no less. It is a grace-filled freedom to act responsibly, but freedom no less. "Companionship" is the near proximity of God, but also the absolute surrender to walk with Jesus in mission. (See my books *Road Runner* and *Mission Mover*.[48])

This is why I love your term *optimystic*. It combines unity with God and co-working with God. The history of twentieth-century Christianity seems to be an attempt to separate mysticism from optimism. Either Christians are passively, personally, and selfishly seeking to merge with God, and letting the world go to hell (in every meaning of that metaphor); or Christians are actively, corporately, and arrogantly trying to create God's kingdom on earth, and letting their souls shrivel into nothingness (in every meaning of *that* metaphor). Why can't it be both? Why can't we be with God and in mission at the same time? Why can't we be "optimystic"?

I think only one thing is stopping us—and therefore, we are only one step away from experiencing powerful, life-changing Christianity. We have failed to find companionship with Christ, and all we need to do is restore companionship with Christ. I do not mean dogmatism about Christ, theories about Christ, books about Christ, trite sayings about Christ, or fantasies about Christ. I do not mean embracing the humanity of Christ without the divinity of Christ, or embracing the divinity of Christ without the humanity of Christ. I mean embracing both together in a single *experience* of Christ that defies logic. I think it can be done. I see it being done. I think more and more Christians are doing it, and God is doing it—and they are meeting in the middle of life's highway. But perhaps I am just "optimystic."

Notes

Introduction: In Dialogue

[1] John Cassian, *Conferences,* trans. Colm Luibheid (New York: Paulist Press, 1985), 137–38.

[2] David Bohm, *On Dialogue* (New York: Routledge, 1996), 6–17.

[3] William van den Heuvel, www.muc.de/~heuvel/papers/on_dialogue.

[4] William Isaacs, *Dialogue and the Art of Thinking Together: A Pioneering Approach to Communication in Business and in Life* (New York: Doubleday, 1999), 9, 19.

[5] Ibid., 79–80.

[6] Ibid., 79–176.

[7] Athanasius, *The Life of Antony and The Letter to Marcellinus,* trans. Robert C. Gregg, The Classics of Western Spirituality, ed. Richard J. Payne (New York: Paulist Press, 1980), 16–17.

[8] Ibid., 30–32.

[9] John van Engen, trans., *Devotio Moderna: Basic Writings,* The Classics of Western Spirituality, ed. John Farina (New York: Paulist Press, 1988), 7–25.

[10] Ibid., 25.

[11] Thomas á Kempis, *The Imitation of Christ* (Garden City, N.Y.: Doubleday, 1955), 75.

[12] Ibid., 104–6.

[13] Charles V. Gerkin, *The Living Human Document: Re-Visioning Pastoral Counseling in a Hermeneutical Mode* (Nashville: Abingdon Press, 1984), 37–38, 56.

[14] *Merriam-Webster's Collegiate Dictionary,* 10th ed., s.v. "theodicy."

[15] *Scout:* to walk along a bank to inspect the river" definition from Jeff Bennett, *The Complete Whitewater Rafter* (Camden, Maine: Ragged Mountain Press, 1996), 193–94. Expressions from the sport of white-water rafting are explained in this excellent guide. "

[16] Gordon Mursell, ed., *The Story of Christian Spirituality* (Minneapolis: Fortress Press, 2001), 367.

Chapter 1: Rafting toward a Crisis of Spirit

[1] *The River Wild* (Hollywood, Calif.: Universal Studios, 1994.

[2] *White water* refers to fast-moving water or rapids. Jeff Bennett explains expressions from the sport of white-water rafting in *The Complete Whitewater Rafter* (Camden, Maine: Ragged Mountain Press, 1996).

[3] *Odyssey is* "(1) a long wandering or voyage usually marked by many changes of fortune; (2) an intellectual or spiritual wandering or quest." Merriam-Webster's Collegiate Dictionary, 10th ed., s.v. "odyssey." The word odyssey is attributed to Homer in his epic poem, The Odyssey, which retells the long wanderings of Odysseus.

[4] Bennett, *Complete Whitewater,* 44. "Simply put, *chaos* is a state of utter confusion."

[5] Ibid., 29–33. A *rescue lifejacket* is "essential riverwear." "*Lifejacket*: a personal flotation device designed to float a swimmer in water."

[6] Ibid., 193–94. A *helmet* is "essential riverwear." "*Helmet*: rigid headgear designed to protect a rafter's head from impact."

[7] Ibid., ix. *River-running* means running the rapids.

[8] Ibid., 194. "*Rapid*: a place where the river leaves its two-dimensional state and enters a three-dimensional state complete with faster currents, rocks, and various types of liquid surface features."

[9] A. E. Thompson, *A. B. Simpson: His Life and Work* (Harrisburg, Pa.: Christian Publications, 1960), 14–15.

[10] Ibid., 13–14.

[11] Ibid., 17.

[12] Ibid., 69.

[13] Ibid., 66.

[14] Ibid., 64.

[15] Ibid., 73–74.

[16] Ibid., 76.

[17]Ibid., 205.
[18]A. B. Simpson, *The Holy Spirit: Volume 2* (Harrisburg, Pa.: Christian Publications, n.d.), 74.
[19]Clark H. Pinnock, *Flame of Love: A Theology of the Holy Spirit* (Downers Grove, Ill.: InterVarsity Press, 1996), 149, 152, 162, 176.
[20]Thompson, *A. B. Simpson: His Life,* 153.
[21]David F. Hartzfeld and Charles Nienkirchen, eds., *The Birth of a Vision* (Beaverlodge, Alberta, Canada: Buena Book Services), 166.
[22]Ibid., 166.
[23]Thompson, *A. B. Simpson: His Life,* 206.
[24]A. B. Simpson, *Holy Spirit: Volume 1* (Harrisburg, Pa.: Christian Publications, n.d.), 160–62.
[25]Andrew Thornton, trans., *Preface to the Complete Edition of Luther's Latin Works (1545)* (Saint Anselm Abbey, 1983). This translation was made by Bro. Andrew Thornton, OSB, for the Saint Anselm College Humanities Program. It is distributed by Project Wittenberg with the permission of the author. This translation may be used freely with proper attribution (http://www.ctsfw.edu/etext/luther/quotes/tower.asc).
[26]Bennett, *Complete Whitewater,* 193. "*Eddy*: a pocket of water downstream of an obstacle that flows upstream or back against the main current."
[27]Harrison Owen, *SPIRIT: Transformation and Development in Organizations* (Potomac, Md.: Abbott Publishing, 1987), 43, 129–30.
[28]Ibid., 132–33.
[29]Harrison Owen, *Leadership Is* (Potomac, Md.: Abbott Publishing, 1990), 51.
[30]I employ "Paddle Captain" in reference to God.
[31]Jim Wallis, "All Together Now," *Sojourners* (May-June, 1997): 16, 21.
[32]Richard J. Foster, *Streams of Living Water* (San Francisco: HarperSanFrancisco, 1998), xv.
[33]Bennett, *Complete Whitewater,* 194. "*Hydraulics*: a change in currents that causes surface features that can deflect, slow, or speed up a raft's descent (e.g., holes, waves, and eddies)."

Chapter 2: Capsized into a Crisis of Morality

[1]River *morphology* refers to "The Dynamics of Running Water," including surface and beneath-the-surface characteristics. Jeff Bennett, *The Complete Whitewater Rafter* (Camden, Maine: Ragged Mountain Press, 1996), table of contents.
[2]This letter has been adapted from "Ignatius of Loyola Speaks to a Modern Jesuit," in *Ignatius of Loyola,* by Karl Rahner, S.J., and Paul Imhof, S.J.: (London: Collins, 1979).
[3]R. Barnes, "Spiritual Exercises of St. Ignatius," Regis College: TST, notes from 1989 lecture.
[4]Marian Cowan and John Carroll Futrell, *The Spiritual Exercises of St. Ignatius of Loyola: A Handbook for Directors* (Cambridge, Mass.: Jesuit Educational Center for Human Development, 1982), 9.
[5]Rahner and Imhof, "Ignatius of Loyola Speaks".
[6]William A. Barry and William J. Connolly, *The Practice of Spiritual Direction* (Minneapolis: Seabury Press, 1982), 8.
[7]Ibid., 46.
[8]Ibid.
[9]Ibid., 27.
[10]Cowan and Futrell, *Spiritual Exercises,* 6–7.
[11]Ibid., 7.
[12]Ibid.
[13]Ibid.
[14]Ibid., 8.
[15]Ibid.
[16]Ibid.
[17]"The foregoing explanation of spiritual consolation could be taken as a commentary on Paul's prayer for the Romans 'May the God of hope fill you with all joy and peace in believing, so that you may abound in hope by the power of the Holy Spirit' (Rom. 15:13); or as a commentary on Paul's statement that 'the kingdom of God is not food and drink but

righteousness and peace and joy in the Holy Spirit' (Rom. 14:17). For righteousness is from faith (Rom. 5:1–2; 3:28). Faith-life grows into fullness of love and hope under the action of the Holy Spirit, who thus brings us a peace and joy that are possible in those who believe." Jules J. Toner, *A Commentary on Saint Ignatius' Rules for the Discernment of Spirits* (St. Louis.: Institute of Jesuit Sources, 1982), 112.

[18]"Associated with gloominess, and even a correlative of it, is 'confusion'…This is a state of mind in which one's own judgments, principles, values, and emotional responses are so jumbled that one cannot discern distinctly or clearly what is going on or why…The desolate feelings tend directly and by their very nature to destroy faith, hope, and charity. Ignatius speaks of the one in desolation as 'tending toward distrust, without hope, without love.'" Ibid., 127, 131.

[19]Kenneth Leech, *Experiencing God* (San Francisco: Harper and Row, 1985), 131.
[20]Walter Wink, *Engaging the Powers* (Minneapolis: Fortress Press, 1992), 8–9.
[21]C. Peter Wagner, *Warfare Prayer* (Ventura, Calif.: Regal Books, 1992), 16–19.
[22]M. Scott Peck, *People of the Lie* (New York: Touchstone, 1983), 183.
[23]Leech, *Experiencing God,* 160.
[24]Evagrius Ponticus, *The Praktikos & Chapters on Prayer,* trans. John Eudes Bamberger (Kalamazoo, Mich.: Cistercian, 1981), 16–18.
[25]Ibid., 25.
[26]Ibid.
[27]Ibid., 20.
[28]Ibid., 18.
[29]James Houston, *The Transforming Friendship: A Guide to Prayer* (Batavia, Ill.: Lion, 1989), 17.
[30]Robert Bly, *Iron John* (New York: Vintage Books, 1990), 205–6.
[31]Ibid., 226–29.
[32]Edwin H. Friedman, *Generation to Generation: Family Process in Church and Synagogue* (New York: Guilford Press, 1985), 6–7.
[33]Ibid., 36.
[34]Ibid., 36–37.
[35]John Cassian, *Conferences,* trans. Colm Luibheid (New York: Paulist Press, 1985), 68.
[36]Henri J. M. Nouwen, *The Way of the Heart: Desert Spirituality and Contemporary Ministry* (New York: Seabury Press, 1981), 28.
[37]Ibid., 22–23.
[38]Cassian, *Conferences,* 49.
[39]Ibid., 33–34.
[40]Walter Rauschenbusch, *Selected Writings,* trans. Winthrop S. Hudson (New York: Paulist Press, 1984), 3.
[41]Gordon Mursell, ed., *The Story of Christian Spirituality* (Minneapolis: Fortress Press, 2001), 302.
[42]Rauschenbusch, *Selected Writings,* 32.
[43]Ibid., 212.
[44]Ibid.
[45]Ibid., 214.
[46]Ibid., 214–15.
[47]Henri J. M. Nouwen, Donald P. McNeill, and Douglas A. Morrison, *Compassion: A Reflection on the Christian Life* (New York: Doubleday, 1982), 16–17.
[48]Ibid., 23–24.

Chapter 3: Submerged within a Crisis of Calling

[1]Vinson Synan, *The Century of the Holy Spirit: 100 Years of Pentecostal and Charismatic Renewal* (Nashville: Thomas Nelson, 2001), 8.
[2]Ibid.
[3]Ibid., 9.
[4]Ibid.
[5]Harvey Cox, *Fire from on High: The Rise of Pentecostal Spirituality and the Reshaping of Religion in the Twenty-First Century* (New York: Addison-Wesley, 1995), 81–83, 91.
[6]Ibid., 105.

Notes to Pages 59–90

[7] Ibid.
[8] Ibid., 100.
[9] Gordon Mursell, ed., *The Story of Christian Spirituality* (Minneapolis: Fortress Press, 2001), 313.
[10] Tom Harpur, *The Uncommon Touch: An Investigation of Spiritual Healing* (Toronto: McClelland & Stewart, 1994), 161.
[11] Francis MacNutt, *Overcome by the Spirit* (Grand Rapids, Mich.: Chosen Books, 1990), 28.
[12] Carol Arnott, "The Purpose of Soaking in His Presence," *Spread the Fire* 7, no. 3 (2001): 6, available through www.tacf.org. 9.
[13] David Pytches, *Come Holy Spirit*, rev. ed. (London: Hodder & Stoughton, 1995), 71.
[14] MacNutt, *Overcome*, 185–187.
[15] Kenneth Leech, *Experiencing God: Theology as Spirituality* (San Francisco: Harper and Row, 1985), 40–41.
[16] Frank Whaling, ed., *John and Charles Wesley: Selected Writings and Hymns*, The Classics of Western Spirituality, ed. Richard J. Payne (Ramsey, N.J.: Paulist Press, 1981), 12.
[17] Ibid., 319.
[18] Ibid., 320.
[19] Ibid., 326.
[20] Colin W. Williams, *John Wesley's Theology Today* (Nashville: Abingdon Press, 1960), 127.
[21] Ibid., 127–28.
[22] Symeon the New Theologian, *The Discourses*, trans. C. J. de Catanzaro, The Classics of Western Spirituality, ed. Richard J. Payne (New York: Paulist Press, 1980), 80–81.
[23] In William R. Barr and Rena M. Yocum, *The Church in the Movement of the Spirit* (Grand Rapids, Mich.: Eerdmans, 1994), 19.
[24] Thomas Merton, *Life and Holiness* (Garden City, N.Y.: Image Books, 1963), 12–13.
[25] Ibid.,13.
[26] Douglas John Hall, *The Future of the Church: Where Are We Headed?* (Toronto: United Church Publishing House (United Church of Canada), 1989), 78.
[27] Henri J. M. Nouwen, Donald P. McNeill, and Douglas A. Morrison, *Compassion: A Reflection on the Christian Life* (New York: Image Books, 1982), 36–37.
[28] Candace R. Benyei, *Understanding Clergy Misconduct in Religious Systems: Scapegoating, Family Secrets, and the Abuse of Power* (Binghamton, N.Y.: Haworth Press, 1998), 51.
[29] Leech, *Experiencing God*, 245.
[30] Clark H. Pinnock, *Flame of Love: A Theology of the Holy Spirit* (Downers Grove, Ill.: InterVarsity Press, 1996), 88.
[31] Thomas R. Kelly, "Testament of Devotion," in *Quaker Spirituality: Selected Writings*, ed. Douglas V. Steere (Ramsey, N.J.: Paulist Press, 1984), 290, 304.
[32] Eugene H. Peterson, *Working the Angles: The Shape of Pastoral Integrity* (Grand Rapids, Mich.: Eerdmans, 1987), 78–82.
[33] Ibid., 86.
[34] Henri J. M. Nouwen, *The Inner Voice of Love* (New York: Doubleday, 1996), 5.
[35] Marcus J. Borg, *The God We Never Knew* (San Francisco: HarperSanFrancisco, 1997), 128–29.
[36] Tommy Tenney, *The God Chasers* (Shippensburg, Pa.: Destiny Image, 1998), 114.
[37] Nouwen, McNeill, and Morrison, *Compassion*, 36.
[38] Kelly, 296.
[39] Ibid., 297–98.
[40] Mary E. Hines, "Rahnerian Spirituality: Implications for Ministry," in *Handbook of Spirituality for Ministers*, ed. Robert J. Wicks (Mahweh, N.J.: Paulist Press, 1995), 135–36.
[41] Avery Dulles, *Models of the Church* (New York: Doubleday, 1974), 27.
[42] Ibid., 32.
[43] "A Covenant Prayer in the Wesleyan Tradition," no. 607 in *The United Methodist Hymnal* (Nashville: United Methodist Publishing House, 1989).
[44] Paul Ricoeur, The Symbolism of Evil, trans. Emerson Buchanan (New York: Harper & Row, 1967).

Chapter 4: River-running the Rapids of Spirit

[1] Jeff Bennett, *The Complete Whitewater Rafter* (Camden, Maine: Rugged Mountain Press, 1996), 77.

[2]Ibid., 77.
[3]Loren B. Mead, *Transforming Congregations for the Future* (New York: Alban Institute, 1994), 72.
[4]Bennett, *Complete Whitewater,* 99–100.
[5]M. Robert Mulholland, Jr., *Shaped by the Word: The Power of Scripture in Spiritual Formation* (Nashville: Upper Room, 1985), 42.
[6]Reginald S. Ward, "Images and Models of the Spiritual Director'" in *Writings on Spiritual Direction by Great Christian Masters,* ed. Jerome M. Neufelder and Mary C. Coelho (New York: Seabury Press, 1982), 29.
[7]Harrison Owen, *Riding the Tiger: Doing Business in a Transforming World* (Potomac, Md.: Abbott, 1991), 28.
[8]Ibid., 29.
[9]Ibid., 45.
[10]Kenneth Leech, *Spirituality and Pastoral Care* (London: Sheldon Press, 1986), 5.
[11]Ibid., 16.
[12]The Book of Resolutions of the United Methodist Church (Nashville: United Methodist Publishing House, 1996), 128. Located in UMC.org, Open Hearts, Open Minds, Open Doors—The People of the United Methodist Church at http://www2.umc.org/interior_print.asp?ptid=4&mid=1080 in January 2006.
[13]Ibid., 130 and online.
[14]*The Book of Resolutions of the United Methodist Church* (Nashville: United Methodist Publishing House, 2000). Located in UMC.org, http://www2.umc.org/interior_print.asp?ptid=4&mid=1080.
[15]Ibid.
[16]*The Book of Discipline of the United Methodist Church* (Nashville: United Methodist Publishing House, 2000), available at http://archives.umc.org/interior.asp?mid=1815.
[17]John Polkinghorne, *The Faith of a Physicist* (Minneapolis: Fortress Press, 1996), 135.
[18]Loren B. Mead, *FIVE CHALLENGES for the Once and Future Church* (New York: Alban Institute, 1996), 36–40.
[19]Harvey Fox, *Fire from Heaven: The Rise of Pentecostal Spirituality and the Reshaping of Religion in the Twenty-First Century* (New York: Addison-Wesley, 1995), 81.
[20]Howard A. Snyder, *Models of the Kingdom* (Nashville.: Abingdon Press, 1991), 106.
[21]Ibid., 106.
[22]Gerald G. May, *Will and Spirit: A Contemplative Psychology* (San Francisco: Harper & Row, 1982), 185, 190.
[23]Ibid., 157–58.
[24]Ibid., 196–97.
[25]Ibid., 196, 199–200.
[26]Thomas C. Oden, *Care of Souls in the Classic Tradition* (Philadelphia: Fortress Press, 1984), 37.
[27]Thomas C. Oden, *Pastoral Theology: Essentials of Ministry* (San Francisco: Harper and Row, 1983), 51–52.
[28]Ibid., 53.
[29]Mary E. Hines, "Rahnerian Spirituality: Implications for Ministry," in *Handbook of Spirituality for Ministers,* ed. Robert J. Wicks (Mahwah, N.J.: Paulist Press, 1995), 134.
[30]Robert K. Greenleaf, *Servant Leadership: A Journey into the Nature of Legitimate Power and Greatness* (Mahwah, N.J.: Paulist Press, 1977), 219–20.
[31]Ibid., 222–24.
[32]Alan Jones, *Sacrifice and Delight: Spirituality for Ministry* (San Francisco: HarperSanFrancisco, 1992), 3.
[33]Roy M. Oswald, *Clergy Self-Care: Finding a Balance for Effective Ministry* (Washington, D.C.: Alban Institute, 1991), 15.
[34]Thomas G. Bandy, *Moving Off the Map: A Field Guide to Changing the Congregation* (Nashville: Abingdon Press, 1998) and *Mission Mover: Beyond Education for Church Leadership* (Nashville: Abingdon Press, 2004).

Chpater 5: River-running the Rapids of Morality

[1]Candace R. Benyei, *Understanding Clergy Misconduct in Religious Systems: Scapegoating, Family Secrets, and the Abuse of Power* (Binghamton, N.Y.: Haworth Pastoral Press, 1998), 47–48.

[2]Ibid., 15.
[3]Ibid., 14–15.
[4]Edwin H. Friedman, *Generation to Generation: Family Process in Church and Synagogue* (New York: Guilford Press, 1985), 1.
[5]Ibid., 1–2.
[6]Ibid., 19.
[7]Ibid.
[8]Ibid., 20.
[9]Alan Jones, *Sacrifice and Delight: Spirituality for Ministry* (San Francisco: HarperSanFrancisco, 1992), 51.
[10]Marcus J. Borg, *The God We Never Knew* (San Francisco: HarperSanFrancisco, 1997), 78.
[11]Benyei, *Understanding Clergy Misconduct*, 70–72.
[12]Douglas John Hall, *The Future of the Church* (Toronto: United Church Publishing House, 1989), 13.
[13]Ibid., 42–43.
[14]Ibid., 95–96.
[15]Jones, *Sacrifice and Delight*, 53.
[16]Ibid., 53–54.
[17]Gerald G. May, *Addiction and Grace* (San Francisco: Harper and Row, 1988), 123.
[18]Ibid., 118, 126.
[19]Henri J. M. Nouwen, Donald P. McNeill, and Douglas A. Morrison, *Compassion: A Reflection on the Christian Life* (New York: Doubleday, 1982), 16–17.
[20]Ibid., 23–24.
[21]Robert Bly, *Iron John* (New York: Vintage Books, 1990), 41–42.

Chapter 6: River-running the Rapids of Calling

[1]Henri J. M. Nouwen, Donald P. McNeill, and Douglas A. Morrison, *Compassion: A Reflection on the Christian Life* (New York: Doubleday, 1982), 14.
[2]Ibid., 88.
[3]Bradley Holt, "Spiritualities of the Twentieth Century," in *The Story of Christian Spirituality*, ed. Gordon Mursell (Minneapolis: Fortress Press, 2001), 352.
[4]Ibid., 353.
[5]Ibid.
[6]Norman Vincent Peale, *Positive Thinking Bible* (Nashville: Thomas Nelson, 1998), 1338.
[7]Ibid., 1316.
[8]William M. Easum and Thomas G. Bandy, *Growing Spiritual Redwoods* (Nashville: Abingdon Press, 1997), 185.
[9]Ibid.
[10]LaMar Boschman, *Future Worship* (Ventura, Calif.: Renew Books, 1999), 96–97.
[11]Ibid., 99.
[12]V. W. Arnold, "Blessing and Benediction," in *Dictionary of Pastoral Care and Counseling*, ed. Rodney J. Hunter (Nashville: Abingdon Press, 1990), 101.
[13]Ibid.
[14]Information obtained from http://www.doj.gov.za/trc November 19, 2005.
[15]Robert D. Dale, *To Dream Again* (Nashville: Broadman Press, 1981), 40.
[16]Ibid., 41–42.
[17]Ibid., 42.
[18]Tom Wright, *The Original Jesus: The Life and Vision of a Revolutionary* (Grand Rapids, Mich.: Eerdmans, 1996), 41–42.
[19]Roy M. Oswald, *Clergy Self-Care: Finding a Balance for Effective Ministry* (Washington, D.C.: Alban Institute, 1991), 71.
[20]Ibid., 75
[21]Edwin H. Friedman, *Generation to Generation: Family Process in Church and Synagogue* (New York: Guilford Press, 1985), 224–28.
[22]Ibid., 229–30.
[23]Ibid., 229.
[24]Howard A. Snyder, *Models of the Kingdom* (Nashville: Abingdon Press, 1991), 16–18.

[25]See Barry Johnson, *Polarity Management: Identifying and Managing Unsolvable Problems* (Amherst, Mass.: Human Resource Development Press, 1997). Johnson offers wisdom on understanding and managing dilemmas in any organization.

[26]Evelyn Eaton Whitehead and James D. Whitehead, *A Sense of Sexuality: Christian Love and Intimacy* (New York: Doubleday, 1989), 59-60.

[27]Henri J. M. Nouwen, preface to *Francis de Sales, Jane de Chantal: Letters of Spiritual Direction*, trans. Péronne Marie Thibert, Classics of Christian Spirituality (Mahwah, N.J.: Paulist Press, 1988), 5.

[28]Robert K. Greenleaf, *Servant Leadership: A Journey into the Nature of Legitimate Power and Greatness* (Mahwah, N.J.: Paulist Press, 1977), 223-24.

[29]Ibid., 225.

[30]Ibid., 224-25.

[31]Ibid., 231.

[32]Ibid., 227.

[33]Jules J. Toner, *A Commentary on Saint Ignatius' Rules for the Discernment of Spirits* (St. Louis: Institute of Jesuit Resources, 1982), 1.

[34]Ibid., 2.

[35]Danny E. Morris and Charles M. Olsen, *Discerning God's Will Together: A Spiritual Practice for the Church* (Bethesda, Md.: Alban Institute, 1997), 19.

[36]Matthew A. Trump, Ilya Prigogine Center for Studies in Statistical Mechanics and Complex Systems, University of Texas at Austin, http://order.ph.utexas.edu/chaos/index.html. "What is Chaos? a five-part online course for everyone," Lesson Five: Manifestations of Chaos.

[37]Ibid.

[38]Marion Cowan and John Carroll Futrell, *The Spiritual Exercises of St. Ignatius of Loyola: A Handbook for Spiritual Directors* (Cambridge, Mass.: Jesuit Educational Center for Human Development, 1982), 36-37.

[39]Thomas G. Bandy, *Mission Mover: Beyond Education for Church Leadership* (Nashville: Abingdon Press, 2004).

Chapter 7: Why I Am an OptiMystic

[1]Saint Augustine, *Confessions,* trans. R. S. Pine-Coffin (Great Britian: Cox and Wyman, 1961), 147, 177-79.

[2]Robert K. Johnston, *Reel Spirituality: Theology and Film in Dialogue* (Grand Rapids, Mich.: Baker Academic, 2000), 83.

[3]William Turner, "The System of Leibniz," in *The Catholic Encyclopedia,* available online at http://www.newadvent.org/cathen/09123b.htm.

[4]Ibid.

[5]Ibid.

[6]John Wesley, *The Works of John Wesley: Volume 4: Sermons IV 115-151,* ed. Albert C. Outler (Nashville: Abingdon Press, 1987), 288-89.

[7]From the Web sitehttp://www.jonathanedwards.com/text/Personal/PNarrative.htm). Published originally in Serene Dwight, *Memoirs of Jonathan Edwards, A.M.* (New Haven, Conn.: Yale University Press). It is taken here from the Works of Jonathan Edwards, 1:xii-xv, xxxiii, xlvi-xlviii.

[8]Rick Warren, *The Purpose Driven Life* (Grand Rapids, Mich.: Zondervan, 2002), 22-23.

[9]William James, *The Varieties of Religious Experience* (New York: Simon and Schuster, 1997), 85, 87-88.

[10]Ibid., 7.

[11]Reinhold Niebuhr, introduction to James, *The Varieties of Religious Experience,* 7.

[12]Ibid., 7.

[13]Norman Vincent Peale, *In God We Trust: A Positive Faith in Troubled Times* (Nashville: Thomas Nelson, 1994), 154-57.

[14]Ibid., 153-54.

[15]Martin E. P. Seligman, *Learned Optimism: How to Change Your Mind and Your Life* (New York: Pocket Books, 1998), 15-16, 44.

[16]Ibid., 204.

[17]Henri J. M. Nouwen, *The Wounded Healer* (Garden City, N.Y.: Image Books, 1972), 19-20.

[18] Bernard McGinn, *The Foundations of Mysticism: Origins to the Fifth Century* (New York: Crossroad, 1991), 265–343. McGinn writes an excellent historical summary covering the dialogue on mysticism among theologians, philosophers, and psychologists. For an insightful piece of work that is essential reading for students of mysticism, see pages xv-xviii.

[19] Ibid., 102.

[20] Ibid., 101–4.

[21] Harvey D. Egan, S.J., *Christian Mysticism: The Future of a Tradition* (New York: Pueblo, 1984), 3.

[22] Peter C. Erb (ed.), *Pietists Selected Writings,* The Classics of Western Spirituality, ed. Richard J. Payne (Mahwah, N.J.: Paulist Press, 1983), xiii.

[23] Ibid., 67–68.

[24] Ibid., 69.

[25] Ibid.

[26] Frank Whaling, ed., *John and Charles Wesley: Selected Writings and Hymns,* Classics of Western Spirituality (New York: Paulist Press, 1981), xix, 1–13.

[27] Robert G. Tuttle, Jr., *Mysticism in the Wesleyan Tradition* (Grand Rapids, Mich.: Francis Asbury Press, 1989), 30.

[28] Ibid., 127.

[29] Gordon Mursell, ed., *The Story of Christian Spirituality* (Minneapolis: Fortress Press, 2001), 198–99.

[30] Tuttle, *Wesleyan Tradition,* 102.

[31] Whaling, *John and Charles Wesley,* 15.

[32] Tuttle, *Wesleyan Tradition,* 101.

[33] W. Reginald Ward and Richard P. Heitzenrater, *The Works of John Wesley Volume 18: Journals and Diaries 1* (Nashville: Abingdon Press, 1988), 248–49.

[34] Ibid., 249–50.

[35] Mursell, *Story,* 199.

[36] John Wesley, *The Works of John Wesley: Volume 1, Sermons I 1–33,* ed. Albert C. Outler (Nashville: Abingdon Press, 1984), 286.

[37] Ibid., 287.

[38] Evelyn Underhill, *Mysticism* (1911; reprint, New York: E. P. Dutton, 1961), 76.

[39] Ibid., 81.

[40] Ibid., 266.

[41] Ibid., 273.

[42] Ibid., 276.

[43] Ibid., 274–77.

[44] Ibid., 278.

[45] Jaroslav Pelikan, *The Vindication of Tradition* (New Haven, Conn.: Yale University Press, 1984), 65.

[46] Ibid., 81–82.

[47] Danny E. Morris and Charles M. Olsen, *Discerning God's Will Together: A Spiritual Practice for the Church* (Bethesda, Md.: Alban Institute, 1997), 45–46.

[48] Thomas G. Bandy, *Road Runner: The Body in Motion* (Nashville: Abingdon Press, 2002) and *Mission Mover: Beyond Education for Church Leadership* (Nashville: Abingdon Press, 2004).